REFLECTIONS IN THE MIND'S EYE:

Reference and Its Problematization in

Twentieth-Century French Fiction

Reflections in the Mind's Eye

Reference and Its Problematization in Twentieth-Century French Fiction

Brian T. Fitch

UNIVERSITY OF TORONTO PRESS

Toronto Buffalo London

© University of Toronto Press 1991
Toronto Buffalo London
Printed in Canada

ISBN 0-8020-5890-6 (cloth)
ISBN 0-8020-6822-7 (paper)

Printed on acid-free paper

Theory / Culture Series 3

Canadian Cataloguing in Publication Data

Fitch, Brian T.
Reflections in the mind's eye : reference and its problematization in
twentieth-century French fiction

(Theory / culture)
Includes bibliographical references and index.
ISBN 0-8020-5890-6 (bound)   ISBN 0-8020-6822-7 (pbk.)

1. French fiction – 20th century – History and criticism.   2. Reference
(Philosophy) in literature.   I. Title.   II. Series.

PQ673.F57 1991   843.91409384   C91-093068-6

This book has been published with the help of a grant from the Canadian
Federation for the Humanities, using funds provided by the Social Sciences
and Humanities Research Council of Canada.

Contents

Preface

The advent of the French New Novel in the 1950s and, even more, of its successor the New New Novel seriously undermined referentiality in the modern French novel. Some ten to fifteen years later, the emergence of the concept of modernity on the French intellectual scene reinforced the subversion of the referential dimension of the novelistic text: at the same time, structuralism in general posited the text as a closed, self-contained system, sufficient unto itself, and the linguistic model in particular banished the problem of the reference, thereby giving rise to what Fredric Jameson has called 'the prison-house of language.'[1]

A distinction, however, needs to be made immediately between, on the one hand, the fictive heterocosm of the literary work and, on the other hand, the more general referentiality of the literary work as a whole, between the extent to which the novel evokes a coherent, recognizable world and the question of whether there exists a relationship between literature and reality. The present study posits the existence of such a relationship while proposing to examine the manner in which the fictive universe emerges or fails to emerge in the French novel between roughly 1930 and 1967.

It is my contention that inasmuch as the reader of any novel or fictional text makes sense of it, the problem of referentiality is always pertinent to the study of literary texts, for referentiality is part and parcel of the reception of the latter.[2] If a text stops making sense, then

---

1 *The Prison-House of Language*
2 As Paul Ricoeur points out, 'une esthétique de la réception ne peut engager le problème de la *communication* sans engager aussi celui de la *référence*' (*Temps et récit*, 117; Ricoeur's emphasis).

the reader will soon put the book down and turn to another, or to some other activity than reading. I have just implied that sense can be made by the book, while having previously stated that it is to be made by the reader. The truth of the matter is, of course, that it is made by both of them, and moreover at one and the same time, arising, as it does, from the meeting or coming together of a book and a reader and from the resulting interaction between the two.

However, it is time to abandon the everyday expression of 'making sense' with the only too appropriate stress it lays on the creative activity involved in the process of reading, which Wolfgang Iser has illustrated in fine detail in what he rightly terms 'the *act* of reading.'[3] For it is important to make the distinction between sense or meaning, on the one hand, and significance, on the other. The sense of language is what is catalogued in the dictionary and activated in discourse, while its significance is what arises from the situation of language in the communicative chain: author–text–reader. It is interesting that the seminal statement in the context of philosophy, that of Gottlieb Frege, drew the distinction between sense (*Sinn*) and nominatum or *reference* (*Bedeutung*).[4] Just as significance concerns the *relationship between* language and its user, whether it be through the act of writing or that of reading, so referentiality, too, bears witness to the manner in which language points outside of itself. Both significance-for and reference-to entail a relationship with *something else* that is hence *non-linguistic* in character: the movement back to the speaker, forward to the addressee (that is, the reader), or towards what is being spoken about is at all events a movement *away from* language and therefore an escape from the text, the prison-house of language. Herein lies the basic distinction between what Northrop Frye has called the centripetal and the centrifugal energy generated by the literary text.[5] This escape from the prison-house of language is effected by the very act of reading: through the act of reading, the reader first enters into the prison-house only to immediately emerge from it again.

We shall be concerned in the following pages with both types or levels of referentiality: the world of the book and the world of the

3 *The Act of Reading*
4 'On Sense and Nominatum,' 85–102
5 *Anatomy of Criticism*: '... verbal structures may be classified according to whether the *final* direction of meaning is outward or inward' (74; Frye's emphasis); '... everything that influences literature from without creates a centrifugal movement in it ...' (75), whereas, poetry, for example, is 'concerned with the centripetal aspect of meaning' (80).

reader. Paul Ricoeur[6] sees the first level, that of the fictive heterocosm in which the novel's characters move and have their being, as corresponding to a kind of suspension of referentiality proper that only subsequently gives way to the full realization of the reference through the act of reading, which, taking up Gadamer's[7] terminology, he sees as being constituted by the fusion of two horizons: that of the work and that of the reader. My concern here is to trace both the movement by which the text generates a fictional world that becomes 'concretized,' – in Roman Ingarden's[8] terminology – in the reader's imagination and that further movement, far more difficult to map out with any certainty or precision, by which the reader appropriates this world or, as Gadamer says so tellingly, 'applies' it to his own existential situation. The stress of my exegesis will quite naturally vary from text to text, since the latter have been selected precisely if not to 'illustrate' the variety of ways in which reference functions in novel texts, to explore and to plumb the process of reference. We shall, in fact, find that the novels I have chosen will tend to render problematic one or more levels of reference. To that extent, they can indeed be seen to constitute an inventory of referentiality in twentieth-century French fiction. More important, however, they will serve to flesh out an account of novelistic reference that should help us better to understand its functioning.

Not the least interesting aspect of such a study is that it is situated at the interface of two fundamental approaches to literature today. For while a theory of the fictive referent might properly take its place within the realm of poetics, the theory of literary referentiality in the fullest sense of that term can only be encompassed within a hermeneutic perspective.

The starting point is always a close reading of the text in question, which, given the language in which I am writing and the continent on which this book is being published, will recall for many nothing more exotic than North American New Criticism. Its true antecedents lie elsewhere, in other climes, francophone with germanic overtones: those of the French *Nouvelle Critique* of the so-called Geneva School with its grounding in German phenomenology. In fact, this study represents an attempt to contribute to a theory of literary representa-

6 *Interpretation Theory*, 23
7 Hans-Georg Gadamer, *Truth and Method*
8 *The Literary Work of Art*

tion and reception based on a hermeneutical critical practice developed in my previous books on Bernanos,[9] Beckett,[10] and Bataille.[11]

The reason for and advantage of such a close textual reading is that I seek to trace the process of reference not only *right through to* its ultimate realization in the world (*Lebenswelt*) of the reader but also *right from* its originating impulse in the syntactic evolution of the text on that level of the work that Roman Ingarden analyses in such fine and discriminating detail in *The Literary Work of Art*. Little attention has been paid to date to the 'concretization' of the work in the reader's imagination starting with the linguistic detail of a given text. It will no doubt be on this level that the following pages will provide their major contribution.

The problem of referentiality is, in fact, central to any theory of literary reception, and that this fact has been lost sight of in recent years is due not only to the prevalence, in the realm of literary studies, of a linguistic model, having its antecedents in Ferdinand de Saussure's *Cours*, but also to the failure, or indeed refusal, to recognize fictional referentiality as having anything whatsoever to do with 'real' (in other words, '*non*-fictional') referentiality. It therefore may be useful if I define my own position in relation to the various schools or proponents of a theory of reception.

Like the work of Wolfgang Iser and contrary to that of his compatriot Hans Robert Jauss,[12] my concern is not with the *collective* reception of the literary work by a given society at a given time but rather with the *individual* reader's reception of the modern French novel. However, in contradistinction to Iser, I situate my initial analysis, as was mentioned above, on the level of the text's microstructures, that is to say, on that of its syntagmatic evolution. While this procedure is more in keeping with the intricate and painstakingly detailed analysis called for by Iser's mentor, the phenomenologist Roman Ingarden, it should be remarked first that Ingarden's *The Literary Work of Art* is a contribution to literary theory and not at all (except, of course, potentially) to the actual textual analysis of given writers' works, and second, that such a close textual analysis has much in common, in this regard, with the formalist contribution to a theory of reception

---

9 *Dimensions et structures chez Bernanos*
10 *Dimensions, structures et textualité*
11 *Monde à l'envers/Texte réversible.* It should be added that this practice was, however, complemented by more formalist concerns in the books on Beckett and Bataille.
12 See, for example, his *Toward an Aesthetic of Reception.*

such as that made by the writings of Michel Charles[13] or Gerald
Prince.[14] My own analysis does not, however, stop short once it has
reached the confines of the text itself. In this respect, therefore, it
more closely resembles the minute analysis undertaken by Stanley
Fish,[15] save that whereas his concern is solely with the effect the text
has upon its reader – what the former actually *does to* the latter, as
he would put it – mine focuses on that intermediary stage or at least
contributory process by which the reader conjures up in his mind's
eye the world of the fiction and its motley inhabitants. My eventual
move beyond the concretization of the fictive referent to the total,
overall, and final impact the novel has upon its reader and the use the
latter makes of the results of that reading is effected primarily thanks
to one of the central concepts not of Iser's mentor, Ingarden, but of
that other philosopher Hans-Georg Gadamer. The concept in question
is that of the 'application' of the literary work. This has been a traditional concept of hermeneutics, arising from its origins in biblical
exegesis and surviving most naturally in one of its other main
branches, that of jurisprudence.[16] But it is Gadamer who has had the
merit of reviving or rather reactivating it in the realm of literary
hermeneutics. However, as the ironic title of his work *Truth and
Method* already suggests, Gadamer does not provide any kind of
method or heuristic tool for the study of actual texts. I turn to the
French philosopher Paul Ricoeur for an appropriate elaboration of
Gadamer's concept within a more linguistically oriented theory of
interpretation than that provided by the German philosopher.

It is in fact to the writings of Paul Ricoeur[17] as well as the work of
Roman Ingarden that I am most heavily indebted in my account of
literary referentiality, which constitutes the first section of the present
study. This does not, of course, prevent me from drawing on a number
of other treatments of this problem when the need arises, such as the
works of Gadamer and Iser, referred to above, not to mention an

13 *Rhétorique de la lecture*
14 'Introduction to the Study of the Narratee,' 7–25
15 *Self-Consuming Artifacts*
16 For an excellent account of the body of modern hermeneutic thought, see Richard
E. Palmer, *Hermeneutics*; for the historical origins of hermeneutics, see Georges
Gusdorf, *Les Origines de l'herméneutique*.
17 Need it be added that until the appearance of the second volume of his *Temps et
récit*, entitled 'La Configuration du temps dans le récit de fiction,' in 1984,
Ricoeur, in his discussion of referentiality, comes no closer than Gadamer did
before him to the actual analysis of the phenomenon of specific literary texts?

important article by Tzvetan Todorov, 'Reading as Construction.'[18] I am also indebted to Leonard Linsky's invaluable synthesis of philosophical accounts of reference in his book *Referring*. For the linguistic perspective on reference needed to complement the latter, I call on Maurice-Jean Lefebve's illuminating *Structure du discours de la poésie et du récit*.

The present study thus aims not only at contributing to a theory of literary referentiality as it functions within the text of the novel – while not itself constituting a full-blown theory of reference nor laying claim to originality in its component parts at least – but also at making the closest possible analysis of the manner in which referentiality functions in several twentieth-century French novels and *récits*. Whereas in some cases, such as the fictional works of Bernanos, Blanchot, Simon, and Bataille, the status of the fictive referent poses specific problems for the reader in the task of concretizing the literary work, in others, such as Camus' *La Chute* and Beckett's *L'Innommable*, the work is very much concerned with the laying bare, through a process the Russian formalists called *la dénudation du procédé*,[19] of the very process of referentiality itself. *La Nausée* lies somewhere between these two positions in that it explicitly thematizes the problematization of reference within the world of the novel, as its narrator-protagonist grapples at first hand with the relationship between language and reality. If I were to sum up in a single statement the aim of the present study, I might claim that it seeks to reveal how the French novel since 1930 tends to problematize the referentiality of the literary text.

18 'Reading as Construction' 67–82
19 See Todorov, Tzevetan, ed., *Théorie de la littérature*.

Acknowledgments

I wish to thank the University of Toronto for awarding me a Senior Connaught Fellowship for 1988–9, which enabled this book to be completed far more expeditiously than would otherwise have been the case. I should also like to thank Vera Grayson and Victor Kocay for their careful reading of the first draft of my manuscript. I am also very much indebted to my friends and colleagues Franc Schuerewegen, Albert Halsall, and Ralph Sarkonak, whose suggestions were invaluable to me in the revision of my original manuscript.

Toronto / Paris
January 1988–April 1990

REFLECTIONS IN THE MIND'S EYE

1

Fictional Referentiality

Although the objective of the present study is to analyse the manner in which the fictive referent is constituted in the twentieth-century French novel and subsequently concretized, together with the problems its concretization poses for the reader, such an analysis necessarily presupposes a certain theory of novelistic and hence literary referentiality in general. It is therefore incumbent upon the author to begin by giving some account of how he conceives reference to function in the novel.

It should be stressed that in relation to the studies of the novels that go to make up the main body of this book the primary function of this chapter is a heuristic one. I give an account of how certain theoreticians deal with the principal stages in the working out of literary reference in fictional discourse. Subsequently these various stages are seen to be problematized in the novels to be studied. In fact, each of the chapters below focuses on one level of the referential process that proves to have an essential role to play in the reception of the novel(s) in question. This means that the exposition of the different levels of reference furnishes the theoretical tools each of which serves in the analysis of one or another of the novelist's works. Although the primary focus is hermeneutic and phenomenological, the concepts involved are not taken from a single discipline, since I draw on the writings of linguists, philosophers, and literary theoreticians; the approach adopted is theoretical and synchronic rather than historical. Inasmuch as the concepts enabling one to map out the evolution of the reference, from the linguistic level of the signifiers and the signifieds through its concretization in the imagination to its appropriation by the reader, prove to be compatible with one another then they can be seen to provide the key elements for a full-fledged theory of novelistic referentiality. The latter is not, however, the objective of these pages, which is distinctly more modest: to provide a theoretical context and background for the studies that follow.

What is more, the content of this account of literary referentiality is as much a result or product of past critical practice as it is a bringing together of various theories of literary reference. Critical practice – over a series of studies of the works of a number of twentieth-century French novelists most of whom are subsequently 'revisited' or re-examined in the rest of this book – preceded the elaboration of theoretical considerations. The result is thus the outcome of a continuing dialogue between (literary) theory and (critical) practice. If only for this reason, the conception of literary reference presented below has to be considered tentative and provisional in character.

Until the present period of literary studies, to state that there exists a relationship between literature and reality would hardly have been considered a programmatic statement. Story-telling and the listening to the telling of stories seem to have been a continuing need throughout the history of human society, and such a need would quite naturally appear to presuppose that literature in general and the novel in particular have some bearing on human life as it is lived. There is little point in going over yet again the way in which structuralism and modern poetics have not only put into question such a relationship, but also, whether for polemical reasons – as most obviously in the case of the brilliantly controversial writings of the French theoretician and novelist Jean Ricardou – or otherwise, have set out systematically to deny its very possibility. Times, however, change and theoretical dogmatism no longer appears to be the order of the day. The appearance of a work such as Andrew Gann's *Social Values and Poetic Acts*[1] is significant in this respect, as is Tzvetan Todorov's dramatic volte-face in his *Critique de la critique*, the tone of which may prompt the reader to wonder what all the fuss was about in the first place: 'Depuis deux cents ans, les romantiques et leurs innombrables héritiers nous ont répété à qui mieux mieux que la littérature était un langage qui trouvait sa fin en lui-même. Il est temps d'en venir (d'en revenir) aux évidences qu'on n'aurait pas dû oublier: la littérature a trait à l'existence humaine, c'est un discours, tant pis pour ceux qui ont peur des grands mots, orienté vers la vérité et la

---

1 See 'The Scandal of Referentiality,' 115–31.

morale. ... Elle ne serait rien si elle ne nous permettait pas de mieux comprendre la vie.'[2]

The concerns of the present book clearly place it at the centre of this debate and in a sense midway between the two positions. For what emerges from its pages is the progressive *problematization* of reference in twentieth-century French fiction over the past fifty-odd years. Since the advent of the French New Novel there has been a certain circularity and reciprocity in the relationship and interaction between literary theorizing and novelistic practice that remain to be studied and to which the influence of Roland Barthes on Robbe-Grillet and subsequently Jean Ricardou on Claude Simon (and vice versa in this latter case, it should be added) bears eloquent witness. It is therefore hardly surprising that the output of the novelist has come to 'confirm', as it were, the claims of the theoreticians, thereby paradoxically, however, perhaps reducing these claims to the status of predictions. Whatever one's ideological position in the debate over reference and the literary text, the studies in the following chapters will offer solace and confirmation to both sides in that the status of the fictive referent is revealed to be central to the critical concerns raised by the novels examined while at the same time becoming progressively more problematic for the reader. A development that was very soon apparent to readers of the French New Novel – the confirmation of what had come to be called the referential fallacy – is here seen to be the culmination of a progressive problematization of reference, beginning with the attempt to depict the undepictable of George Bernanos, foreshadowing the later analogous enterprise of Maurice Blanchot, and highlighted quite explicitly in a novel, *La Nausée*, that seeks to rise from the ashes of the collapse of any necessary relationship between language and the objects it seeks to designate.

Reference most properly, of course, belongs to the domain of philosophy, for it is the philosopher who has traditionally concerned himself with the problem of how language relates to reality. In order to assure itself of a clearly definable and – more important – manageable object of study, linguistics decided to exclude such complex, albeit fundamental considerations from its purview. And so once literary theoreticians, beginning with the Russian formalists, took as their premiss a linguistic model, thereby abandoning once and for all those concerns that had exercised the philosophy of language, and the poetician replaced the literary critic, then the question of reference could, quite

2 *Critique de la critique*, 188

naturally, no longer be seen to have any relevance for the student of literature.

Any discussion of reference has to take as its starting point Frege's fundamental distinction between *Sinn* or sense, on the one hand, and *Bedeutung* or reference on the other, which Paul Ricoeur reformulates thus: 'The sense is the ideal object which the proposition intends, and hence is purely immanent in discourse. The reference is the truth value of the proposition, its claim to reach reality.'[3] In other words, 'the sense is *what* the proposition states; the reference or denotation is *that about which* the sense is stated.'[4] What the key philosophical texts on reference have to tell us about literary texts, however, is meagre in the extreme, as becomes readily apparent from Leonard Linsky's useful survey *Referring*,[5] and we have soon to turn to the work of linguists in order to begin to clarify the situation. Now among linguists, there is general agreement that the term *reference* applies to what J. Lyons, in his work *General Linguistics*,[6] calls the 'relationship which exists between words and the objects, events, actions and qualities that the words represent.'

The first point that needs to be established for the purposes of the present study is that, like everyday discourse and all other forms of discourse, literary discourse possesses a reference. The second point is that it does not, however, possess the same form of reference as the latter, or rather, that while what it ends up, so to speak, by referring to is the same – the extralinguistic 'reality' that constitutes the space that determines man's existential condition – the manner in which it goes about referring to that reality is quite different. Literary discourse refers in a much less direct manner than ordinary discourse so that the process involved is a more roundabout one. Rather than referring to those objects, events, actions, and qualities that its words represent

---

3 'The Hermeneutical Function of Distanciation,' 140
4 Paul Ricoeur, *The Rule of Metaphor*, 217
5 Mention should also be made here of Thomas Pavel's work *Fictional Worlds*, which is essentially concerned with the status of such worlds rather than the manner of their textual embodiment. Pavel deals with the problem of the reference of literary works on a more general level than I do. He provides an extensive and invaluable bibliography of work done in this area, not only by philosophers but also by linguists and semioticians.
6 Cited by George Lavis in his article 'Le Texte littéraire, le référent, le réel, le vrai,' 9

as they exist in the 'real' world, it refers in the first instance to those same objects, events, actions, and qualities in the form they would take on in an imaginary world; in other words, initially it refers to imaginary equivalents of those phenomena. Indeed, literary discourse never does get around to referring to those constitutive elements of reality in any *literal* sense of the word for, as we shall see in our subsequent examination of the second and final stage of literary reference, the way in which its ultimate reference is realized is not through the designation of specific phenomena as such but rather through recourse to human experience in general and as a whole. It functions referentially by calling on the reader's own existential situation.

It is because the immediate, first-level reference of literary discourse is not real but imaginary that one can be led to believe that it is a form of language that has the peculiarity of not possessing a referent. To recognize that in the literary text the referent is fictive in character can well appear to be tantamount to acknowledging that it has no referent at all. In an article in which he addresses directly the status of literary reference, George Lavis emphasizes that this does not mean that 'parce que le texte littéraire est ... un univers signifiant imaginaire n'implique pas ... que la réalité, le monde des choses et des idées (en général), ou, plus précisément, l'expérience que moi, lecteur, j'ai de cette realité, de ce monde, n'ait aucune influence sur l'appréhension que je peux avoir de ce texte.'[7] An exponent of a psychoanalytical theory of literature, Michel Picard, concurs with the linguist on this point when he stresses that as well as referring to logico-semantic structures of signifieds that are dependent upon contemporary culture and ideologies, the signifiers of any literary text at the same time refer the reader to his own personal history: 'Par le jeu des connotations et des glissements paradigmatiques, les signifiés sont *aussi* ceux de ses préoccupations les plus secrètes, les moins conscientes ... De plus des *référents*, sous forme de flashes 'visuels' dont l'affect compte plus que la précision, lui sont également fournis, parfois à sa grande surprise, par des souvenirs ... fugitifs, partiels, mais vécus.'[8] In fact, whatever the particular intent or strategy of its author, no text can be totally non-referential for, as is conclusively demonstrated by Catherine Kerbrat-Orecchioni, 'tout texte réfère, d'une certaine manière; "réfère," c'est-à-dire renvoie à un monde (préconstruit, ou construit par le texte

7 Ibid., 17
8 *La Lecture comme jeu*, 51; Picard's emphasis

lui-même) posé hors langage; "d'une certaine manière," variable selon les textes ..."[9]

The crux of the matter here, of course, is the nature of the referent concerned. It is only when the referent is conceived of from within a purely practical perspective, whereby it designates real-life objects and directly relates to the everyday world in which we function, that it is legitimate to speak of literary discourse being cut off from its referent. Such is not the case once one considers reference to call upon our *experience and knowledge* of those objects and that world and thereby to be synonymous with what Maurice-Jean Lefebve calls the reactivation of our experience of the latter.[10] Just as the ultimate reference the text points towards is none other than the total existential situation of its reader, so it is the total text, taken in its entirety, that alone possesses a reference that goes beyond the individual *fictive* referents constituting the world of the novel and is able and intended to be fully realized in the final outcome of the reading process, once the mere perception and decoding of the words on the page give way to reflection. On the level of its constituent parts, the individual words and sentences of a given novel's text, however, the normal process of reference is, at it were, blocked so that the latter are, in effect, cut off from their normal referents, which have been replaced by their fictional counterparts. In other words, it is only when the various fictive referents coalesce to form a new entity, a coherent fictional universe, that the text's real or full referential potential becomes activated. It is the totality of actions, situations, characters, objects, feelings that go to make up the fiction and that, in spite of their fictional character, are presented to us as real that constitute the novel's referent. It is a referent that is marked out and defined by its natural context: the novel seen as a whole. At the same time, precisely because of its fictive nature, such a referent acquires a generality the referent of everyday discourse normally lacks, thereby calling upon our knowledge of the world and our experience as human beings.[11] All the *fictive* referents come together to form a new signifying entity that is the world of the book, corresponding to the whole of the literary text in question.

It is Lefebve who provides the most detailed account of the referentiality of the literary text. As a consequence of its being cut off from

9 'Le Texte littéraire'
10 See *Structure du discours*, 111.
11 Lavis, 'Le Texte littéraire,' 19

the practical reference that characterizes everyday language, literary language takes on, according to this theoretician, two specific attributes. [12] In the first place, literary language points to its own materiality so that the work announces itself as such in all its literariness. In the second place and in accord with the latter, being deprived of its normal function and in order to fill the resulting void, literary discourse calls on and emits new, secondary meanings that go beyond its ordinary sphere of application: these are the *connotations*, which are as difficult to enumerate as their content is to define. The very imprecision resulting from their superabundance of meaning brings about what Lefebve calls 'presentification,' that is to say, the impression of being in the presence of a certain reality (30). Now, the first of these two attributes, the materialization of the signifier, which is none other than the opacity referred to above or the self-reflexivity of literary language – what Northrop Frye would call its centripetal tendency – whereby language makes us aware of its existence as a visual and audible phenomenon, figures only briefly in these pages, particularly in the chapters devoted to Claude Simon's *Histoire* and Georges Bataille's *Histoire de l'œil*, although it is tangentially relevant to the analysis of Beckett's *L'Innommable*. The second, the presentification of the signified – or what Frye would call its centrifugal tendency – plays the key role in the referential process. The image evoked by the signified takes the place of the referent and in a way takes on the presence of the latter (32), that is, creates a referential illusion. Consequently, the referent takes on the status of 'un signifié où une *certaine expérience que nous possédons de l'objet se trouve rappelée, recréée, réactivée.*' Contrary to the situation in ordinary, non-literary discourse, rather than being 'une simple notion évoquée par le signifiant,' it arises from 'une *intention tournée vers les choses*, ... une *approche concrète du monde*' (109). [13] Lefebve sees it as 'une sorte de réservoir contenant la totalité des expériences que nous avons de l'objet, le terreau où le signifié s'enracine et puise ses sens' (109–10). Moreover, he concurs with Lavis in considering the totality of the text's fictive referents as constituting what is in effect a new *signifier*, which gives rise to a new referent through 'l'interaction des réalités représentées (décor, personnages, événements).' The latter thus takes

---

12 There is, in fact, a third characteristic according to Lefebve, which need not concern us here, the phenomenon of 'incarnation,' whereby the realization of the indefinite signifieds seeks to take on form and substance in the signifiers.
13 Lefebve's emphasis

on all the appearance of a language in its own right, 'comme les signifiants ordonnés d'un nouveau discours' (112).[14] This does not mean, however, that the referent has thereby ceased to exist: it has merely receded behind the totality of the represented realities (in the form of the fictive referents) constituting the fictive universe – what the poetician calls the diegesis. It is going to draw on the latter for the substance of its actualization, for it is the diegesis (considered as a discourse) that actualizes the referent, through both denotation and connotation, by making it present to the imagination with the immediacy that characterizes all mental images, through the phenomenon of what Lefebve terms 'la présentification imaginale' (113).

Having established that the literary text is not without reference, albeit of a very particular kind, and having at the same time established the linguistic bases for the two-stage process involved therein, I shall now examine in some detail the first of those two stages situated on the level of the fictive referents and the imaginary universe they bring into being. This involves scrutinizing and accounting for the exact process by which the picturing of this universe in the mind's eye of the reader is effected. This next step in my account of literary referentiality entails focusing on the actual reading process itself and hence calls for a shift from the linguistic perspective adopted so far to a phenomenological one. It also brings us a step closer to the main concern of the present study, since its object is the *reception* rather than the *description* of the literary text. In fact, the manner in which the reader is led to conjure up the world of the novel within his imagination constitutes the central concern of the analysis of each novel studied in the chapters that follow. That is why it is necessary to give detailed attention to the nature and, ultimately, to the theoretical status of the process involved. This is rendered even more necessary by the paucity of studies devoted to the phenomenon by either critics or theoreticians, for reasons that will become apparent in the course of my analysis.

One of the rare theoreticians to study this dimension of the literary experience is the phenomenologist Roman Ingarden in his invaluable work *The Literary Work of Art*.[15] However, he does not refer to it as

14 In more technical, linguistic terms, Lefebve formulates the situation thus: '... tandis que le langage quotidien abolit le Sa [*signifiant*] au profit du Sé [*signifié*], le langage littéraire n'abolit pas le Sé au profit du Sa: simplement il a tendance à maintenir la présence du Sa et de faire de tout Sé un nouveau Sa, du moins en puissance' (28; Lefebve's emphasis).

15 For a detailed account of Ingarden's work, see Eugene H. Falk's invaluable exegesis

presentification but speaks rather of the 'concretization' of the literary work.[16] The first problem raised by the activity in question is due to the fact that the concretization effected by any given reader of any given work never corresponds exactly, in every detail at least, to that actualized by any other given reader. Even more disconcerting is the realization that even readings made at different points in time by the same reader, while being necessarily far more similar to one another, inevitably manifest some differences – notwithstanding the fact that each new reading, thanks to a cumulative process, has been strongly influenced, or rather partly determined by every previous reading. What this means, of course, is that no two concretizations of the same literary work are ever identical. That being so, the question then arises as to what extent the process of concretization gives rise to something that is susceptible to study and analysis? If no two concretizations of a work are the same, what is there left to study? That this question should arise is of course one of the reasons why literary theoreticians, not to mention contemporary poeticians, have been distinctly loath even to talk about the concretization involved in the activity of reading, let alone study it.[17] I shall return to the problem posed by the criterion of intersubjective verifiability in a moment.

First of all, however, let us look more closely at the process itself. Concretizations form what Ingarden calls 'the mode of appearance of a work, the concrete form in which the work ... is apprehended' (332) and are therefore to be distinguished from the work itself. They are made up of all those sense impressions – visual, tactile, etc. – that come to us through our five senses, although more precisely the resulting mental images, being the product not of perception but of ideation, are *analogous to* (as opposed to identical with) those sense impres-

---

in *The Poetics of Roman Ingarden*. See also Robert R. Magliola, 'Roman Ingarden,' 107–41.

16 Within this study, the terms *présentification* and *concretization*, together with *actualization (of the reference)*, are employed interchangeably and refer to what actually takes on shape and form in the mind's eye of the reader while being constituted not only by visual images, however, but also by images related to the other four senses. They involve the decoding of the words read. They are to be distinguished from the terms *appropriation* (Ricoeur) and *application* (Gadamer), also synonymous, which correspond to the subsequent process by which the reader makes the work his own by relating it to his own existential situation. The further term *reception* encompasses both these preceding processes.

17 With, of course, the notable exception of those theoreticians working in the hermeneutic tradition and directly influenced by the work of Ingarden himself, such as Wolfgang Iser in particular in his *The Act of Reading*

sions. That is not all that concretizations consist of, however, as is brought out by Ingarden's more technical account of their composition when he lists the following constitutive elements: 'various cognitive acts, such as perceptual acts, in which word signs or word sounds and phonetic formations of a higher order are apprehended ... meaning-apprehending acts that are based on cognitive acts, and, finally, acts of imaginative beholding of represented objectivities and situations and, if need be, of metaphysical qualities manifested in them' (332–3). For the complexity of the form that the work takes on within the reader's imagination naturally mirrors the structure of the literary work itself. The phenomenologist conceives of the latter as a *polyphonic* phenomenon consisting of four strata or levels, all of which contribute to its concretization: the first is the level of phonetics, '*word sounds* and *phonetic formations* of higher order built on them,' which include rhythmic effects and rhyme; the second is the level of '*meaning units* of various orders,' that is, words, sentences, and multiples of sentences; the third is the level of 'schematized *aspects*,' which are schematized structures with various degrees of indeterminateness by which objects appear; and the fourth is the level of '*represented objectivities*,'[18] or the objects themselves. It is understandable therefore that, given the complexity of the sum of phenomena encompassed within a given concretization, only a few are focused upon as central within the reader's imagination at any particular moment (333–4), so that the parts and strata of the work that are clearly perceived are always different: what is foregrounded at one moment will be backgrounded a moment later. The result is that the work is never grasped in its entirety, in all its strata or components, but always only partially in what Ingarden calls a 'perspectival foreshortening' (334). This is why concretizations not only differ from reader to reader but are never identical from one reading to the next.

Although the work differs from its concretization with regard to all of its strata to some extent (337–9), the most important differences are to be found on the stratum of schematized aspects, for 'from mere preparedness [*Parathaltung*] and schematization in the work itself, aspects attain concreteness in the concretization and are raised to the level of ... imaginational experience' so that the schematic structures become 'fleshed out,' so to speak, in the reader's imagination. These 'completions,' which although programmed to a certain degree by the

18 Roman Ingarden, *The Literary Work of Art*, 30. The emphasis is Ingarden's as in all other quotations from this text unless otherwise indicated.

schematized aspects are never wholly determined by the latter, are another reason why any two concretizations of one and the same work necessarily differ from each other (339). They tend to reduce the number of what are referred to as 'spots of indeterminacy,' a concept that we shall subsequently see Wolfgang Iser put to good use. It is the existence of these blanks that distinguishes represented objectivities – that is, objects offering themselves up for visualization in the imagination – from real objects. As these spots of indeterminacy tend to disappear through concretization, represented objects 'appear in a much fuller form than they possess *de facto* in the work itself,' for the objects represented in a literary work are, according to their identity, almost exclusively of the nature of real objects, that is to say, fully determined objects, and so the reader is predisposed to apprehend them as such in his concretization of the work (341–2). This is, however, only an impression or illusion since, in fact, spots of indeterminacy can never be eliminated entirely and in the passage between the work and its concretization, represented objects can never be completed (341), that is, wholly 'filled in,' as it were, by the reader's imagination. This impression nonetheless suffices to facilitate the suspension of disbelief[19] that is indispensable to all novel reading. A

19 Catherine Kerbrat-Orecchioni provides a useful definition of the concept of 'suspension of disbelief' when she gives the following account of the fictional trope:
'[Le trope fictionnel] contraint ... son récepteur
– à identifier d'abord le sens littéral,
– à le reconnaître comme trompeur, dissimulant en fait un sens dérivé qui fonctionne en contexte comme le *vrai* sens de la séquence,
– de telle sorte qu'une fois atteint ce vrai sens, le sens littéral, quoique invalidé par cette découverte, ne soit pas pour autant oblitéré totalement, ainsi que le dit fort bien Fontanier: "... il faut que celui qui écoute puisse partager jusqu'à un certain point l'illusion, et ait besoin d'un peu de réflexion pour n'être pas dupe." Le récepteur d'un trope doit à la fois partager l'illusion (que constitue le sens littéral), et n'en être pas dupe (savoir que le vrai sens est ailleurs): c'est un sujet dédoublé – nous dirons même, usant ici d'un concept freudien, un sujet *clivé: je sais bien* que c'est le sens dérivé qui est le bon, *mais quand même*, je persiste à croire, même après répudiation, au sens littéral. Ce qui donne, appliqué au cas particulier du trope fictionnel: je sais bien qu'il s'agit d'une fiction, mais quand même, je persiste à croire "quelque part" que tout cela s'est passé "pour de vrai".'
('Le Statut référentiel des textes de fiction,' 137). With regard to this 'sujet dédouble' or 'clivé,' see Ricoeur's concept of a 'split' reference, which he substitutes, in *The Rule of Metaphor* (224), for that of the 'suspended' reference. His treatment of metaphor (see 'Metaphor and Reference' in *The Rule of Metaphor* 216–55) will be considered in more detail in the chapter devoted to Blanchot's *Au Moment voulu.*

further factor militating in favour of the reader's being able to subscribe to the reality of what he is experiencing through concretization is that, because of the complexity of the demands the work makes on its reader, he is obliged to mask off everything *other than* his apprehension of the work, and 'there is ... an involuntary thrusting-aside and suppression of all those experiences and psychic states belonging to the rest of the given reader's real world.' This enables what is depicted to constitute a quite separate world for him, existing independent of everyday reality (334–5).

Although every concretization is quite distinct from the work,[20] this does not mean, Ingarden is at pains to stress, that concretizations are 'anything psychic or in any way an element of experience' (335). This point is, of course, a crucial one as far as the intersubjective verifiability of the product of concretization mentioned earlier is concerned and hence the possibility of its constituting a feasible object of study, whether it be for the critic – as in the subsequent chapters of this book – or for the theoretician: '... just as a rainbow is not something psychic, even though it exists concretely only when a visual perception is effected under certain objective circumstances, so also the concretization of a literary work, though it is conditioned in its existence by corresponding experiences, has at the same time its second ontic basis in the literary work itself; and with respect to the experiences of apprehension, it is just as transcendent as the literary work itself' (335–6). Such then is Ingarden's response to this important matter of the concretization's status. No less important – this time for the validity and indeed feasibility of Ingarden's whole enterprise – is the point made by Sartre at the outset of his analogous enterprise in formulating, in *L'Imaginaire*, a phenomenological psychology of imagination itself when he states that it is 'nécessaire de répéter ... ce qu'on sait depuis Descartes: une conscience réflexive nous livre des données absolument certaines.'[21] It is this fact that indeed makes concretization accessible and available to us for the purposes of analysis.

20 Here, however, it should be noted that as readers, we are generally not aware of the difference between our concretization and the actual work for the simple reason that 'we do not turn our attention to the concretization *as such* but to the work *itself*' (337).

21 *L'Imaginaire*, 16. Sartre goes on to develop this point thus: 'D'où vient alors, dira-t-on, l'extrême diversité des doctrines? Les psychologues devraient tomber d'accord pour peu qu'ils se réfèrent à ce savoir immédiat. Nous répondons que la plupart des psychologues ne s'y réfèrent pas d'abord. Ils gardent le savoir à l'état implicite et préfèrent bâtir des hypothèses explicatives touchant la nature de

I do not, however, wish to leave the question of the possibility of verifying the content of a given novel's concretization at that, for it is too crucial a matter for the task I have set myself in the following chapters. What it is essential to establish here is the existence of some form of common denominator to be found within *all* the concretizations a particular novel may give rise to. Such a common denominator is to be located in the distinction between signification and symbolization made from within a linguistic – as opposed to Ingarden's philosophical – perspective by one of the major contemporary French poeticians, Tzvetan Todorov. At the same time, such a distinction – articulated in an essay constituting one of the rare occasions on which a poetician has addressed the problem of concretization in the novel[22] – will enable us subsequently to make the transition to the second stage of the referential process, articulating, as it does, the interface between the first and second levels of reference. For those two reasons, I shall present Todorov's argument in some detail.

His opening remarks as he situates the problem already conclude by making a point that could not be more pertinent for present purposes: 'In literary studies, the problem of reading has been posed from two opposite perspectives. The first concerns itself with readers, their social, historical, collective, or individual invariability. The second deals with the image of the reader as it is represented in certain texts: the reader as character or as "narratee." There is, however, an unexplored area situated between the two: the domain of the logic of reading. *Although it is not represented in the text, it is nonetheless anterior to individual variations*' (67).[23] This 'domain of the logic of reading' is none other than that marked out by the activity of constructing a fiction that, of course, lies at the core of any act of concretization, and the poetician sees it as *preceding* any individual variations in the act in question. There is thus posited a distinction, a line of demarcation, *within* the concretization process itself between what is common to all readers of a given text and what is particular to each one of them. This distinction rests on the further distinction, mentioned earlier, between signification and symbolization. The lat-

---

l'image. Celles-ci, comme toutes les hypothèses scientifiques, n'auront jamais qu'une certaine probabilité: les données de la réflexion sont certaines' (16).

22 'Reading as Construction,' 67–82. Owen Miller's discussion of this essay, 'Reading as a Process of Reconstruction,' 19–27, is pertinent from the present perspective in that it attempts to situate (re)construction in relation to both structuralist and hermeneutic principles.

23 My emphasis

ter results from the two different ways in which a text evokes the facts that go to make up or 'to construct an imaginary world' (68). Taking Constant's *Adolphe* as an illustration, Todorov comments: 'Ellénore's trip to Paris is *signified* by the words in the text. Adolphe's (ultimate) weakness is *symbolized* by other factors in the imaginary universe, which are themselves signified by words. For example, Adolphe's inability to defend Ellénore in social situations is signified; this in turn symbolizes his inability to love.'[24] And he sums up the distinction thus: 'Signified facts are *understood*: all we need is knowledge of the language in which the text is written. Symbolized facts are *interpreted*[25] and interpretations vary from one subject to another' (73).[26] For this theoretician, what is signified arises from what he calls 'the author's account' and constitutes 'the imaginary universe evoked by the author,' whereas what is symbolized arises from 'the reader's account' and constitutes 'the imaginary universe constructed by the reader' (73), the former being 'richer' – an unexpected epithet to come from a poetician's pen – than the latter, owing of course, one might add, to the polysemous nature of the text from which the reader derives a particular Gestalt, here a coherent and consistent fictional universe. Todorov makes my point quite explicitly here when he says: 'We could question whether there really is a difference between stage 2 [the universe evoked by the author] and 3 [that constructed by the reader] ... *Is there such a thing as a nonindividual construction? It is easy to show that the answer must be positive*' (73). In other words, here Todorov's account of the 'construction' of the fictional universe by the reader concurs with Ingarden's analysis of concretization in establishing that the process in question is indeed open to intersubjective verification. The poetician thus confirms the phenomenologist while at the same time usefully elucidating for us this dimension of the phenomenon.

At this point, I would draw the reader's attention to the fact that in the analyses of specific novels in the chapters that follow – up to and including the chapter devoted to *Au Moment voulu* at least – I endeavour to situate the 'reading' of the text on the level of what is signified, leaving aside, as far as that is possible, what is symbolized.

24 Todorov's emphasis
25 Later in the article, he unfortunately and inexplicably speaks rather of *reinterpre-tation*: 'After we have constructed the events that compose a story, we begin the task of reinterpretation' (75).
26 Todorov's emphasis

It would then appear to follow from Todorov's remarks that I deal not with 'the reader's account' of the text but with 'the author's account.' Does this mean therefore that, by the same token, 'the imaginary universe constructed by the reader' is not my concern? Clearly not, since such an 'imaginary universe' is precisely the form that concretization necessarily takes. The nature of the problem now becomes clear: the distinction *between* the two levels of what is evoked by any text is very difficult to establish with any degree of precision, and they are both a part of what is concretized. Moreover, it is, in my view, virtually impossible to *maintain* – that is to respect – such a distinction within a given analysis of a work's reception.[27] To do so would, at the very least, call for an even more detailed and fastidious form of minute analysis than that found in the following pages and would have resulted in a book easily twice as long. Why one needs, nonetheless, to recognize this fine distinction between what one might call, in the manner of Ingarden, these two 'layers' of concretization is that without it, the 'readings' below could be considered to be particular to the author of this study alone and to shed no light on the way anyone else might read the same works. What is at stake then is nothing less than the precise status of the proposed 'readings' – the ambiguity of the very term 'reading' (when does a reading become an interpretation?) could not be more revealing in this respect. And the status of the 'readings' cannot be divorced from that of the 'reader.'

A word then about the 'reader' who figures in the following chapters. It is precisely because of the need to focus on the initial level of concretization corresponding to what is signified that our 'reader' no doubt, at times, gives the impression of being exceptionally literal-minded. The fact of the matter is that to concentrate on the *referential* dimension of any literary text means to concentrate on its *literal* meaning, on what it refers to (albeit in a fictional mode) most directly and obviously. It is my awareness of the 'literal-mindedness' of the analyses below that leads me to speak of 'a certain perversity' in the discussion of Simon's *Histoire*. The same might well be said of the study of Blanchot's *Au Moment voulu*, the concretization of which, if it were to be read as a poem rather than as a work of fiction, would not pose a problem either to the same degree or in the same manner. For this reason stress must be laid on the very particular perspective

---

27 Owen Miller quite rightly questions whether 'in any practical manner the two processes [signification and symbolization] can be distinguished' ('Reading as a Process of Reconstruction,' 24).

adopted in the studies of the novels considered here and the concomitant fact that *none of them either seeks or claims to give an overall, comprehensive account of the novel under scrutiny*. In other words, a certain literal-mindedness is inseparable from any concern for referentiality and is to be viewed in these pages as a heuristic device.

How, then, does the transition between the first and second levels of reference come about? The transition is crucial to the account of literary referentiality presented here, for there can be no disputing the existence or character of the first level of reference that has been my concern so far. Just as 'ways of worldmaking,' to use Nelson Goodman's expression,[28] engage the attention of the philosopher, so the 'fictional worlds' discussed by Thomas Pavel[29] are necessarily central to any reflection on the phenomenon of literature. Novels, in particular, are inseparable from the worlds they invite their readers to inhabit. What is more problematic is the reference that lies beyond and outside the world of the fiction as such, on the way to which the latter is but a transitional stage and for which it is the necessary prerequisite. It is this level of reference that directly engages the existential being of the reader and marks the crossing-over from fictional reference to 'real' reference, that is, reference as it functions in non-literary language. As can be seen subsequently, the conceptualization of the passage between the two levels of literary reference is essential for any adequate account to be given of a work such as Camus' *La Chute*, and Beckett's *L'Innommable* validates in an exemplary manner the second and final stage in the referential process at work in all fiction. That is why this present sketching out of the way reference functions in literary discourse is an essential prerequisite and preparation for the studies of the novels below. What needs to be emphasized, however, is the *inter*dependence of this chapter and those that follow. For the present pages are in no wise to be construed as an aprioristic model that, in any sense *determines* the content or nature of the analyses of the novels. They can more appropriately be conceived of as the result of – as opposed to the reason for – the latter.[30] Consequently, the extent to which the reader finds the analyses of the coming chapters convincing will determine, in my view, the validity of the present

28 *Ways of Worldmaking*
29 *Fictional Worlds*
30 My reader will recognize here a manner of proceeding characteristic of the literary critic in contradistinction to the strategy of most contemporary theoreticians.

exposition, for they alone will be able to illuminate and flesh out this brief account of reference in the novel.

Let us now return briefly to the first level of reference. Before scrutinizing the process of concretization, we noted a kind of blocking off of the normal (non-literary) functioning of reference that operated on the level of the individual word. This has led Paul Ricoeur to describe the referential process as having been 'suspended'[31] in the case of the literary text, or, if one prefers, deferred to a later point in time. What reactivates the process is the act of reading, for 'it is precisely the task of reading, as interpretation, to actualize the reference.'[32] While the initial act of reading actualizes the fictive referents, producing their concretization in the mind's eye of the reader, the act of interpretation completes the work's reference since it is through the reader's interpretation of the work that the world of the novel and that of the reader merge into each other. It becomes a question of 'imaginatively actualis[ing] the potential non-ostensive references of the text in a new situation, that of the reader.'[33] That is why the perspective that now has to be adopted to pursue this exposition is a hermeneutic one as elaborated by the author of *Interpretation Theory*. The final stage in the process of the realization of the reference can be succinctly explicated thus: 'In one manner or another poetic texts speak about the world. But not in a descriptive way ... The effacement of the ostensive and descriptive reference liberates a power of reference to aspects of our being in the world which cannot be said in a direct descriptive way, but only alluded to, thanks to the referential values of metaphoric and, in general, symbolic expression.'[34]

To sum up my argument so far, whether one considers that all the fictive referents combine to form, in George Lavis's terms, a new referent or, as Maurice-Jean Lefebve puts it, a new signifier,[35] or

---

31 See *Interpretation Theory*, 80.
32 Ricoeur, 'What Is a Text? Explanation and Interpretation,' 138
33 *Interpretation Theory*, 81
34 Ricoeur, 'Writing as a Problem for Literary Criticism and Philosophical Hermeneutics,' 10
35 This two-level functioning of the reference is in keeping with the analogous multi-level semantic functioning of the text as analyzed by Iouri Lotman whereby 'un élément syntagmatique à un niveau de la hiérarchie du texte artistique devient un élément sémantique à un autre niveau.' Likewise the coalescing of all the fictive referents/signifiers to form a new global referent/signifier is due precisely to the fact that 'le texte est un signe achevé, et tous les signes isolés du texte linguistique général y sont ramenés au niveau d'éléments du signe' (*La Structure du texte artistique*, 50, 53).

whether, like Paul Ricoeur, one speaks of a suspended reference, the result is fundamentally the same: rather than being devoid of any referent, the literary text clearly possesses not *one* but *two* levels of reference, each being activated in turn.[36] The first functions in a solely imaginative mode as the reader conjures up for himself the world originally conceived of by the novelist, with its imaginary inhabitants and the events and experiences making up their lives. The second is the sequel and the logical consequence of the first, as the reader relates the total experience afforded by his reading of the novel to his own existential situation.

Let us now turn our attention to the second level of reference. The philosopher Nelson Goodman makes the point that worlds are always made from other pre-existing worlds. This calls to mind Hans-Georg Gadamer's[37] concept of the fusion of horizons that, in my view, has to inform any contemporary hermeneutic conception of the reception of the literary work.[38] This means that the reader inevitably brings to the horizon – or world – of the novel he is reading his own horizon – or world – and that the two come together to form a new horizon. Now the creation of a new world for the reader as a result of the experience afforded him by the novel is the direct result of the realization of the second level of reference, of the falling away of the parentheses that fictivity or literariness placed around the normal, everyday reference of the text's discourse.

36 Although in an admittedly less obvious way, Nelson Goodman's point about the reality of fictional worlds is in keeping with this conception of reference in fiction functioning on two levels: 'Fiction ..., whether written or painted or acted, applies truly neither to nothing nor to diaphanous possible worlds but, albeit metaphorically, to actual worlds ... the so-called possible worlds of fiction lie within actual worlds. Fiction operates in actual worlds in much the same way as nonfiction. Cervantes and Bosch and Goya, no less than Boswell and Newton and Darwin, take and unmake and remake familiar worlds, recasting them in remarkable and sometimes recondite but eventually recognizable – *re-cognizable* – ways' (*Ways of Worldmaking*, 104–5; Goodman's emphasis). Just as the 'real' reference *recedes behind* the fictive reference, so 'possible worlds of fiction *lie within* actual worlds.' Tzvetan Todorov remarks in a similar vein that 'there does not seem to be a big difference between construction based on a literary text and construction based on a referential but nonliterary text' and that ' "fiction" is not constructed any differently from "reality" ' (see 'Reading as Construction,' 80–1).

37 See *Truth and Method*. For an excellent exposition of his thought, see Robert Palmer's chapter on Gadamer in *Hermeneutics*.

38 See Robert Palmer's excellent presentation of this traditional branch of literary studies in *Hermeneutics*.

Paul Ricoeur's writings best illuminate this second level of reference, which is contingent upon the effacement or thwarting of the
first level, for it is the resulting 'abolition of a first order reference'
that 'is the condition of possibility for the freeing of a second order
reference, which reaches the world not only at the level of manipulable objects, but,' as Ricoeur puts it, 'at the level that Husserl designated
by the expression *Lebenswelt* [life-world] and Heidegger by the expression "being-in-the-world."'[39] What is implicated here is the reader's
overall and fundamental existential situation. It should be noted that
the concept of the 'world' of which Ricoeur speaks in a number of
places in his works (as when he states that 'hermeneutics can be
defined ... as the explication of the being-in-the-world displayed by
the text' or that 'what is to be interpreted is a proposed world which I
could inhabit and in which I could project my ownmost possibilities'[40])
appears to correspond neither to the world that is the final outcome
of the merging of the work's horizon and the reader's nor to the fictive
universe in the form of what is immediately and directly evoked by
the fictive referents as mental images in the concretization of the
work. However, what is clear from his statement that understanding
a text involves grasping 'the world-propositions opened up by the
reference of the text' and following 'its movement from sense to reference: from what it says, to what it talks about'[41] is that in relation
to Gadamer's horizons, Ricoeur's world[42] or 'being-in-the-world' is

39 'The Hermeneutical Function of Distanciation,' 141
40 'Phenomenology and Hermeneutics,' 112
41 *Interpretation Theory*, 87
42 Since this will be relevant to our study of Blanchot's *Au Moment voulu*, I would
like to add that with the appearance of *La Métaphore vive* in 1975, a more
detailed account of the nature of this proposed world was provided by the French
philosopher in the context of his discussion of the reference of metaphor. He
speaks of the world of the work arising from the *structure* of the work, its structure
being its sense and its world its reference, and says that a work refers to a given
world 'by virtue of its "arrangement," its "genre," and its "style" ' ('Metaphor
and Reference,' 220), these features therefore being synonymous with its structure. Now whereas the work's 'arrangement' could conceivably include the topog-
raphy of its fictive universe, that is clearly not the case with regard to either its
'genre' or its 'style.' He also defines the work's structure as being 'to the complex
work what sense is to the simple statement' just as the world of the work 'is to
the work what the denotation is to the statement' (220). The final realization of
reference that had been suspended on the level of the fiction is now seen to be
achieved through the functioning of metaphor or, as Ricoeur puts it, 'it may be,
indeed, that the metaphorical statement is precisely the one that points out
most clearly this relationship between suspended reference and displayed refer-

clearly situated on the side of the work's rather than the reader's horizon.[43]

It is important to appreciate that the world proposed by the work is in fact not an *actual* world at all but a *potential* world, which the reader only eventually comes to actualize once he embarks upon his reading of the novel: it is a latent possibility waiting to be realized. 'Through fiction and poetry,' as Ricoeur puts it, 'new possibilities of being-in-the-world are opened up within everyday reality. Fiction and poetry intend being, not under the modality of being-given, but under the modality of power-to-be.' So it is therefore that 'everyday reality is ... metamorphised [sic] by what could be called the imaginative variations which literature carries out on the real.'[44] The world offered up by the work should not be construed as somehow lying beyond or behind the text as a kind of meaning that can only be reached by passing through language (or the signifier) to reach the meaning (or signified). On the contrary, it is situated on this side of the text, which is why it allows ready access to the reader. In fact, it is as though it unfurled in front of the text, offering itself up to and coming halfway to meet its reader. Thus it is that it becomes subject to appropriation: 'Ultimately, what I appropriate is a proposed world. The latter is not *behind* the text, as a hidden intention would be, but *in front of* it, as that which the work unfolds, discovers, reveals.' When the reader's horizon engages with the work's horizon, the reader finds himself embarked upon a voyage of self-discovery as he attempts to come to grips and to terms with a new reality embodied in the world of the work. To understand involves nothing less than '*to understand oneself in front of the text.*' The term *appropriation* suggests the action of taking hold of something in the manner one grasps an object. Here, however, there is a reciprocal, dialectical relationship involved whereby the reader makes himself available to the work just as the

---

ence': 'Just as the metaphorical statement captures its sense as metaphorical midst the ruins of the literal sense, it also achieves its reference upon the ruins of what might be called ... its literal reference' (221). Here reference functions not at the level of units of discourse or sentences but at the level of the totality of a work: 'If the metaphorical statement is to have a reference, it is through the mediation of the "poem" as *an ordered, generic, and singular totality*' (221–2; my emphasis).

43 Ricoeur, in fact, makes this clear when he writes: 'Above all, the *vis-à-vis* of appropriation is what Gadamer calls "the matter of the text" and what I call "the world of the work" ' ('The Hermeneutical Function of Distanciation,' 143).

44 Ibid., 142

work offers itself to the reader. Thus 'it is not a question of imposing on the text our finite capacity of understanding, but of exposing ourselves to the text and receiving from it an enlarged self,[45] which would be the proposed existence corresponding in the most suitable way to the world proposed.' And this new 'self is constituted by the "matter" of the text.'[46] Just as the world of the work presents itself to us in the mode of the potential, so it calls upon the potential of the reader himself, his potential as being-in-the-world.

This is why there is no appropriation of the work by the reader that is not accompanied, if not preceded, by the disappropriation of his self: 'To appropriate is to make what was alien become one's own. What is appropriated is indeed the matter of the text. But the matter of the text becomes my own only if I disappropriate myself, in order to let the matter of the text be. So I exchange the me, master of itself, for the self, disciple of the text.'[47] This latter distinction is clarified elsewhere when Ricoeur distinguishes between 'the self which emerges from the understanding of the text' and 'the ego which claims to precede this understanding.' It is this pre-existing ego that is left behind when the reader approaches the text the reading of which reveals to the reader his own self: '... the text, with its universal power of unveiling ... gives a self to the ego.'[48] So it is that paradoxically appropriation involves a process of self-discovery by giving 'the subject new capacities for knowing himself.'[49] What is involved here is perhaps best grasped by the image of foregrounding and backgrounding, whereby the pre-existent ego is backgrounded. Wolfgang Iser develops the concept of the interplay between appropriation and disappropriation occurring within the reading experience itself when he writes: 'In thinking the thoughts of another' conveyed by the text, the reader 'temporarily leaves his own disposition, for he is concerned with something which until now had not been covered by and could not have

45 Lefebve would no doubt speak rather of an *essential* self, for he remarks that the fact that the signified is cut off from its practical referent 'permet ... à l'œuvre de s'ouvrir sur la totalité de notre expérience, mais en en dégageant par là même de cette expérience ce qu'elle a d'essentiel' (*Structure du discours*, 111).
46 'The Hermeneutical Function of Distanciation,' 143–4; Ricoeur's emphasis
47 'Phenomenology and Hermeneutics,' 113; Ricoeur's emphasis. Ricoeur expresses the same idea more succinctly when he says that 'it is in allowing itself to be carried off towards the reference of the text that the *ego* divests itself of itself' ('Appropriation,' 191).
48 'Appropriation,' 193; Ricoeur's emphasis
49 Ibid., 192

arisen from the orbit of his personal experience;'[50] he 'has to make himself present to the text, and so leave behind him that which has hitherto made him what he is' (156–7). Iser thus enables us to trace back to its origin in the actual manner of 'presentification' of the novelistic universe in the reader's imagination the grounding of the new self born of what this theoretician sees as 'a kind of artificial division as the reader brings into his own foreground something which he is not.' This 'does not mean, though, that his own orientations disappear completely' since 'they still form the background against which the prevailing thoughts of the author take on thematic significance' (155).

If the texts of novelists such as Bernanos and Beckett possess the power to change the existence[51] of those who live in their presence over the years, it is because they call upon the depths of their reader's being, revealing to him previously inaccessible dimensions of which he had been unaware. In this sense, what we read in the text is ultimately ourselves, so that, in Ricoeur's words, 'we understand ourselves only by the long detour of the signs of humanity deposited in cultural works.'[52] What I have been describing here is, of course, none other than the hermeneutic activity itself.[53]

From the foregoing exposition, it would appear that Ricoeur, contrary to Iser, places the process of appropriation as the last in a series of procedures the reader is involved in through his reading of a given work, and that the 'lifting' of the suspension of reference brought about by the fictional character of the novel's discourse can only be effected subsequent to its initial suspension. If this is so, then his position clearly differs from that of Gadamer also, for whom the fusion

50 *The Act of Reading*, 156
51 Iser speaks of 'the impressions readers sometimes have of experiencing a transformation in reading,' which he attributes to the 'forgetting [of] oneself' (156). He essentially concurs with Ricoeur's account of appropriation, although he locates it, as I do (see below), at the very first level of the decoding of the text: '... the constitution of meaning not only implies the creation of a totality emerging from interacting textual perspectives ... but also, through formulating this totality, it enables us to formulate ourselves and thus discover an inner world of which we had hitherto not been conscious' (158).
52 'The Hermeneutical Function of Distanciation,' 143; Ricoeur's emphasis
53 This is made explicit when he speaks of 'the *power of a work* to project a world of its own and to set in motion the hermeneutical circle, which encompasses in its spiral both the apprehension of projected worlds and the advance of self-understanding in the presence of these new worlds' ('Metaphor and the Problem of Hermeneutics,' 171; Ricoeur's emphasis).

of horizons (*Horizontverschmelzung*) is operative from the very out-set of one's reading of the text and continues to evolve hand in hand with the latter, so to speak. Moreover, it will be clear to my reader from the initial discussion of the fictive referent within a linguistic perspective that I concur with Gadamer here in holding that the fusion of horizons already plays a role in our actualization of the referent through the concretization of the world of the fiction. As we read on on our way through the novel this merging of horizons gradually takes on greater scope through a cumulative effect, its sweep progressively broadening to encompass more and more of the two horizons as they interface with each other, even if their final consolidation[54] is brought about only when the reading has come to an end and given way to reflection.

Just as there emerged from Todorov's distinction between significa-tion and symbolization an awareness of a limit to the degree of inter-subjective verifiability possible in any discussion of concretization, similarly as I have plotted the course of the referential process in the preceding pages I have gradually moved step by step *away from* what can be demonstrated text in hand, so to speak, and agreed upon as being subject to objective verification. As was pointed out earlier, this explains why, in the present intellectual climate marked by a striving for scientificity and the recourse to linguistic models, so little atten-tion has been given to the phenomenon in question by theoreticians, poeticians, or literary critics.[55] At all events, we have now reached a point in the mapping out of the referential process beyond which it is doubtless impossible to proceed. In fact, the studies of *La Chute* and *L'Innommable* below represent, in my view, the only possible way to take the discussion further, that is to say, through the analysis of particular texts that go so far as to problematize the very act of

---

54 Here the term *consolidation* should be qualified with Jean-Paul Resweber's word of warning, with regard to this Gadamerian concept, against 'toute conception dialectique qui ferait, de l'horizon nouveau, la synthèse de l'horizon de l'auteur (thèse) et de celui de l'herméneute (anti-thèse). Car le nouvel horizon, né du glissement des deux horizons l'un sur l'autre, témoigne de la relation polémique que ceux-ci entretiennent. Il exprime leur différence comme étant le lieu de leur identité. De ce point de vue, on dira plus volontiers que l'interprète vient éveiller l'horizon de l'auteur, inscrire l'efficacité symbolique du texte et du comportement à l'horizon de ses préoccupations et, par conséquent, éveiller son propre horizon au contact de l'autre' (*Qu'est-ce qu'interpréter?*, 20).

55 It should be noted that even Ricoeur leaves aside the problem of concretization as such. Lefebve's study is an outstanding exception here, as is, of course, Wolfgang Iser's *The Act of Reading*, itself heavily indebted to Ingarden's work.

appropriation itself, thereby shifting the focus from the work to the reader and illuminating the ultimate reference of all literature. The fact that with this final development in the working out of the novel's reference we are dealing with not an actual but a potential world already suggested such a limitation. And nowhere is the power of the work to disclose a potential world, the potency of which derives for its reader precisely from its latency, more manifest than in Beckett's *L'Innommable*. The realization of this potential world comes about only through the reading process, and each reader brings to his reading his own world or *Weltanschauung*. It is the fascinating alchemy of the coming together of the two horizons about which it is, in the final analysis, impossible to generalize: the theoretical must yield to the empirical. Or in simpler terms, who would presume to be able to recognize the person who will finally walk away from the novel one is reading?

2

The Problematization of
Reference: Sartre's *La Nausée*

Sartre's *La Nausée*, like Bataille's *Histoire de l'œil*, represents the most extreme example of the problematization of reference in the novel, and it is therefore fitting that the studies of these two novels open and close respectively the series of chapters devoted to the analysis of specific works of fiction that make up the body of the present study. Whereas Bataille's text reveals how it is possible for the novel's reference to turn in upon itself and thus to be caught up in a process of linguistic *auto*-referentiality, Sartre's first novel thematizes the very topic this book addresses: the relationship between language and what it designates, non-linguistic reality. This gives rise to a situation that could not be more delicate in terms of the problems it poses in order to be able to take its place within and to be integrated into the present study. However, at the same time, *La Nausée* most conveniently lays out and analyses in the fictional mode the initial and most fundamental task faced by every writer who has ever taken up his pen to begin a novel or indeed any work of fiction: the use of language to create for his reader an imaginary universe analogous to the real world.

Thanks to the existence of this remarkable work that attempts to rise, like a phoenix, from the ashes of a language that has collapsed back into its original condition of aural and scriptable materiality to assume its most fundamental status as *matière langagière*, we are able to begin this series of novel studies in the self-referential mode just as we shall end it in like manner with Bataille's no less remarkable novel. In other words, I shall be analysing a work that itself sets out to do exactly what we are intending to undertake. The prospect faced is all the more daunting because the perspective adopted both by the author of *La Nausée* and by myself is a phenomenological one.[1] In this

---

1 'A Berlin [en 1933–1934] Sartre travaillait le matin sur Husserl ... et l'après-midi

particular sense and within the present context, one might say that Sartre attempts to make of the literary discourse of the novel a *meta-language*[2] inasmuch as his character and narrator, Roquentin, not only *experiences* the phenomena involved but also *comments upon* what he has experienced and is experiencing: 'la nausée' furnishes the *occasion* for Roquentin's writing of the text we have before us. Such is, of course, the fiction of the novel's narration and, in this case, of the diary(-novel)'s writing.

In fact, *La Nausée* – a work that pre-dates the advent of the French Nouveau Roman by more than a decade – brings into being and to aesthetic fruition a conception of literary self-reflexivity or auto-representation that is far more radical or fundamental than that which was later to hold sway in the novels of that younger generation of novelists whose works were promoted by a single publisher, Jérome Lindon of Les Editions de Minuit. In fact, Samuel Beckett is the only one of the latter writers who attains in his works the same degree of what one might call self-undermining self-referentiality. Thus, not until we broach *L'Innommable*, which, as we shall see, goes even further than Sartre's greatest novel in that it not only undermines but dissolves the very distinction between discourse and metalanguage, between literary language and all language, do we again encounter the phenomenon of auto-representation. However, auto-representation will

---

il écrivait *La Nausée* ... Qu'il y ait eu ... une certaine osmose entre le travail philosophique et le roman, que celui-ci ait bénéficié de la découverte de la phénoménologie, notamment par l'aquisition d'une formulation philosophique plus précise, cela n'est guère douteux au vu du texte final: *La Nausée* est bien un roman phénoménologique; elle l'est par le statut de la conscience qu'elle établit à travers le personnage de Roquentin, par la dissolution du sujet qu'elle opère, par son refus de la psychologie: Roquentin n'a pas de "caractère", pas d'ego substantiel, il est pure conscience *du* monde, son expérience n'est pas un voyage dans les profondeurs de l'intériorité, c'est au contraire un éclatement vers les choses; tout est dehors: la Nausée n'est pas *dans* Roquentin, c'est lui qui se dissout en elle' (Michel Contat and Michel Rybalka in Jean-Paul Sartre, *Œuvres romanesques*, 1664). It should be noted that it is precisely because of this 'éclatement vers les choses' that objects are centre-stage in this novel and that 'for the reader, as for the protagonist-narrator, the spotlight plays unceasingly on the fictive referents corresponding to the objects.

2 Here it is highly ironic that the editors of the new Pléiade critical edition of the text have defined the concept of 'la contingence' by citing the text of the novel: 'la meilleure définition de la contingence est sans doute celle donnée dans le texte même de *La Nausée*' (1660, n. 4). They thereby abolish the fictional status of the novel's *literary* discourse and ultimately place themselves within the world of the fiction.

continue to occupy us throughout our examination of Simon's *Histoire* and will culminate in that ultimate paroxysm of self-referentiality, *Histoire de l'œil*, where language becomes analogous to the fingers of a clenched fist.

Like Beckett's finest achievement, the diary of Antoine Roquentin puts into question the very possibility of literature itself and, by the same token, its own existence as literature. It does so, however, in a slightly more roundabout manner than its successor was later to do. That is partly because it reveals a more explicit and persistent parodic intent; that is true from its very first page with its 'Avertissement des éditeurs'[3] which echoes the 'Avis de l'éditeur' of a work such as *Adolphe*, for example, and is immediately followed by the first page of the novel proper, so to speak, headed 'Feuillet sans date' (5) with, at the bottom of the page, two footnotes: 'Un mot laissé en blanc.' and 'Un mot est raturé (peut-être "forcer" ou "forger"), un autre, rajouté en surcharge, est illisible.' This is, of course, a reflection of the literary convention, employed in many a traditional novel, whereby the first fictive referent the existence of which is posited by the text is none other than the actual physical document and book one is reading. In the case of Sartre's text, however, – and this must be stressed here – given the parodic mode of its discourse, what *would have been* in any eighteenth- or nineteenth-century novel the fictive referent yields to a purely literary referent: that category of traditional novelistic text that resorted to such a device in order to attempt to establish in its reader's mind the authenticity of what he was reading as a real, historical as opposed to fictional document. The difference between the two novels in this respect can be readily measured by the fact that corresponding to the passage taken from Balzac's *Eugénie Grandet* (58–9)[4] and cited in full in *La Nausée* is the single sentence in the first volume of Beckett's trilogy (of which *L'Innommable* is, of course, the third), *Molloy*: 'Mais ce n'est pas arrivé à ce point de mon récit que je vais me lancer dans la littérature.'[5]

It is no doubt because the parody of literature follows so naturally and inevitably on the heels of any critique – and hence potential parody – of language as a designator of anything other than itself that

3 All page references are to the latest Pléiade critical edition of the text, *Œuvres romanesques*, 3–210.
4 I do not suggest, however, that all the parodic elements of this novel are as explicit; see, for example, the Malrucian echoes in Jonathan Dale, 'Sartre and Malraux,' 335–46.
5 *Molloy*, 235

the focus of the present topic has become blurred for critics writing on Sartre's novel. The other reason why the auto-referentiality of *La Nausée* functions in a more roundabout manner than in *L'Innommable* is that the problem posed *explicitly* by the text through its commentary or metadiscourse in the fictional mode is a *philosophical* one. This has served to obscure the fact that the embodiment of the problem of referentiality within a literary work poses a subtly different *implicit* problem concerning the status of all literary discourse. The philosophico-linguistic problem posed by the non-necessary or arbitrary relation between signifier and signified (for the linguist), between language and reality (for the philosopher), naturally supersedes the literary problem of the status of the fictive referent. It goes without saying that to put the referent in question is, by terminological definition, to put the *fictive* referent in question – the one following from the other. When, however – and this is the crux of the matter here – the referent is put in question within the world of the literary work itself, a situation arises for which even the concept of 'problematization' is clearly inadequate. For when the problematization that is thematized, as it were, within the novel concerns the very possibility of language referring to anything other than itself, that problemization becomes reactivated to the point of undermining the vehicle of its original thematization. One might, therefore, speak here of a kind of metaproblematization process where the problematization itself becomes self-reflexive. This last formulation has the advantage of rendering the measure of the complexity of the situation. In simpler terms, if language is irreparably divorced from what it ostensibly signifies, how can such a situation be spoken or written about? And if language proves to be impotent, literary language would appear, in a sense, to be doubly so ...

What has so far hidden from critical view the crucial question of the fictive referent in *La Nausée* is that up to now the critics writing on this novel have focused on the *production* of language. This is only natural given the fact that Roquentin is himself writing a diary and is therefore confronting head-on, so to speak, the dilemma created for him who finds that language no longer signifies anything whatsoever. Within such a perspective, all that matters is that one receive some intimation of the distance Roquentin experiences as separating him not only from all that surrounds him physically but also from his very emotions and thoughts[6] – once language no longer serves to bridge

6 This intimation was analysed in detail in Fitch, *Le Sentiment d'étrangeté*, 95–139.

that gap by domesticating all that is other than human consciousness, that is, by labelling it and thus dissipating or at least attenuating its otherness. However, only when one shifts one's attention to the *reception* of the novel is the full nature of the dilemma brought home to one. At the same time, the examination of its implications for the reader draws attention to the challenge presented to that other writer, the novelist, Sartre himself. Given his main project to convey to his reader Roquentin's realization that there is no 'match' between the things around him, or indeed within his mind, and the names or linguistic labels intended to designate them, the question of what precise form Sartre *would have*, or might have, intended[7] the fictive referent to take in his novel – and I say 'would have' since his actual intentions are inaccessible to us – is not easy to answer. A better way to formulate the problem – since recourse to the author himself in any way is unacceptable to most contemporary literary theoreticians and critics – would be to remain resolutely within the context of the actual novel and ask ourselves exactly what kind of fictive referent would likely be evoked for the reader by Roquentin's self-interrogation concerning the nature of matter and its contingency, that is, the very thingness of things that is the source of their otherness and hence of man's potential sense of alienation not only from the world he lives in but also from his own corporeal existence.[8] Does it suffice for the reader to share Roquentin's dilemma of being unable to relate language to reality, in which case the fictive referent of the tree trunk the contemplation of which bemuses the protagonist would fail to materialize for the reader? But then how could this fail to affect the reader's concretization of Roquentin himself and the situation he finds himself in? And is it not necessary for the reader to concretize the tree trunk in all its materiality in order for the full force of its impact, of its thingness and hence otherness, on Roquentin to be brought home to him? Moreover, how can the reader be led to the realization of language's failure to exercise any referential function at the very moment that his reading and understanding of the novel and his concretization of Roquentin's dilemma resulting therefrom is constituting irrefutable proof of the contrary? In short, the referential power of language that ensures its functioning in everyday discourse is no different from that which is at work in literary discourse and ensures

---

7 I have profited here from the documentation in Contat and Rybalka's fine critical edition of the text.

8 Roquentin's subsequent further alienation from his own thoughts and emotions need not concern us here.

that novels can be read and understood: as was pointed out earlier, the latter presupposes the former.

We are now in a position to appreciate better the complexity of the situation confronting the critic who sets out to analyse the status of the fictive referent in *La Nausée*, a situation that leads me to maintain that this novel constitutes nothing less than an *aesthetic paradox* and its study a critical conundrum. It would, in fact, take a book-length study to do justice to the problems posed by Sartre's novel in this regard. The attempt above to shed some light on the matter does, however, for the purposes of the rest of the present study, go some way towards laying bare the complexity and subtlety of the linguistic, philosophic, and aesthetic issues at stake in any adequate account of the status and role of the fictive referent in the process of a text's concretization. There can be no doubt of the crucial place that *La Nausée* must occupy in any study of reference in the modern novel: in the most remarkable manner, it already problematizes the novels that were to succeed it and that most fundamental characteristic of the French novel from the 1950s onwards: its auto-referentiality – albeit in the form of linguistic[9] self-referentiality in contradistinction to the formal self-referentiality constituted by textual devices such as *mise en abyme*, which characterizes the French Nouveau Roman.

My previous study of Sartre's first novel[10] analysed in minute detail the nature and the gradual evolution of Roquentin's alienation as recorded in his diary. His alienation begins as a purely visual phenomenon but goes on to encompass all five senses. The story he tells is that of a world in which objects (begin to) exist for their own sakes and end up taking on the form of a kind of proliferating matter that progressively eliminates not only the *Lebensraum* of the human body but also that of the human consciousness. Such a proliferation recalls analogous phenomena in Ionesco's theatre, where, for example, it characterizes the existence of the corpse in *Amédée*. However, what concerns us here is rather the fact that a text that seeks, through its evocation of Roquentin's experience, to convey to the reader the realization of the autonomous existence of inanimate, or rather non-human objects, not to mention the philosophically more significant

---

9 That is, pertaining to language, as in the French term *langagière*, rather than to linguistics as a discipline.
10 'Le Mirage du moi idéal: *La Nausée* de Sartre,' in *Le Sentiment d'étrangeté*, 93–139

gratuitousness of the latter, would at first sight appear to need to offer up for concretization a fictive referent in its 'purest' form, in all the immediacy of its real-life equivalent, so that its impact upon the reader not be attenuated in any way and nothing be felt to stand between it and the reader.

The project Roquentin sets himself in undertaking to keep a diary is the following: 'Tenir un journal pour y voir plus clair ... Il faut dire comment je vois cette table, la rue, les gens, mon paquet de tabac, puisque c'est *cela* qui a changé' (5). 'Y voir plus clair' entails just that: elucidating the new way he now *sees* the things around him. 'Par exemple,' he continues, 'voici un étui de carton qui contient ma bouteille d'encre. Il faudrait essayer de dire comment je le voyais *avant* et comment à présent je le* ['Un mot laissé en blanc,' the 'editors' ' note at the bottom of the page tells us] Eh bien! c'est un parallélépipède rectangle, il se détache sur – c'est idiot, il n'y a rien à en dire' (5). Having identified the object ('un étui de carton') for the reader by designating its presence ('voici'), he attempts to describe it in abstract geometric terms and immediately realizes the futility of such an endeavour. The fact is that contrary to what may appear to be the case at first sight, mathematical discourse, although not representing a *personification* of the object as such in that it produces an *abstract representation* of the latter, does nonetheless constitute a *humanization* of material reality in that mathematics are a product of the human intellect.[11] What matters in the present context is that Sartre first posits the existence/presence of the cardboard container for the reader, allowing him to concretize the object *before* inciting him to share Roquentin's realization of the inadequacy of any verbal description of that object: having pictured the holder in his imagination, he[12] is then the better equipped to compare what he has imagined with the abstraction that characterizes any kind of geometric description. The latter can then only reinforce the impression the reader has of the material object's immediacy. In other words, in this passage the author, far from undermining or frustrating the reader's initial concretization of the object in question, builds on that initial concreti-

11 Robbe-Grillet failed to appreciate this when he attacked both Camus and Sartre for their recourse to humanizing metaphoric language in *L'Étranger* and *La Nausée* (see 'Nature, humanisme et tragédie'), while himself continuing to indulge in geometric descriptions in his own novels.

12 The occasional, stylistically unavoidable masculine personal pronoun and possessive adjective is intended to refer to both female and male readers in accordance with traditional linguistic usage.

zation in order subsequently to bring home to his reader the realization that detailed description fails to capture the reality of the object. The *logical* conclusion to be drawn from the reader's experience here – although it is not one that he will be likely to draw at this point – has to be that naming is a more effective vehicle for evocation than describing. For the novelist is himself *relying* on the power of naming to evoke what is named in the reader's consciousness precisely in order to convey to him Roquentin's realization.

Naming or direct designation is, however, soon abandoned, as in the scene where Roquentin looks into the mirror: 'Au mur, il y a un trou blanc, la glace' (22). Here identification follows immediately on the heels of the image of a white hole. But then the same procedure is repeated at more length: 'C'est un piège. Je sais que je vais m'y laisser prendre. Ça y est. *La chose grise* vient d'apparaître dans la glace. Je m'approche et je la regarde, je ne peux plus m'en aller.'[13] And then – but only then – we learn what this grey thing is: 'C'est le reflet de mon visage.' A whole page of description leads up to the following evocation: '... ce que je vois est bien au-dessous du singe, à la lisière du monde végétal, au niveau des polypes.' And this strange object is appropriately designated by the neutral 'ça': 'Ça vit, je ne dis pas non; mais ce n'est pas à cette vie-là qu'Anny pensait: je vois de légers tressaillements, je vois une chair fade que s'épanouit et palpite avec abandon. Les yeux surtout, de si près, sont horribles. C'est vitreux, mou, aveugle, bordé de rouge, *on dirait des écailles de poisson*' (23).[14] The metaphor, when it finally arrives, definitively divorces the eye from any conceivable human association; as in any enlarged close-up photograph of a part of the human body, the latter, with its immediate context masked off, loses all recognizable human attributes: '... j'approche mon visage de la glace jusqu'à la toucher. Les yeux, le nez disparaissent: il ne reste plus rien d'humain.' This is human life reduced to a painter's still life, and thus it is that the reader is led to picture it. The remainder of this evocation with the transformation of the non-human into the inanimate reminds one not so much of a painting as of another work of literature, Swift's *Gulliver's Travels*, where the hero contemplates close-up the physiological features of the giant inhabitants of Brobdingnag: 'Des rides brunes de chaque côté du gonflement fiévreux des lèvres, des crevasses, des taupinières. Un soyeux duvet blanc court sur les grandes pentes des joues, deux poils

13 My emphasis
14 My emphasis

sortent des narines: c'est *une carte géologique en relief.* Et, malgré tout, ce *monde lunaire* m'est familier' (23).[15]

The device by which an object is evoked, paradoxically, before being identified, in other words in an unrecognizable form, is characteristic of any phenomenological vision of reality.[16] It recurs, moreover, during one of the episodes in the café Mably: '… je vois de temps en temps, du coin de l'œil, un éclair rougeaud couvert de poils blancs. C'est une main' (25–6).

Earlier in his diary, Roquentin had in fact sought to avoid looking directly at a given object, which was only natural in view of the fact that it is the new and disconcerting manner in which things have begun to appear to him that he finds so disturbing. This gives rise to an intriguing situation when the reader attempts to concretize the fictive referent: '… voilà une demi-heure que j'évite de *regarder* ce verre de bière. Je regarde au-dessus, au-dessous, à droite, à gauche: mais *lui,* je ne veux pas le voir' (13). We are thus led to imagine all the space surrounding the beer glass – and hence what is tantamount to the silhouette of the latter – but not the glass itself, which we, following Roquentin's example, imagine averting our gaze from *in spite of the fact* that the beer glass has been explicitly designated as such. What we are, in fact, now led to imagine is none other than the *absence* of that glass, the volume of space it occupies as though it were not, however, actually occupying it! The rest of this passage is no less remarkable in that although an actual description of the beer glass is given, Roquentin puts it into the mouths of the other people in the café with him: '[Tous les célibataires qui m'entourent] me diraient: "Eh bien, qu'est-ce qu'il a, ce verre de bière? Il est comme les autres.

---

15 My emphasis
16 Sartre has himself commented on this feature of such a description of one's own face in his non-fiction work *L'Imaginaire* (see *Œuvres romanesques,* 1746, p. 26, n. 1). An analogous scene is to be found in Malraux's *La Condition humaine* when Clappique grimaces in the mirror: 'Il … s'approcha encore, le nez touchant presque la glace; il déforma son masque, bouche ouverte, par une grimace de gargouille … Il transforma son visage, bouche fermée et tirée vers le menton, yeux entrouverts, en samouraï de carnaval. … il commença à grimacer, se transformant en singe, en idiot, en épouvanté, en type à fluxion, en tous les grotesques que peut exprimer un visage humain. Ça ne suffisait plus: il se servit de ses doigts, tirant sur les coins de ses yeux, agrandissant sa bouche pour la gueule de crapaud de l'homme-qui-rit, tirant ses oreilles' (372). However, this evocation gives rise to a quite different comparison as when Paul-Raymond Côté writes: 'L'étonnante similitude avec les démons de Goya tels qu'exprimés dans *Les Caprices* n'est certainement pas fortuite' (*Les Techniques picturales chez Malraux,* 95).

Il est biseauté, avec une anse, il porte un petit écusson avec une pelle et sur l'écusson on a écrit 'Spatenbräu'.'' ' Let us note the introductory verb in the conditional tense here ('diraient'): Roquentin is only *imagining* the reaction of the other people. Nonetheless, through this device, the reader's concretization of the beer glass has been reinforced *without* this detracting from Roquentin-the-narrator's inability to verbalize his perception of the glass: 'Je sais tout cela, mais je sais qu'il y a autre chose. Presque rien. Mais je ne peux plus expliquer ce que je vois' (13). And the reader is thus able to share the character's own perplexity as he contemplates the glass. Let me spell this out even more explicitly: the reader is thereby able to concretize *both* the presence of the beer glass experienced in all its perceptual immediacy *and*, at the same time, the character's *in*ability to see that glass in any way comparable to the way in which he has been in the habit of seeing material objects – or, indeed, in any way comparable to the way the *reader* is used to perceiving them.

Pieces of paper play a very particular role in the experiences Roquentin has set out to record in his diary. He has always liked to pick them up when he has found them lying on the ground: 'En été ou au début de l'automne, on trouve dans les jardins des bouts de journaux que le soleil a cuits, secs et cassants *comme des feuilles mortes*, si jaunes qu'on peut les croire passés à l'acide picrique' (15).[17] This first comparison is an obvious one given the fact that in French the same word *feuille* serves to designate both a sheet of paper and the leaf from a tree. 'D'autres feuillets, l'hiver, sont pilonnés, broyés, maculés, ils retournent à la terre. D'autres tout neufs et même glacés, tout blancs, *tout palpitants*, sont posés *comme des cygnes*, mais déjà la terre les englue par en dessous.'[18] This second comparison is far more striking, and since all the sheets of paper can possibly share with swans is their immaculate whiteness, possessing as they do a quite different shape, it is, as with the beer glass (that is, at the beginning of the latter's evocation), through its absence, through the concretization of what it is *not* – the image of a swan – that the reader is led to imagine the sheet of paper. And the comparison is extended in the form of a metaphoric evocation of animation, completely in keeping with the life of a swan: 'Ils se tordent, ils s'arrachent à la boue, mais c'est pour aller s'aplatir un peu plus loin, définitivement' (15).

Another sheet of paper takes the form of that on which Roquentin

17 My emphasis
18 My emphasis

is writing and with which the ink from his pen fuses inseparably as it dries: '... je restai, la plume en l'air, à contempler ce papier éblouissant: comme il était dur et voyant, comme il était présent. Il n'y avait rien en lui que du présent. Les lettres que je venais d'y tracer n'étaient pas encore sèches et déjà elles ne m'appartenaient plus' (114). We can appreciate how the spatial phenomenon of presence and its temporal counterpart, the present, combine and complement each other to produce the effect of *immediacy*. (They are, in fact, linguistically inseparable in their common adjective.)

Previously,[19] I was at pains to show how this experience of Roquentin's illustrates the way in which our own thoughts no longer belong to us once they are set down in writing. This explains the fundamental distinction between oral discourse and written language, as was later to be stressed by theoreticians such as Paul Ricoeur,[20] although the perspective adopted by Ricoeur is that of the reader rather than that of the writer – in other words, the way we relate to the language of *another*. Once our thoughts, ideas, and feelings are externalized through their materialization in the form of paper and ink, all sense of intimacy with them is lost. It is memory alone that enables us to establish that we were responsible for their transcription. However, the moment we let ourselves become visually fascinated by their present presence, so to speak, all causal relationship with the words on the sheet of paper is lost. Our only link with them is then that which links any contemplating subject with any contemplated object: 'Cette phrase, je l'avais pensée, elle avait d'abord été un peu de moi-même. A présent, elle s'était gravée dans le papier, elle faisait bloc contre moi. Je ne la reconnaissais plus. Je ne pouvais même plus la repenser. Elle était là, en face de moi; en vain y aurais-je cherché une marque d'origine. N'importe qui d'autre avait pu l'écrire. Mais moi, *moi* je n'étais pas sûr de l'avoir écrite' (114).[21] Paradoxically, the effect of immediacy is contingent upon an awareness of an intact and uncrossable space separating one from the object concerned. For if the space in the first instance distances us from the object, it is nonetheless necessary in order to ensure the object's existential autonomy, guaranteeing its independent existence without which it would lack any specific identity. Thus the 'drawing back' of the self that is insisted

---

19 See *Le Sentiment d'étrangeté*, 121.
20 In *Interpretation Theory* in particular
21 Emphasis in the text, as for all other quotations from *La Nausée* unless otherwise indicated.

upon in the above passage is a prerequisite for any real appreciation of the presence of these traces of ink on paper in all their immediacy.

In spite of the fact that we are here concerned with a phenomenon of language, the concretization of this episode of the novel does not pose any of the problems foreseen in my introductory discussion of Sartre's novel above. This is because what is to be conveyed and evoked is precisely the *materialization* of language, and that can only facilitate the concretization of the phenomenon in question. Here the fictive referent in the form of the sheet of paper with writing on it is readily actualized within the reader's imagination. The stress on the sheer *presence* of the sentence on the sheet of paper, as an integral part of the latter, militates in favour of an impression of *immediacy*, and immediacy is no doubt the primary characteristic of all images produced by and experienced within the imagination and hence of fictive referents likewise.

It goes without saying that in a first-person diary narrative incarnating an existentialist *Weltanschauung*, an impression of immediacy is inseparable from an impression of otherness. The conclusion Roquentin comes to is the realization of the sheer *contingency* of things: 'Maintenant, je savais: les choses sont tout entières ce qu'elles paraissent – *et derrière elles...* il n'y a rien' (114). However, contingency, the arbitrariness of the existence enjoyed by all existing things, is a philosophic concept with philosophical consequences and it does not, in itself, affect the readiness with which the fictive referent can be actualized any more than the materialization of language did. As we shall see later, it is only when language itself becomes tarred with the same brush and its gratuitousness reduces it to impotence that the process of concretization is jeopardized.

The diary page is not the only sheet of paper to come to Roquentin's attention and to be submitted to his fascinated gaze. There are also the historical documents that are intended to serve in his writing of M. de Rollebon's biography: 'Pour expliquer la présence de ces papiers dans ma chambre, il n'eût pas été difficile de trouver cent autres histoires plus croyables: toutes, en face de ces feuillets rugueux, sembleraient creuses et légères comme des bulles' (115). Again the very materiality of the papers imposes their presence upon him and effaces the accessibility of the past, rendering the latter subject to interpretation and hypothetical reconstruction, there being no *necessary* reason for their presence at that time and place. We may note here that the fictive referent is no longer merely named – that is, evoked directly –

but is also designated by the narrator's spelling out what it is not in a procedure we shall see figuring prominently in Bernanos's novels: what the sheets of paper are *not* is 'creuses et légères comme des bulles.' It should be noted that this device already allows for the inadequacy of any form of direct or positive designation, that is, for the coming collapse of language's power to refer. In short, if language is no longer, for the mind and the imagination, a pointer to anything non-linguistic in character, it is only logical to use it to designate precisely those phenomena whose *non-existence* is being posited.

Then there is the seat Roquentin is sitting on in the streetcar before he gets off to enter the park. This is the object that sets off his most devastating experience of alienation, culminating in his awareness of all the implications of the existence of the famous chestnut tree, which I shall come to in a moment: 'Ils l'ont faite tout exprès pour qu'on puisse s'asseoir, ils ont pris du cuir, des ressorts, de l'étoffe, ils se sont mis au travail, avec l'idée de faire un siège et quand ils ont eu fini, c'était *ça* qu'ils avaient fait ... Je murmure: c'est une banquette, un peu comme un exorcisme. Mais le mot reste sur mes lèvres: il refuse d'aller se poser sur la chose' (148). Here all the demonstrative force of the indeterminate and indeterminable 'ça,' already encountered earlier, bears the brunt of conjuring up the object in question within the reader's imagination, the sense of immediacy being reinforced by its deictic function as a part of speech whose semantic content is wholly dependent on the circumstances in which it is employed by the writer (here, the fictional writer Roquentin and not the novelist). Not only does his reminding himself of how such a thing came into being – of the materials from which it has been made and the stages it has gone through before assuming its final form – fail to explain its present existence, the past revealing itself once again to be undeducible from the present, but the pristine purity of its sheer presence holds at bay even the very words that would seek to encompass and contain it through the process of naming: 'Les choses se sont délivrées de leurs noms. Elles sont là, grotesques, têtues, géantes et ça paraît imbécile de les appeler des banquettes ou de dire quoi que ce soit sur elles ...' (148). Naming will prove to be no less problematic in Bernanos's novels. Language has peeled away, as it were, from the brute reality of matter that it has heretofore served to domesticate by neutralizing its otherness, by translating it into properly human terms – language, of course, being man's creation. The potential set of problems outlined in the introduction to this analysis now begins to emerge. The fictive referent, once it is deprived of its normal, indeed its *only* vehicle, has to emerge *in spite* of its escaping its dependency on language, through other means yet to be explored.

Roquentin's observation that things have been freed of their linguistic labels was directly preceded by an evocation of what the streetcar seat is *not*: '[La chose] reste ce qu'elle est, avec sa peluche rouge, milliers de petites pattes rouges, en l'air, toutes raides, de petites pattes mortes. Cet énorme ventre tourné en l'air, sanglant, ballonné – boursouflé avec toutes ses pattes mortes, ventre qui flotte dans cette boîte, dans ce ciel gris, ce n'est pas une banquette' (148). The seat has become unrecognizable for the protagonist, as has therefore the referent conjured up by the reader's imagination. However, it must be stressed that the referent concerned does not correspond to any material object (in the fictional mode) whatsoever: what the reader concretizes here is a mental image produced by Roquentin's imagination. '... ce n'est pas une banquette,' – that is, not only is it impossible to associate such a phenomenon with the word *banquette*, but what the character is *visualizing* is not the object in front of him. Perceived real space – since Roquentin is still contemplating the seat, not having for a moment closed his eyes – has become intermingled with imaginational space: 'Ça pourrait tout aussi bien être un âne mort, par exemple, ballonné par l'eau et qui flotte à la dérive, le ventre en l'air dans un grand fleuve gris, un fleuve d'inondation ...' (148). It is because of the reader's inevitable awareness that Roquentin's senses are at this point betraying him and that he is no longer *seeing* what he is looking at, that the (fictionally) real, material referent is here evoked indirectly through the (direct) evocation of its absence, the imaginational space occupied by the donkey.

As he stands in front of the tree a moment later, it, too, becomes unnamable, just as man himself will subsequently take on, for Beckett, the anonymous traits of 'l'innommable': 'La racine du marronnier s'enfonçait dans la terre, juste au-dessous de mon banc. Je ne me rappelais plus que c'était une racine. Les mots s'étaient évanouis et, avec eux, la signification des choses, leurs modes d'emploi, les faibles repères que les hommes ont tracés à leur surface' (150). The veil of linguistic nomination devised by man to make things more livable-with, to tame and domesticate their innate otherness, has fallen away from its object to reveal the latter in all its strangeness, as it really is:

Jamais, avant ces derniers jours, je n'avais pressenti ce que voulait dire 'exister.' J'étais comme les autres ... Je disais comme eux 'la mer *est* verte; ce point blanc, là-haut, *c'est* une mouette,' mais je ne sentais pas que ça existait, que la mouette était une 'mouette-existante'; à l'ordinaire l'existence se cache ... Si l'on m'avait demandé ce que c'était que l'existence, j'aurais répondu de bonne foi que ça n'était rien, tout juste une forme vide qui venait s'ajouter aux choses du dehors, sans rien changer à leur nature. Et puis voilà, tout d'un coup, c'était là, c'était clair comme le jour: l'existence s'était soudain dévoilée. Elle avait perdu son allure inoffensive de catégorie abstraite: c'était la pâte même des choses, cette racine était pétrie dans de l'existence. (150–1)

We can now begin to appreciate what, in novelistic terms, is at stake here. The task of the fictive referent is, at the moment of concretization, to present the object – whether it be the root and trunk of the tree, the streetcar seat or the sheets of paper – in all its nakedness, divested of all those attributes that normally serve to reassure us of its innocuousness. Although words – in this case: 'exister,' 'la mer,' 'verte,' 'une mouette' – have lost their meaning, it is at the expense of the very things, ontological states, and attributes they are intended to designate of whose reality there is nonetheless not the slightest doubt – on the contrary. Paradoxically, in the first instance, *in spite of* the sudden failure of language to signify, this merely emphasizes, by contrast as it were, the *immediacy* of the phenomena in question. At the same time – and compounding the paradox – those phenomena have become no less meaningless than the words that sought to refer to them:

... devant cette grosse patte rugueuse, ni l'ignorance ni le savoir n'avaient d'importance: le monde des explications et des raisons n'est pas celui de l'existence ... Cette racine ... existait dans la mesure où je ne pouvais pas l'expliquer. Noueuse, inerte, sans nom, elle me fascinait, m'emplissait les yeux, me ramenait sans cesse à sa propre existence. J'avais beau me répéter: 'C'est une racine' – ça ne prenait plus. Je voyais bien qu'on ne pouvais pas passer de sa fonction de racine, de pompe aspirante, à *ça*, à cette peau dure et compacte de phoque, à cet aspect huileux, calleux, entêté. La fonction n'expliquait rien: elle permettait de comprendre en gros ce que c'était qu'une racine, mais pas du tout *celle-ci*. (153)

However, meaninglessness is not an attribute that affects in any way the facility with which those phenomena lend themselves to concretization by the reader. Nonetheless, it is true that the fact that their linguistic *vehicle* has become meaningless *should* very much affect concretization: in fact, were the reader to share fully Roquentin's experience of language here, concretization would be simply *impossible*. The key to this logical conundrum lies in the fact that the only way the reader *could*, or rather *can* share in Roquentin's realization that the signifier bears no necessary relation to the signified, is through the signifying capacity of the words he is reading.

Now the crucial distinction that emerges from the preceding analysis is the distinction between words (that is, language) that are *the vehicle* of concretization and words that are *the object* of concretization, as is the case of the words *exister, la mer, verte*, and *une mouette* in the above passage. Once words themselves constitute the fictive referent, then through the elimination or evacuation of the signified in favour of the signifier – the perception or awareness of either one rendering the simultaneous perception or awareness of the other impossible – they, by the very fact of their concretization, become devoid of any meaning and by the same token divorced from any referent whatsoever: they have, in fact, become *their own referent* (which is exactly the situation we shall be confronted with in Bataille's *Histoire de l'œil*). However, it is because the surrounding words, their textual context, has in the first instance functioned *meaningfully* [sic] that this result has been possible. And it is only if the arbitrary character of the aforementioned signifiers, as perceived in common both by Roquentin and the reader, were to end up by contaminating, through mere contiguity, the words around them (and between them) that the whole text of *La Nausée* would itself become meaningless and fail to give rise to any concretization whatsoever of its potential fictive referents by being reduced to a series of linguistic signs. In that case, the workings of the reader's imagination in the task of (re)creating would give way to his sense of sight, and the printed page would no longer be the gateway to a fictional world but a barrier to it, refusing the reader access – an end in itself, frustrating all concretization.

This particular root in its existential specificity is perceived as not being reducible to the type of being to which it ostensibly belongs: it eludes the very quality of being a root. The passage continues thus: 'Cette racine-ci, avec sa couleur, sa forme, son mouvement figé, était... au-dessous de toute explication. Chacune de ses qualités lui échappait un peu, coulait hors d'elle, se solidifiait à demi, devenait presque une chose; chacune était *de trop dans* la racine ...' (153). Here one is reminded of Meinong's 'principle of the independence of so-being (*Sosein*) from being (*Sein*),'[22] whereby, as Leonard Linsky puts

22 'The Theory of Objects,' 76–117, cf. 82

it, 'an object's having such and such characteristics is independent of
its existence.'[23] The root loses those very qualities that, on the contrary, it becomes reduced to in Malraux's novels, as we shall see. What
the novelist seeks to convey to the reader is pure being independent
of any 'so-being,' and it is in such a form that the fictive referent is
intended to be concretized.

The reader had, in fact, very early in his reading of Roquentin's
diary been led to focus precisely on the *appearance* of certain objects,
that is, on their *superficial* appearance characterized by their actual
surfaces: '[Le soleil] dore vaguement de sales brumes blanches ... il
coule dans ma chambre, tout blond, tout pâle; il étale sur ma table
quatre reflets ternes et faux' (20). Here the fictive referents are identical with those we shall encounter in Malraux's revolutionary novels:
the surface of objects seen under particular climatic conditions and
transformed thereby: 'Ma pipe est badigeonnée d'un vernis doré qui
attire d'abord les yeux par une *apparence* de gaieté';[24] but in this
novel of Sartre the surface appearance suddenly disintegrates and
decomposes – 'on la regarde, le vernis fond, il ne reste qu'une grande
traînée blafarde sur un morceau de bois. Et tout est ainsi, tout, jusqu'à
mes mains.' This means that for the reader the initial fictive referent
conjured up in the mind's eye – the light playing on the surface of the
object – breaks down and is seen to dissolve. This leaves the reader to
imagine for himself what is then revealed: the object in all its materiality until then concealed by its own shining surface.

An even more striking example of the same phenomenon is the
passage that evokes the pair of mauve braces. Here colour is the
object's attribute that disintegrates beneath Roquentin's gaze: .

Les bretelles [mauves] se voient à peine sur la chemise bleue ... mais c'est de
la fausse humilité: en fait elles ne se laissent pas oublier, elles m'agacent par
leur entêtement de moutons, comme si, parties pour devenir violettes, elles
s'étaient arrêtées en route sans abandoner leurs prétentions. On a envie de
leur dire: 'Allez-y, *devenez* violettes et qu'on n'en parle plus.' Mais non, elles
restent en suspens, butées dans leur effort inachevé. Parfois le bleu qui les
entoure glisse sur elles et les recouvre tout à fait: je reste un instant sans les
voir. Mais ce n'est qu'une vague, bientôt le bleu pâlit par places et je vois
réapparaître des îlots d'un mauve hésitant, qui s'élargissent, se rejoignent et
reconstituent les bretelles.' (26)

23 *Referring*, 13
24 My emphasis

In this case, the colour – the result of the way the object's surface reflects the light falling on it – does not dissolve completely and ends up by reconstituting the surface of the braces. It is as though the surface were on the point of breaking up to reveal the substantiality of the object beneath it, but had, to adopt Roquentin's own manner of describing the phenomenon, a change of heart, thus restoring the initial fictive referent in the reader's imagination.

Here, too, as in the previous passage quoted, it is the precarious character and instability of the fictive referent that is revealed. The undermining of the latter is, of course, due to the fact that it corresponds to the way in which Roquentin *used to* perceive the things around him *before* he began to experience *la nausée* and therefore before the beginning of the events recounted in his diary. In spite of Roquentin's earlier observation that 'les choses sont tout entières ce qu'elles paraissent – *et derrière elles...* il n'y a rien' in the sense that there is no metaphysical reason at the back of things justifying in any way their existence, the surface of things does have to peel away in order for their reality as sheer, brute matter to be apprehended. Appearances, the so-being of things, *are* deceptive, concealing as they do their very thingness: 'La *vraie* mer est froide et noire, pleine de bêtes; elle rampe sous cette mince pellicule verte qui est faite pour tromper les gens. Les sylphes [those strolling along the sea front] qui m'entourent s'y sont laissés prendre: ils ne voient que la mince pellicule, c'est elle qui prouve l'existence de Dieu. Moi je vis le dessous! les vernis fondent, les brillantes petites peaux veloutées, les petites peaux de pêche du bon Dieu pètent de partout sous mon regard, elles se fendent et s'entrebaillent' (147). It is the apprehension of the immediacy of the inexplicable presence of everything that exists in all its gratuitousness that can only come about once the surface structure of things – their veil of attributes through which we normally perceive them without seeing them for what they really are – has broken up and disintegrated: '... l'existence s'était soudain dévoilée ... c'était la pâte même des choses, cette racine était pétrie dans de l'existence. Ou plutôt la racine, les grilles du jardin, le banc, le gazon rare de la pelouse, tout ça s'était évanoui; la diversité des choses, leur individualité n'étaient qu'une apparence, un vernis. Ce vernis avait fondu, il restait des masses monstrueuses et molles, en désordre – nues d'une effrayante et obscène nudité' (151).

The challenge that Sartre set himself in attempting to create for his reader a fictive referent that would convey to him the intimation of the sheer existence of brute matter, that is, pure contingency, can be measured by the complexity and fine distinctions of the preceding discussion. In the final analysis, it is no doubt an impossible one, since the only 'thing' that *can* be conveyed to the reader of any novel is a referent whose nature is by definition *fictional*.[25] What is involved, in Ingardenian terms, is a merging for the reader of 'represented space' (as evoked by the novel) and 'imaginational space' (within the mind of the reader): the latter has to be taken for the former or, in more traditional terms, the reader has to feel or have the impression that there *is* no 'suspension of disbelief,' on his part, involved in the process he is engaged in as a reader. Interestingly, such a phenomenon is envisaged by Ingarden thus: '... despite the dissimilarities between represented space and the "imaginational space" of a particular imagining conscious subject, there exists the possibility that in reading the work we can see, by means of a lively intuitive imagining *directly* into the given represented space and can thus in a way bridge the

---

25 The novel itself gives an account of the complexity of the process involved, albeit with reference to another form of imagining: that required not to conjure up, while reading, the imaginary referents of the novel but to remember past events and experiences. In this passage, we see the subtle interplay between signifier and signified, between words and the mental images they evoke. They alternate within consciousness, since both – words and their corresponding images – can never be experienced contemporaneously: in the reading process, when the former predominate we have a *literary text* and when the latter predominate we have a *fictional universe* composed of fictive referents: 'Pour cette place de Meknès, où j'allais pourtant chaque jour ... : je ne la vois plus du tout. Il me reste le vague sentiment qu'elle était charmante, et ces cinq mots indissolublement liés: une place charmante de Meknès. Sans doute, si je ferme les yeux ou si je fixe vaguement le plafond, je peux reconstituer la scène: un arbre au loin, une forme sombre et trapue court sur moi. Mais j'invente tout cela pour les besoins de la cause. Ce Marocain était grand et sec ... Ainsi je *sais* encore qu'il était grand et sec ... Mais je ne *vois* plus rien: j'ai beau fouiller le passé je n'en retire plus que des bribes d'images et je ne sais pas très bien ce qu'elles représentent, ni si ce sont des souvenirs ou des fictions.

  'Il y a beaucoup de cas d'ailleurs où ces bribes elles-mêmes ont disparu: il ne reste plus que des mots: je pourrais encore raconter les histoires, les raconter trop bien ... mais ce ne sont plus que des carcasses ... Quelquefois, dans mon récit, il arrive que je prononce de ces beaux noms qu'on lit dans les atlas, Aranjuez ou Canterbury. Ils font naître en moi des images toutes neuves, comme en forment, d'après leurs lectures, les gens qui n'ont jamais voyagé: je rêve sur des mots, voilà tout' (41). Concretization of a literary work is merely imagining set in motion not by memory but by the printed word alone: all readers of novels 'rêve[nt] sur des mots' but the reader of *La Nausée* does so in more senses than one.

gulf between these two separate kinds of space.'[26] However, he adds significantly that we are thus capable of 'viewing the represented objects directly – even though clearly *not in the perceptible corporeal self-givenness that is fundamentally precluded here.*'[27] And it is nothing less than this that Sartre is aiming to achieve, or more precisely, create the illusion of for his reader. For when all is said and done, no image created by the human imagination can be mistaken for nor rival, ontologically speaking, what is perceived through the five senses: reading and hallucinating are incompatible activities.

26 Roman Ingarden, *The Literary Work of Art*, 225; Ingarden's emphasis
27 Ibid. my emphasis

3

The Fictive Referent
at One Remove:
Malraux's Revolutionary Novels

The situation with regard to the fictive referent in *Les Conquérants,* *La Condition humaine,* and *L'Espoir* could not be more different from that obtaining in *La Nausée.*[1] Far from attempting to convey to us the brute materiality of objects existing fully in their own right, Malraux depicts a world in which objects are always at one remove and can rarely be apprehended directly.

Sometimes they are physically removed, in space that is, because of the distance separating them from us. In the case of a pilot flying high over the landscape, this is not surprising: 'La route devant eux était piquée de points rouges à intervalles réguliers, toute droite, sur un kilomètre ... Trop petites pour être des autos, d'un mouvement trop mécanique pour être des hommes.'[2] From the sky, the nature of the objects can only be guessed at: '... à trois cents mètres ... on devinait la couleur des maisons ... et les formes des camions ...' (*E,* 519). Such is also the case for the narrator of *Les Conquérants,* as he attempts to catch sight of the participants in a procession: '... le catafalque passe, traditionnel, longue pagode de bois sculpté rouge et or, élevé sur les épaules de trente porteurs très grands dont j'entrevois les têtes, et dont *j'imagine* la marche rapide, la claudication, les jambes lancées d'un coup, toutes à la fois ... Qu'est-ce donc qui la suit?... *On dirait* une maison de calicot ...'[3]

More often climatic phenomena create a barrier that is hardly

---

1 It should be pointed out, however, that this is not true of *La Voie royale,* where the evocation of the stone Claude struggles to dislodge has distinct affinities with the Sartrean *être en soi* (see Fitch, *Les Deux Univers romanesques d'André Malraux*).
2 *L'Espoir* in *Romans,* 516
3 *Les Conquérants* in ibid., 128

penetrable. '... les camarades arrivaient, informes dans le brouillard comme des poissons dans de l'eau trouble ...'[4] A wall is momentarily hidden by the smoke of an explosion, and when it finally appears it is still obscured by the blood and flesh with which it is covered: 'Une explosion intense retentit sur le trottoir; malgré la fumée, une tache de sang d'un mètre apparut sur le mur. La fumée s'écarta. Le mur était constellé de sang et de chair' (CH, 254). Dust often has the effect of attenuating forms and destroying the third dimension of things: 'Dans la poussière qui montait vers le grand soleil, épaulements et coteaux faisaient des silhouettes plates ...' (E, 515). Such, too, is the effect of the procession at the beginning of Les Conquérants: 'Un tourbillon d'enfants qui courent en regardant derrière eux ... un nuage de poussière sans contours qui avance, une masse indistincte de corps vêtus de blanc, dans laquelle semblent piquées des oriflammes de soie cramoisie, pourpre, cerise, rose, grenat, vermillon, carmin ...' (C, 127).

Lighting effects producing a play of light and shadow, particularly those created by artificial light, are what gives these novels their cinematographic quality, often commented upon by the critics: '... les phares avaient éclairé soudain les mains que l'aveugle étendait devant lui, grandies par leur projection jusqu'à l'immensité à cause de l'inclinaison de la Gran Via ...' (E, 858). And here, too, the effect is to break up the normal forms and shapes of things. Either objects are obscured by shadow: 'Ils se regardèrent; l'ombre ne permettait pas de voir l'expression des visages' (CH, 293), or they are reduced to their own shadow: 'Plaqué contre l'ampoule électrique, un gros papillon projette sur le mur une large tache noire' (C, 108). And a shadow playing on an object will necessarily serve to break up the surface of the image the object offers to the senses: 'A côté de lui, l'épicier du village était mort: l'ombre d'un papillon dansait sur sa figure' (E, 488). As for actual events, they can be reduced to the mere sounds of which they are the cause: 'Il se retournait pour aller retrouver Katow: à la fois deux coups de sonnette précipités, un coup de feu et le bruit d'une suffocation, puis, la chute d'un corps' (CH, 371).

However, the analogy posited early on by the critics[5] between Malraux's revolutionary novels and the cinema poses fundamental problems. Käte Hamburger, in one of the seminal works of German literary theory, Die Logik der Dichtung, classifies the cinema, with the third-

4 La Condition humaine in ibid., 371
5 W.M. Frohock, André Malraux and the Tragic Imagination and René Carduner, La Création romanesque chez Malraux

person novel and drama, as fiction (while, at the same time, excluding from fiction both lyrical poetry and the first-person novel) because by virtue of 'l'animation de l'image' (193), the film does not belong, phenomenologically speaking, within the domain of the plastic arts. However, as far as its representational function is concerned, the novelist's art cannot be likened to that of the film director. If the precise role of mimesis in the genre of the novel has been the subject of endless debate, there is no doubt of the mimetic nature of the cinema as an art-form. Any photo, whether it be the product of the photographer or the film director, reconstructs reality in the form of a reflection of the latter inscribed on a two-dimensional sheet or roll of film while at the same time attesting to the independent existence of that reality at the moment the photograph was taken. There is, of course, no way that this could be true of the novel:[6] First, because contrary to the roll of film, the novelist's medium, language, inasmuch as it is a two-dimensional visual phenomenon, is representative of nothing other than itself; and second, because even if the novelist, like the journalist, has been able to be present when certain historical events depicted in his novel took place, he certainly was not in the presence of those events at the time he was writing his work. The first factor is obvious: it results from the arbitrary relation between language and reality – in linguistic terms, between any signifier and its signified. It is this that differentiates literature from the plastic arts, for example, and every reader is immediately aware of the fact. The second factor is perhaps less obvious due to the fact that the world of the movie, the story projected on the silver screen, is no less imaginary than is the world of the novel. In other words, the fictional character of the meaning the movie-goer makes of the movie and the reader makes of the novel tends to obscure the fundamental differences between the role of the film director and that of the novelist in their respective creative capacities. *In comparison with the movie director* (but only relative to him), the novelist can be said to create *ex nihilo*. In light of this distinction, it is curious, to say the least, that Malraux's

---

6 Hamburger is of the same opinion: 'dans la description du monde matériel ... les fictions épique et cinématographique se distinguent nettement ... la fonction narrative épique produit un monde fictif par le biais de l'interprétation; il s'agit d'un monde qui vit et qui n'existe que par le mot, ce mot capable d'ériger un monde ... À l'opposé, le récit cinématographique ne peut que présenter, même si le metteur en scène a effectivement le pouvoir de prêter à l'image des fonctions interprétatives. Parce que ... cette interprétation n'est pas consolidée par le concept, elle reste à la charge de la perception ...' (ibid., 195).

creations as a novelist have been confused with the products of the film director's art – notwithstanding the fact that in one instance Malraux was himself director of the film of *L'Espoir*.

The confusion can be explained by the fact that the peculiar status of the fictive referent in these novels had been lost sight of by the critics in favor of the status of the subject implied by such and such a narrative perspective. And this is not surprising, for it is precisely through the role of narrative perspective that the situation of the novel reader is comparable to that of the movie-goer. The narrative viewpoint of the novelistic text is like the keyhole in the door that permits the intruder to discover what is taking place in the room on the other side: it furnishes the reader with the only possible means of access to the world of the novel. And this keyhole situated at the threshold of the text and the limited field of vision it provides is in every respect analogous to that other field of vision that is determined by the cameraman's choice of lens during the shooting of a movie: 'Il regarda par le judas: la rue embrumée était toujours calme et vide: les camarades arrivaient, informes dans le brouillard comme des poissons dans l'eau trouble, sous la barre d'ombre que projetaient les toits' (*CH*, 371).

That is why all the passages quoted earlier can suggest to the reader that he is following the line of vision of one of the novel's characters, for the series of sense impressions evoked are precisely the form in which the character would necessarily take cognizance of the objects in question. Because at such moments we are aware of 'reading' a subjectivity, as it were, on the surface of the objects depicted, all our attention is concentrated on the subject in question and by the same token distracted from the fictive referents existing for their own sake.

This is, however, not always the case. For example, the conversation between Colonel Ximénès and Puig in the hotel Colon, in *L'Espoir*, is interrupted by the evocation of events in the town that neither of them could have witnessed: 'Les derniers clients, délivrés des lingeries, des cabinets, des caves et des greniers où les avaient enfermés les fascistes, sortaient, le reflet orangé de l'incendie sur leurs visages ahuris' (*E*, 460). Nonetheless the characters are indeed reduced to a series of close-ups of their faces 'orangés de l'incendie' that the reader is led to picture in his imagination. Not dissimilar is the following canvas featuring a number of splashes of colour: 'Clappique gagna le grand salon: dans une brume de tabac où brillaient confusément les rocailles du mur, des taches alternées – noir des smokings, blanc des épaules – se penchaient sur la table verte' (*CH*, 357). The effect here is clearly analogous to that created by an impressionistic painting: 'Sous ses yeux, deux rides profondes, parallèles à celles qui vont du nez aux extrémités de la bouche, limitent de larges taches violettes ... et une tache bleue s'étend des sourcils à la moitié des joues' (c, 137).

What happens is that the detail of the particular surface of a given object becomes subordinated to its interrelationship with other surfaces of different colours. The result is an interplay of shapes and colours where the status of any given object is reduced to its contribution to the sum total of the resulting pattern produced by those shapes and colours: 'La lumière frisante du soleil joue autour des arêtes des sampans et détache violemment de leur fond brun les blouses et les pantalons des femmes, taches bleues, et les enfants grimpés sur les toits, taches jaunes. Sur le quai, le profil dentelé des maisons américaines et des maisons chinoises: au-dessus, le ciel sans couleur à force de lumière ...' (c, 56). As recourse to the adjective *impressionistic* already suggested, here the novelist is no longer a movie-maker but a painter: '... la masse du rocher fameux, puissante, d'un noir compact à la base, monte en se dégradant dans le ciel, et finit par arrondir au milieu des étoiles sa double bosse asiatique entourée d'une brume légère' (c, 29). Such word paintings figure frequently in *L'Espoir* in particular: 'Les assiettes et les carafes à col d'alambic réverbéraient comme des vers luisants les mille points de lumière des briques trouées, à travers *l'énorme nature morte*. Le long des branches brillaient les fruits, et les courtes lignes bleuâtres des canons des revolvers' (e, 604).[7] One of the most striking passages is the following:

A côté de Ramos, un milicien paysan dont le pansement s'était défait, regardait son sang descendre tout le long de son bras nu et tomber goutte à goutte sur l'asphalte: dans cette sombre lumière, la peau était rouge, l'asphalte noir était rouge, et le sang, brun clair comme du madère, devenait en tombant d'un jaune lumineux, comme celui de la cigarette de Ramos ... D'autres blessés, avec les bras des plâtrés, glissèrent comme un ballet lugubre, noirs d'abord en silhouette, puis leurs pyjamas clairs de plus en plus rouges, au fur et à mesure qu'ils traversaient la place dans la sombre lueur de l'incendie.' (e, 722)

The harmony of the various colours all partaking of a common tonality

---

7 My emphasis

could not be more striking. The concluding paragraph of this description is no less interesting:

> ... Dans le faisceau mince de la torche de Ramos, fébrile comme une antenne d'insecte, en avant des corps allongés le long du mur, apparut un homme étendu sur un perron. Il était blessé au côté et gémissait ... La torche l'éclairait de haut, promenait sur son visage l'ombre des graminées qui poussaient entre les pierres du perron; Ramos, dans l'inlassable frénésie des coqs, regardait avec pitié ces fines ombres indifférentes, *peintes avec une précision japonaise* sur ces joues qui tremblaient.
> A l'extrémité de la bouche tomba la première goutte de pluie. (E, 724)[8]

As is explicitly pointed out, given the precision and the delicacy of its lines, this scene could have been taken from a Japanese painting. In the words of a critic, 'le monde que nous propose le narrateur est un monde rectifié à la manière des peintres.'[9]

It is, in fact, quite common for the comparison to be made within the text between what is being evoked and a particular painterly effect: 'A droite, Kyo Gisors; en passant au-dessus de sa tête, la lampe marqua fortement les coins tombants de sa *bouche d'estampe japonaise* ...' (CH, 187);[10] 'Maintenant, sur les meubles et les rideaux, aux coins du plafond, les oiseaux des îles voletaient, mats dans cette faible lumière comme *ceux des fresques chinoises*' (CH, 344).[11] Often, the effect in question is even associated with a particular painter: '... dès qu'il se trouva sous l'ampoule électrique du couloir, Scali s'aperçut que les poils modifiaient ce Greco comme l'eût fait la copie d'un peintre baroque ...' (E, 698).

It is not only dramatic colour effects that recall the painter's art but also the studied composition of certain scenes such as the following tableau of street fighting, which is not viewed from the perspective of any of the protagonists in spite of an angle of vision that is clearly delimitated spatially: 'Le premier rang de soldats ... tira sur une des rues, se déploya sous un vol de pigeons clairs ... Le second rang tira sur une autre rue, se déploya ... Le premier rang prit le pas de course, arriva sur le fusil-mitrailleur du Négus et, comme une vague retombe en abandonnant ses galets, reflua vers l'avenue dans les rafales ra-

8 My emphasis
9 Paul-Raymond Côté, *Les Techniques picturales chez Malraux*, 20
10 My emphasis
11 My emphasis

geuses, laissant un feston de corps allongés ou boulés' (*E*, 449). Here it is the fixed, static angle of vision[12] from which the world of the fiction is viewed together with the broad area depicted, which would, if this were in a movie, be panned or swept over by the camera, that incite one to abandon any comparison with the cinema in favour of the painter's art. Likewise in the following fresco-like evocation, the movement of the soldiers is wholly subordinated to the movement of the lines espousing the topology of the landscape that go to make up a strikingly harmonious composition:

Sous un grand voile de pluie oblique, la brigade de Manuel avançait de la Sierra de Guadarrama dans un paysage de 1917 aux clochers démantelés. Les silhouettes se détachaient pesamment de la boue, descendaient peu à peu. Un horizon de soir en plein matin, de longues lignes d'anciens labours orientées vers une vallée basse qui remontait jusqu'au ciel en charpie et derrière laquelle la plaine de Ségovie dévalait sans doute à l'infini, comme la mer derrière une falaise. La terre semblait s'arrêter à cet horizon; au-delà, un monde invisible de sommeil et de pluie grondait de tous ses canons. (*E*, 729)

The only adequate term that comes to mind to describe such a passage is a *tableau*. It is the studied composition of such an evocation that is the most striking with the interplay of lines and outlines – that, together with its two-dimensionality. The reader's eye focuses on the oblique streaks of the falling rain driven by the wind from which the shapes of the belfries barely emerge. Thence the eye is drawn to the horizon, towards which all the other lines converge. Finally, it follows the ploughed furrows as they descend towards the valley below, only to continue up the other side of the valley and to come to rest at its original point of departure: the ragged sky. The last sentence creates the impression that the line of the horizon – the only horizontal line here – at the same time blocks our view and cuts the picture in two; for it creates a tension between two different images: one, two-dimensional, consisting of what is actually perceived, and the other, three-dimensional, being merely imagined, since it is reduced, in its physical absence, to a series of auditory sense impressions.

Malraux's contemporaries were themselves aware of this aspect of his art. Already in 1930, Léon Daudet observed: 'Malraux peint avec sa

---

12 It is precisely because of the static nature of the image involved that Käte Hamburger classifies the photograph, contrary to the movie, with painting and the plastic arts in general (see *Logique des genres littéraires*, 189).

plume,' avec un 'téméraire et dangereux talent ... incisif et languide, à la fois sombre et lumineux comme un clair-obscur et dont certaines pages imposent à votre mémoire la vision de Rembrandt ...';[13] more recently, Edouard Morot-Sir went as far as to maintain that 'il reste indiscutable que Malraux a été, au xxe siècle, l'artiste qui vécut le plus intensément l'expérience complice de la peinture et de la littérature.'[14] However, by far the most extensive treatment of this aspect of the novelist's art is in Paul-Raymond Côté's *Les Techniques picturales chez Malraux: Interrogations et métamorphose*, which provides a systematic and virtually exhaustive account of the interrelationship between Malraux's novels and the world of art.

Côté draws our attention to the emphasis placed, in many an evocation in the novels, on geometric shapes, as in the famous opening passage of *La Condition humaine:* 'La seule lumière venait du building voisin: un grand rectangle d'électricité pâle, coupé par les barreaux de la fenêtre dont l'un rayait le lit ...' (*CH*, 181). However, the rest of this sentence – 'juste au-dessous du pied *comme pour en accentuer le volume et la vie*' – gives a different complexion to the description by placing the stress rather on its cinematographic[15] character, with the lighting effect throwing the foot into three-dimensional relief and giving it something of the immediacy of the objects in *La Nausée*.[16] Analogous descriptions are to be found in the same novel: 'L'homme était en face de Kyo, le corps coupé verticalement par un barreau' (*CH*, 391). However, a better example of geometric description is the following passage from *Les Conquérants*: '... la rue semble fermée comme une cour. Partout, à tous les étages, des caractères: noirs, rouges, dorés, peints sur des tablettes verticales ou fixés au-dessus des

13 Quoted by Jean Lacouture in *André Malraux: Une vie dans le siècle*, 143
14 'Imaginaire de peinture et imaginaire romanesque dans l'œuvre d'André Malraux,' 249. Two other works have a direct bearing on this topic: Geoffrey T. Harris's *André Malraux: L'éthique comme fonction de l'esthétique* and Pascal Sabourin's *La Réflexion sur l'art d'André Malraux*.
15 Elsewhere Côté makes this remark: 'Il n'est pas dans notre intention d'opposer les techniques cinématographiques et les techniques de la peinture, de développer les unes au détriment des autres' (19) – which is fine as far as it goes, except for the implication that the differences between the two techniques are somehow without consequence. These pages attempt, of course, to prove the contrary.
16 It is true that elsewhere Côté does come back to this sentence, quoting its ending and drawing attention to what it has in common with a Caravaggio painting. He cites the art critic René Huyghe's remark that 'Caravage met en évidence les parties les plus matérielles du corps humain, les pieds en particulier' (*Dialogue avec le visible*, 282; cited by Côté, 113).

portes, énormes ou minuscules, fixés à hauteur des yeux ou suspendus là-haut, sur le rectangle du ciel, ils m'entourent comme un vol d'insectes. Au fond de grands trous sombres limités par trois murs, les marchands aux longues blouses, assis sur un comptoir, regardent la rue' (*c*, 31). Côté comments that 'ce penchant pour la géométrie a une parenté certaine avéc les origines artistiques de Malraux qui fut très influencé par le milieu cubiste qu'il fréquentait à Paris au début des années vingt' (29). Although there seems no doubt about this influence nor about the fact that such scenes appear to be verbal equivalents of cubist paintings, it should be noted that the reader – at least initially – is unlikely to see them as such, since he is explicitly viewing the scene *through the eyes of a particular character*. This means, as in the case of all of the last three passages quoted, that any cubist leanings are to be attributed, in the first instance at least, to the workings of that character's imagination and *only subsequently* to the novelist himself.

The same critic goes into considerable detail in the analogies he establishes with a number of painters, grouping these analogies under four main headings: 'La Mise en relief de la matière: Penchant caravagiste' (110–16); 'La Lampe de Latour: Lumière harmonique et lien avec l'éternel' (117–23); 'L'Ombre tragique de Goya' (124–36); and 'Sous le signe de Rembrandt' (137–44); and we have already seen that the texts of the novels themselves evoke the names of particular painters. Let us note just three examples here. The first one recalls Caravaggio: 'Les hommes emmêlés s'agitaient dans la pleine lumière des lampes – il n'y avait pas de soupiraux – et le volume de ces corps épais autour de la caisse, rencontré après les ombres qui filaient sous les ampoules voilées du corridor, le surprit comme si, devant la mort, ces hommes-ci eussent eu droit à une vie plus intense que celle des autres' (*CH*, 371). Côté remarks: 'Le "fameux soupirail" du Caravage était assurément présent à l'esprit de Malraux quand il a composé cette image où lumière et obscurité se disputent' (115). The second suggests Latour: 'Un affreux petit Chinois resta debout devant eux, mal éclairé par derrière: de l'auréole de lumière qui entourait sa tête, son moindre mouvement faisait glisser un reflet huileux sur son gros nez criblé de boutons. Les verres de centaines de lampes-tempête accrochées reflétaient les flammes de deux lanternes allumées sur le comptoir et se perdaient dans l'obscurité, jusqu'au fond invisible du magasin' (*CH*, 194). The critic's comment here is to the effect that 'ce reflet huileux rappelle la qualité translucide des figures de Latour qui semblent faites de cire' (119). And finally, there is the influence of the war drawings of

Goya with their 'corps sectionnés' (126): 'Encore une fusée entre les arbres; au-dessous, les taches convulsives des grenades, des branches, et un bras arraché, les doigts écartés' (E, 805). In addition to the four painters mentioned, this critic also identifies a Degas (42): '... la porte était déjà à demi-écartée, et coupait en deux le corps nu d'une femme de haute taille, le bras appuyé au chambranle le plus haut possible pour rendre le sein plus beau, au-dessus d'un visage de Sémaris fatiguée ...'[17] and the frequent use of a framing effect à la Velasquez 'pour isoler un objet ou un être dans l'intemporel' (56): 'A travers la porte ouverte de la grande salle, avec leurs profils d'éclopés des Grandes Compagnies, les blessés dont le bras était plâtré marchaient, avec leur bras saucissonné de linge tenu loin du corps par l'attelle, comme des violinistes, violon au cou. Ceux-là étaient les plus troublants de tous: le bras plâtré a l'apparence d'un geste, et tous ces violinistes fantômes, portant en avant leurs bras immobilisés et arrondis, avançaient comme des statues qu'on eût poussées, dans le silence d'aquarium ...' (E, 514).

It is now time to consider the pertinence of all this for present concerns. First of all, it should be pointed out that the author of Les Techniques picturales chez Malraux cites countless passages not only from the three revolutionary novels but also from La Voie royale and Les Noyers de l'Altenburg, the only novel absent from his study being Le Temps du mépris, since, as he points out, 'la simplification structurale du Temps du mépris élimine pratiquement toute référence à la réalité reconnue ainsi qu'à l'art' (39). However, the other two novels have been left aside from the present discussion, because in the case of La Voie royale almost every evocation of external reality is a direct reflection of Claude's or Perken's state of mind, while Les Noyers de l'Altenburg is rightly considered by most critics to possess a very different aesthetic status from all the other novels. Second, a number of devices studied by Côté could have figured equally well in any study of cinematographic technique in the novel (as Côté's remark cited earlier already suggested). I am thinking here of the technique of 'l'encadrement,' 'la vue plongeante,' 'le miroir,' and 'l'éclairage.' This is not to invalidate in any way that critic's main argument. It does, however, mean that all the material from the novels he deals with does not by any means have the same relevance for the point being

---

17 Taken from a chapter of La Condition humaine not included in the definitive version (see 'À l'hôtel des sensations inédites,' 4)

made in the present chapter, which concerns what is a very particular status of the fictive referent.

At stake here is the actual *reception* by the reader of a given passage from one or another of the novels, and in this respect the narrative perspective plays a crucial role. Whenever the reader finds himself sharing the perspective of an identifiable protagonist as he perceives what is being evoked, the fictive referent takes the form of a series of mental images produced by the character's five senses. In short, the resulting description of the fictional reality is nothing more extraordinary than a *subjective account* of the latter, dependent upon a subject that is itself a part of that fictional world. That the various scenes depicted bear a striking resemblance to the paintings produced by certain artists does, of course, tell us something important about Malraux's art as a novelist; it does not, however, *in itself*, change the manner in which the reader will be led to concretize the fiction: for it to do so, he would have to stand back, so to speak, from the object of his concretization and have the impression of actually looking at so many canvases of paintings. And that would inevitably rob his concretization of any illusion of (fictional) reality. In other words, an awareness of the painterly qualities of the descriptions cannot come about while the reader is taken up in and by the events of the novels. That is why I am insisting here on the existence of evocations that cannot be attributed to the perception of any identifiable character of the novel in question, for it is precisely such passages that are most likely to bring to the reader's awareness the peculiar situation that is produced by the concretization of the scene – which is none other than that of the painter sitting in front of his easel.

Not all of the previously cited 'word paintings' (where a painterly effect is created by means of a linguistic medium), therefore, induce such an awareness in the reader. It is those descriptions that not only testify to the studied composition of the overall picture but also reveal a clearly two-dimensional character that are of concern here. Except for certain of the examples cited by Côté, in the passages I quoted before the consideration of his study, all the real-life objects evoked indeed lack their third dimension, their material volume: they are, in that sense, the mere shadow of their real selves – which would never have done, as we have seen, for the author of *La Nausée*. To go one very significant stage further, it is almost as though the fictive referent were itself a painting, analogous to the postcards that occupy the fictive universe of Claude Simon's *Histoire* – a possibility we shall, in fact, come back to later. More precisely, it is as though the novelist were himself sitting in front of a landscape he is rendering by resorting to his linguistic palette and thereby necessarily being subject to the perspective he has on the scene that unfolds before his eyes.

The analogy with painting is, however, far from resolving the paradox inherent in the previous comparison of Malraux's novelistic technique to the cinema. It merely substitutes for the original paradox a quite different paradox, albeit a more interesting and fundamental one. It is true that in phenomenological terms, the *mental space* represented by the narrative perspective implicit in the images of the objects making up the fictive referents of the world of the novel and registered by the senses of a given protagonist has thus been replaced by the *material* space in which those objects are situated, the fictional counterpart of that space in which we live out our lives from day to day. For what conceivable reason, however, would the novelist adopt the situation of the painter sitting in front of his easel with, stretched out before him, the landscape he is seeking to render on his canvas? Or to be more precise, how has he managed to convey such an impression to us, his readers, given the fact that neither landscape nor still life (in spite of the reference to 'l'énorme nature morte' in *L'Espoir* cited earlier) is or was in front of him to meet his gaze and that he is not called upon to *render* a pre-existing universe but rather to *create* a fictional and hence imaginary world? The aesthetic situation we are confronted with is even more unsettling and perplexing than that arising from the analogy with the cinema, where the impression we had of directly experiencing sense perceptions could be attributed to the fact that we were sharing the subjective experience of one or another of the protagonists of the novel. Here the alchemy of the novelist's art is such that language has been woven into a text that has taken on all the attributes of the painter's canvas.

It is clear that from an aesthetic point of view, such a state of affairs tells us much about the way in which Malraux's imagination as a writer functions. However paradoxical the result may be from the reader's perspective, the novelist's writing technique and artistic creativity is intimately bound up with the process the outcome of which we have been analysing. It is not surprising that throughout his career, from his earliest activities amongst the *bouquinistes*, working for the Swiss fine art publisher Skira, to his later book-length essays on the plastic arts with their highly innovative use of photographic reproductions,[18] Malraux's interest in the plastic arts has had precedence over

18 See Fitch, 'La Navette et l'ellipse chez Malraux,' 95–105, for some of the aesthetic implications of the layout of the photographic reproductions of those books.

his literary interests. Nor is it surprising that the novelistic technique of these revolutionary novels is not only to be found in *La Voie royale* but is also present in his earliest fictional writings, the surrealistic short stories 'Lunes en papier' and 'Royaume farfelu.'[19] For present purposes, however, in order better to appreciate how the fictive referent has been able to acquire such a particular, if not peculiar status, we shall have to abandon once and for all the analogy between literature and the other art-forms and resort to the more technical terminology provided by phenomenological analysis.

In these novels then, the fictive referent does not exist for its own sake either as *Sein* or *Sosein*. For its very characteristics are constantly transformed, that is to say, either completely distorted or merely modified, its form being either veiled by some kind of atmospheric or climatic filter or thrown into relief so that its surface detail is completely sacrificed in favour of its silhouette or profile; alternatively its shape disappears completely as it becomes reduced to a single one of its attributes in the form of an undifferentiated blob of colour. Accompanying these tendencies is the loss of the third dimension so that the fictive referents here, due to their lack of volume, can be clearly differentiated from real objects. As a consequence the existence or presence of such a fictive referent does *not* presuppose or imply the existence, in the fictional mode, of actual objects analogous to their real-life counterparts. The 'real' objects corresponding to the series of sense data that essentially constitute the fictive referent never come into actual fictional existence, for they have never, in fact, been created, that is, evoked as such by the novelist. The fundamental difference between the author of these novels and a painter sitting at his easel in front of a landscape is a crucial one: it is that the former's landscape does not actually exist. Nonetheless through his activity as a writer he acts as though it did.

Curiously, the status of the fictive referent here is very much analogous to the status of the unreal object for the philosopher Alexius Meinong, who points out that 'any particular thing that isn't real (*Nichtseiendes*) must at least be capable of serving as the object for those judgements which grasp its *Nichtsein*' so that 'in order to know that there is no round square, I must make a judgement about the round square.'[20] Meinong continues:

19 See 'The Imagery of Malraux's *Royaume farfelu* and Its Significance for the Novels,' 20–9.
20 'The Theory of Objects,' 82–3

If I say, 'Blue does not exist,' I am thinking just of blue, and not at all of a presentation and the capacities it may have. It is as if the blue must have being in the first place, before we can raise the question of its being (*Sein*) or non-being (*Nichtsein*) ... Blue or any other Object whatsoever, is somehow given prior to our determination of its being or non-being, in a way that does not carry any prejudice to its non-being ... if I should be able to judge that a certain Object is not, then I appear to have had to grasp the Object in some way beforehand, in order to say anything about its non-being, or more precisely, in order to affirm or deny the ascription of non-being to the Object.[21]

Strange though it may seem, the fictive referent has a status comparable to that of the word *blue* in the sentence 'Blue does not exist.'

In these revolutionary novels, the fictive referent has receded out of reach. What we are left with is, as it were, the reflection of a fictional object that *does not exist*, in the sense that nowhere does it exist within the fictive universes of the novels concerned for the simple fact that it has never been created by the novelist. And yet this reflection is by no means synonymous with the image reflected in the eye of one or another of the characters of the novels. In Ingardenian phenomenological terms, the reader is called upon to concretize a represented material space that stops short of the space occupied by the fictive referent, the ostensible object of the evocation. That is to say, the object concerned lies *beyond* any space that is evoked. In the fullest sense of the expression, its existence is taken for granted, its presence is merely implied. This means that although there can be no doubt of the existence of a fictional world corresponding to each of Malraux's novels, that world is not occupied by objects enjoying ontological autonomy, that is, existing in their own right as objects. In fact, the space circumscribed by the parameters of that world is that which separates the subject from the object, the space *between* the two.

There exists, as was implied earlier, an alternative manner of conceiving of the fictive referent's status in these novels. That is to conceive of them as *painted images*, existing in the material form of paint on canvas. In that case, the fictive referent of the words in the text would not be the fictional equivalent of a real object but an artistic medium – paint on canvas – in its own right, and Malraux's novels could then be seen to be precursors of Simon's novel *Histoire* – *were it not for the crucial fact that there exist, for Malraux, no real-life*

21 Ibid., 83–4

equivalents of Simon's postcards (since the particular paintings referred to in Côté's study are never *copied* as such by Malraux but have, at most, served to work on his imagination as a novelist). What would then be concretized would be painterly effects, certain attributes particular to the painter's artistic medium, and hence constitutive elements of visual *representations* of 'reality.' But that reality, rather than being a representation of a verbal character – which is, of course, the case with all literature – would be a visual representation in paint. This means that the fictive referent would itself have the status of a representation, bringing us back to the concept of a fictive referent at one remove. However, once the novels were perceived by the reader as so many paintings in words, then the fictional worlds evoked would not be those of the Chinese Revolution and the Spanish Civil War but that of the museum analogous to the Bouville museum with, hanging on its walls, the portraits described by Roquentin in *La Nausée*. And so these novels confer, in advance, a rather different sense on a concept that was to be central to the subsequent evolution of Malraux's work, *le musée imaginaire*.

Such a fictional world is, of course, in reality unlikely to materialize for Malraux's reader. What is more likely is, as was suggested earlier, that any concretization of the novels would be frustrated, given the fact that the novels are clearly *about* revolution – and not at all about paintings in museums. Rather than *concretizing the world of the novel*, the reader would *become aware of the novelistic technique* involved and, to use Barthes' terminology, the *lisible*[22] would yield to the *scriptible*, albeit in the unique and paradoxical form of what could only be termed *the paintable*, or more precisely the capacity of language to simulate painting. In other words, the reader's consciousness of the process he is involved in – reading a novel – would come to the fore to the detriment of the normal outcome of that process: the picturing of an imaginary world.

22 Roland Barthes, *S/Z*, 7

4

The Supernatural Referent: Bernanos's *Sous le soleil de Satan* and *L'Imposture*

Few novelists in the history of French literature have set themselves a task as formidable as that undertaken by Georges Bernanos. Although there have always been certain writers who have seen their religious beliefs as central to their artistic vocation, there are many different ways in which a work of literature can come to embody particular religious beliefs. To take two of the most prominent exponents of what is conveniently classified as the French Catholic Novel, François Mauriac and Julien Green, it is clear that the supernatural does not have to figure as such for a work of fiction to serve as a vehicle for a Christian *Weltanschauung*. Neither Mauriac's psychological novels of manners set in the traditional Catholic community of the Landes south of Bordeaux nor Green's Celtic tales of the individual's endless struggle between the soul and the flesh make particular, extraordinary demands on the reader in terms of the credibility of the world they depict.[1] This is not the case with Bernanos's fiction, which places the supernatural at the centre of its universe and whose whole artistic purpose is to depict an ontological dimension probably unknown to many if not most of his readers and certainly unknown to the author of the present study. His whole enterprise as a novelist seeks to evoke supernatural phenomena as a perceptible reality within the imagination of the reader, perceptible in the sense that they be experienced by the latter in all their immediacy.

Given the challenge the attainment of such an objective constitutes, it should come as no surprise to discover that to this end Ber-

---

1 With the notable exception of Green's novel *Varouna*, which is founded on the belief in the reincarnation of the same person throughout the ages in different bodily forms

nanos resorts to many different novelistic strategies. In fact, the progression of his work reveals a continual and continuous evolution in the means deployed to depict the supernatural, an evolution that never retraces its steps. As we move from *Sous le soleil de Satan* to *L'Imposture* and *La Joie* and thence from *Journal d'un curé de campagne* to *Monsieur Ouine*[2] and *Nouvelle Histoire de Mouchette*, we gradually progress from the more obvious to the more subtle, from the explicit to the implicit.[3] As for the problem posed by the concretization of the fictive referent, the most interesting texts are obviously those where the depiction of the supernatural is most explicit and most detailed. This is why I have chosen to examine the two earliest novels, *Sous le soleil de Satan* and *L'Imposture*, the former being by far the most explicit in this respect and the latter by far the most detailed. Within each of these novels, we shall focus exclusively on what appears to me to be at the heart of the portrayal of the supernatural – where that portrayal is most explicit in the first novel, the scene of the encounter between l'abbé Donissan and the horse dealer, and most detailed in the second, the evocation of l'abbé Cénabre's inner turmoil.

The main purpose in beginning by looking at the dramatic encounter between the hero and the cattle dealer in Bernanos's first novel and in particular the manner of its evocation is first to examine what is no doubt the most extreme situation regarding the treatment of the supernatural within the genre of the novel: the depiction of the Devil himself, Lucifer; and second, to appreciate better thereby the considerably greater technical sophistication employed by the novelist in his next novel *L'Imposture* to convey to the reader the spiritual crisis undergone by its protagonist, l'abbé Cénabre.

The scene in question is found in the second of the three parts into which *Sous le soleil de Satan* is divided, entitled 'La Tentation du désespoir.' Although the supernatural would appear to be wholly absent from the first part, 'Histoire de Mouchette,' it should be noted

---

2 The reader will discover no further mention of this novel in the present chapter. In this his most complex and subtle work, Bernanos doubtless comes up against the limits of what is expressible in this domain; the supernatural is everywhere and nowhere, so that its treatment eludes any technical analysis of the text in the present mode.

3 See Fitch, *Dimensions et structures chez Bernanos*, in which the study of the supernatural was at the heart of the proposed reading of Bernanos's fiction, although the concern of that work was far removed from the present technical topic of the status of the fictive referent.

that the reader is to some extent prepared for the drama that is to unfold by the initial presentation of the young priest, Donissan, later to be known as 'le saint de Lumbres,' at the beginning of part 2. His first appearance is dramatic: 'Au seuil du vestibule obscur, sa silhouette, prolongée par son ombre, parut d'abord immense, puis, brusquement – la porte lumineuse refermée – petite, presque chétive' (124).[4] The narrator tells us that this strange character 'entre dans les âmes comme par la brèche' (137), that the 'volonté de Dieu sur sa pauvre âme l'accablait d'une fatigue surhumaine' (142), and that he is possessed by a singular kind of joy: 'Aucun signe extérieur n'avait annoncé cette joie et il semblait qu'elle durât comme elle avait commencé, soutenue par rien, lumière dont la source reste invisible, où s'abîme toute pensée, comme un seul cri à travers l'immense horizon ne dépasse pas le premier cercle de silence...' (141–2). Together with the reactions he provokes in his ecclesiastical superiors, such as l'abbé Menou-Segrais's 'prévision d'un événement singulier, inévitable' (126) and his impression that there is something of the saint about him ('Son extérieur est d'un saint ...' [141]), these indications do constitute a portent of things to come. Moreover, the reader comes to share in Donissan's inner experience: 'Dans un éclair, tout lui parut possible ... Du fond de l'abîme où il s'était cru à jamais scellé, voilà qu'une main l'avait porté d'un trait si loin qu'il y retrouvait son doute, son désespoir, ses fautes mêmes transfigurées, glorifiées ... La main qui l'avait porté s'écartait à peine, se tenait prête à sa portée, ne le laisserait plus... Et le sentiment de cette mystérieuse présence fut si vif qu'il tourna brusquement la tête, comme pour rencontrer le regard d'un ami' (146). This means that when the priest encounters the cattle dealer, the reader's perspective on the strange events that unfold is that of Donissan himself, which serves to make them that much more readily credible.

It is significant that in this first novel, the supernatural protagonists who contribute to Donissan's inner turmoil are clearly identified:

La volonté déjà cabrée échappe à la main qui la sollicite: une autre s'en empare, dont il ne faut attendre pitié ni merci.

Ah! que l'autre est fort et adroit ... Le saint de Lumbres, un jour, connaîtra la face de son ennemi. (147)

The reader is left in no doubt as to which is the force of Good and

4 Page references within parentheses refer to the Pléaide edition.

which is the force of Evil: 'Comme l'autre, qui s'est glissé entre Dieu et lui, se dérobe avec art!' (147). There is nothing here to announce the complexity, subtlety, and ambiguity of the evocation of the powers of the supernatural that will be found in *L'Imposture*.

As Donissan, one dark cold night, is stumbling through the muddy countryside on his way home, he is suddenly aware of another's presence: 'Car depuis un moment ... *il n'est plus seul.*[5] Quelqu'un marche à ses côtés. C'est sans doute un petit homme, fort vif, tantôt à droite, tantôt à gauche, devant, derrière, mais dont il distingue mal la silhouette ... ' (167). Donissan is reassured to hear another human voice: 'C'est certainement un jovial garçon,' we are told, 'car sa voix, sans aucun éclat, a un accent de gaieté secrète, véritablement irrésistible' (168). As they walk together, his companion helping the priest to slip under a barbed wire fence by lifting it up for him, they converse together, and by far the greater part of this episode is taken up by their dialogue, so that the characterization of the 'petit homme' (168), this stranger encountered in the night, is effected more by the words he speaks than by the description of his person. And it should be noted that there is far more latitude with regard to the credibility of dialogue as long as it follows its own internal logic in the interplay between the two speakers. Whereas the depiction of material reality labours under the constraints of the basic laws of physics, biology, etc., which have to be respected for any depiction of that reality to be believable, and a social tableau has, in the final analysis and notwithstanding the undoubted relevance of the laws of human psychology, to observe the laws of economics, demography, etc., the only laws that language has to obey to be credible are those of linguistics itself, the reason being that language is neither a state nor a form of being but rather a tool of human creativity.

When asked if he comes from those parts, the stranger replies: 'Je n'habite nulle part, autant dire ... Je voyage pour le compte d'un marchand de chevaux du Boulonnais' (169). Donissan is touched by the other's apparent solicitude towards him and shakes off some of his fatigue: 'Mais à mesure que la fatigue se dissipe une autre faiblesse s'insinue en lui, prend possession, pénètre sa volonté d'un attendrissement si lâche, si poignant! ... – Le bon Dieu vous récompensera de votre peine, dit-il. C'est lui qui vous a mis sur mon chemin, en un moment où le courage m'abandonnait' (169). One is struck by the fact that the horse dealer significantly avoids any direct response to this

5 Italicized in the text

remark, replying 'évasivement' (170). He offers to shelter Donissan for the rest of the night in a hut nearby, but his invitation appears hesitant to the priest: ' "Il redoute bien que je n'accepte, pense-t-il avec tristesse ..." Cette humble évidence verse tout à coup dans son cœur un flot d'amertume. Sa déception est de nouveau si grande, son désespoir si soudain, si véhément qu'une telle disproportion de l'effet à la cause inquiète tout de même ce qui lui reste encore de bon sens ou de raison, à travers son délire grandissant' (170). Donissan's progressive delirium goes some way towards rendering the rest of this episode more believable to the reader, facilitating his concretization of the events, in that what is evoked can be put down to his subjective vision of what is happening to him.

As tears come into his companion's eyes, the horse dealer lays out his coat on the ground and virtually obliges him to lie down on it: 'Que le geste de ce rude Samaritain est attentif, délicat, fraternel! Quel moyen de résister tout à fait à cette tendress inconnue? Quel moyen de refuser à ce regard ami la confidence qu'il attend?' (171). While the irony of Donissan's earlier reference to God's having sent him his strange companion was clearly perceived by the reader as unconscious, the irony of the present reference to the Good Samaritan is more likely to make him uncomfortably aware of an authorial presence. His discomfort arises from the difficulty he experiences here in maintaining that suspension of disbelief that all fiction demands of its reader. Needless to say, the narrating author's presence cannot but distract from and indeed undermine the concretization of the fictive referents.

Donissan feels unable to refuse the outstretched hand of this 'homme de bonne volonté qui, en l'assistant, pratique, sans la pouvoir nommer peut-être, la charité de l'Évangile': 'Il la prend, cette main, il la presse, et aussitôt son cœur s'échauffe *étrangement*[6] dans sa poitrine' (171). As he begins to confide in the stranger, he involuntarily rests his head on the other's shoulder without letting go of his hand. Thereupon, 'le vertige ceignait sa tête d'une couronne souple, et pourtant, resserrée peu à peu, inflexible' (172). The reader can hardly fail to perceive the analogy with Christ's crown of thorns. 'Puis il défaillit, les yeux grands ouverts, parlant en rêve...' (172). He feels as though he is falling: 'Il lui sembla qu'il glissait dans le silence, d'une chute oblique, très douce. Puis, tout à coup, la durée même de ce glissement l'effraya; il en mesura la profondeur.' And instinctively, he pulls himself up towards the other's shoulder, which remains firm as a rock:

6 Unless otherwise indicated, all emphasis in quotations from the novels is my own.

La voix, toujours amicale, mais qui sonna *terriblement* à ses oreilles, disait:
– Ce n'est qu'un étourdissement... là... rien de plus ... Appuyez-vous sur
moi: ne craignez rien!

Whereupon he adds ambiguously: 'Il y a longtemps que je vous suis,
que je vous vois faire, l'ami!' But no, there is a perfectly natural
explanation for this remark: 'J'étais sur la route, derrière vous, quand
vous la cherchiez à quatre pattes... votre route... Ho! Ho!... ' The
falling sensation returns and 'les ténèbres où il s'enfonçait sifflaient à
ses oreilles comme une eau profonde': 'En une seconde, pour une
fraction presque imperceptible de temps, toute pensée l'abandonna –
seulement sensible à l'appui rencontré – à la densité, à la fixité de
l'obstacle ... Son vertige, comme dissous au creux de sa poitrine par
un feu *mystérieux*, s'ecoulait lentement de ses veines' (172).

It is now, for the first time, that Donissan, unlike the reader, who
has not been oblivious to the ironical undertones of the text, has some
intimation of the significance of what is happening to him: 'C'est
alors, c'est à ce moment même, et tout à coup, bien qu'une certitude
si nouvelle ne s'étendît que progressivement dans le champ de la
conscience, c'est alors, dis-je, que le vicaire de Campagne connut
que, ce qu'il avait fui tout au long de cette exécrable nuit, il l'avait
rencontré' (173). And the scene draws to a climax as his companion
clasps him around the waist 'd'une étreinte lente, douce, irrésistible'
and his head buries itself between his neck and his shoulder 'si étroitement qu'il sentait sur son front et sur ses joues la chaleur de l'haleine.'
For the first time too, the horse dealer's words betray his true identity:
'– Dors sur moi, nourrisson de mon cœur ... Tiens-moi ferme, bête
stupide, petit prêtre, mon camarade. Repose-toi. Je t'ai bien cherché,
bien chassé. Te voilà. Comme tu m'aimes! Mais comme tu m'aimeras
mieux encore, car je ne suis pas près de t'abandonner, mon chérubin,
gueux tonsuré, vieux compagnon pour toujours!' There is no longer
any doubt possible, either for Donissan or for the reader, who to his
astonishment has to acknowledge that the fictive referent in the form
of the horse dealer is none other than the Devil himself – in other
words, that he is being called upon by this text to concretize within
his imagination a being whose existence in all probability he cannot
even conceive of – and certainly not in any incarnate form... 'C'était
la première fois que le saint de Lumbres entendait, voyait, touchait
celui-là qui fut le très ignoble associé de sa vie douloureuse ... ' For it
is important to note that Donissan's companion is evoked in all his
bodily presence, truly existing in flesh and blood; what is being forced

upon the priest is a form of physical communion: 'lorsque, par une dérision sacrilège, la bouche immonde pressa la sienne et lui vola son souffle, la perfection de sa terreur fut telle que le mouvement même de la vie s'en trouva suspendu, et il crut sentir son cœur se vider dans ses entrailles' (174).

The full force of the horror of this scene now comes home to the reader as he listens to Lucifer's words: '– Tu as reçu le baiser d'un ami, dit tranquillement le maquignon ... Je t'ai rempli de moi, à mon tour, tabernacle de Jésus-Christ, cher nigaud! Ne t'effraye pas pour si peu: j'en ai baisé d'autres que toi, beaucoup d'autres ... Vous me portez dans votre chair obscure, moi dont la lumière fut l'essence – dans le triple recès de vos tripes – *moi, Lucifer...*' In the middle of this scene, he takes out a handkerchief, and 'le plus simplement du monde, s'essuya le cou et les joues' before giving the priest a friendly clap on the back (174), just as any real-life (from the reader's point of view) or human (from the novelist's[7]) acquaintance might do.

It is at this point that Donissan counter-attacks, although probably not in any conscious, voluntary manner but rather in spite of himself: '... sans qu'aucun des traits de son visage se détendît, commença de couler entre ses paupières un regard noir et fixe' (175).[8] His companion becomes more and more agitated as the priest's eyes fixedly follow his every movement:

Tout à coup l'étrange marcheur s'arrêta net, comme s'il eût, dans ses gesticulations, resserré d'invisibles liens, tel qu'un taureau garrotté. Sa voix, un moment plus tôt montée jusqu'au ton le plus aigu, reprit son habituel accent, et il prononça les paroles suivantes, avec une certaine simplicité:
– Laisse-moi. Ton expérience est finie. Je ne te savais pas si fort ... Depuis une minute, je n'ai plus aucun pouvoir sur toi. (176)

The fact that this curious stranger is not one person but two, and that the Devil has taken possession of the horse dealer, borrowing his earthly being for his own purposes, now becomes clear as he says: '– Cette guenille commence à me peser ... Je me sens mal dans ma gaine de peau... Donne un ordre, et tu ne trouveras plus rien de moi, pas

---

7 For there is no doubt in my mind – that of a non-believer – of the reality of the supernatural for Bernanos (see *Dimensions et structures*)
8 See 'Un Thème: le regard' (in ibid., 27–48) for an analysis of the way the look serves as a kind of lightning-rod of divine intervention of which its owner is only aware after the event.

même une odeur..." ' (177). This does, in a sense, facilitate the reader's task: what he is being asked to imagine is not, *in the first instance*, the Devil in the flesh, so to speak, but the very ordinary person of the horse dealer. The powers of the imagination are far less put to the test in picturing in the mind's eye a person apparently possessed by a malignant force than in visualizing the Devil himself as perceptible to the five senses.

Having evoked God, He whom he calls Donnisan's 'maître': 'Ah! si vous saviez le salaire que ton maître vous réserve ...' (177), he proceeds to mime the blessed sacrament: 'Se baissant avec une agilité singulière, il prit au hasard un caillou du chemin, le leva vers le ciel entre ses doigts, prononça les paroles de la consécration, qu'il termina par un joyeux hénissement...' (178).

This marks the eruption within the natural universe of the world beyond that known to man – and more important, to countless readers. 'L'écho du rire parut retentir jusqu'à l'extrême horizon. La pierre rougit, blanchit, éclata soudain d'une lueur furieuse. Et, toujours riant, il la rejeta dans la boue, où elle s'éteignit avec un sifflement terrible.' Donissan dismisses him from his presence in a low, calm, soft voice tremulous with pity: 'Va-t-en!' Thereupon the behaviour of his companion takes on all the appearance of someone demented: 'L'affreuse créature fit un bond, tourna plusieurs fois sur elle-même avec une incroyable agilité, puis fut violemment lancée, comme par une détente irrésistible, à quelques pas, les deux bras étendus, ainsi qu'un homme qui chercherait en vain à rattraper son équilibre.' As though sensing that through this evocation of the creature's strange contortions he risks provoking a sense of disbelief in his reader concerning the significance, heavy with import, that these events are meant to convey, the novelist quickly adds: 'Si grotesque que fût cette cabriole inattendue, la succession des mouvements, leur violence calculée, plus encore leur brusque arrêt avaient je ne sais quelle singularité qui ne prêtait pas à rire.'

What tends to undermine the *intended*[9] concretization of this scene is indeed that there is something potentially comical about this description of the Devil's antics as he finally concedes: 'Vous me tenez donc ...' The events depicted can be pictured with little difficulty, but it is the precise response they occasion in the reader that becomes problematic. Rather than being filled with fear, fright, and foreboding,

9 For no reader possessing any familiarity with the Bernanosian universe as revealed in his novels could possibly perceive any comic intent behind this text.

the reader is no longer inclined to take the events seriously once the dramatic has been undercut by the *melo*dramatic, as it is once again when Donissan tells Satan that he sees him 'écrasé par [s]a douleur, jusqu'à la limite de l'anéantissement' (179): 'A ce dernier mot, le monstre roula de haut en bas du talus sur la route, et se tordit dans la boue, tiré par d'horribles spasmes. Puis il s'immobilisa, les reins furieusement creusés, reposant sur la tête et sur les talons, ainsi qu'un tétanique.' One notes that from the innocuous 'étrange marcheur' (176), the horse dealer had become 'l'affreuse créature' (178) before becoming transformed purely and simply into 'le monstre.' And the comparison with a victim of tetanus merely underscores what has been explicitly referred to by the text itself as the grotesque character of the scene. The monster ends up lying on the ground 'pareil à une dépouille' (179), groaning and gnashing his teeth.

Since the main concern of my analysis is with the evocation of the Devil rather than with l'abbé Donissan's inner struggle and spiritual torment, Donissan's experience during the remainder of his dialogue with his companion can be passed over rapidly. It is enough to point out that 'de la dépouille immobile [his companion has become] une nouvelle voix monta,' indicating that a change is taking place in the monster. This transformation only gradually culminates in Donissan's witnessing 'la dépouille s'agiter, s'enfler, reprendre une forme humaine, et ce fut le jovial compagnon de la première heure ...' (182). The metamorphosis back into human form is now complete: '... l'être étrange se dressa lentement, s'assit avec un calme affecté, boutonna posément sa veste de cuir. Le maquignon picard était à la même place, comme s'il ne l'eût jamais quittée.' The world of the supernatural has once again given way to the banality of the everyday with the return to the reality familiar to every reader: '[Donissan] osait à peine lever les yeux sur cette apparence inoffensive, ce bonhomme si prodigieuse-ment semblable à tant d'autres.' And the novelist-narrator adds tell-ingly: 'Et le contraste de cette bouche à l'accent familier, au pli canaille, et des paroles monstrueuses était tel que rien n'en saurait donner l'idée.' For what has he been attempting ever since he intro-duced the character of the horse dealer if not to evoke within the reader's imagination the full impact of this contrast? Whether in the final analysis he has altogether succeeded is another question ...

And this other question is not what is most important in the present context. What *is* important is for us to realize the dimensions of the task the novelist set himself. It is an eloquent testimony both to his confidence in his powers as a novelist and to the uncompromising character of his art that Bernanos would undertake to convince his reader that he is actually witnessing a real human being – as 'real', that is, as any other character owing its existence to the writer's pen – becoming metamorphosed into the Devil only to finally change back into himself once again – and all this before the bemused inner eye of the reader's imagination. Of one thing there can be no doubt: here the novelist taxes that imagination to its limit – if not beyond.

Let us turn now to a very different depiction of the supernatural in the pages of *L'Imposture*, which in some respects was to be carried over into Bernanos's following novel, *La Joie*.[10] It is obvious that *naming* supernatural phenomena is a major problem. For the reader who holds no religious beliefs and whose situation has been adopted in these pages, the traditional vocabulary – primarily but not exclusively biblical in origin – is, in the most precise and literal sense of the word, meaningless and hence of no help whatsoever in the task of concretizing the work. And as for his opposite, the believer more or less versed in or at least familiar with such terms, the existential experience associated with the terms will vary to a far greater extent than is the case with language in general, ranging, for example, from the direct experience of the mystic to the second-hand knowledge of the lapsed church-goer. The novelist therefore has every reason to limit his naming of these particular fictive referents to the minimum.

The author of *L'Imposture* was clearly much more aware of this problem than was the author of *Sous le soleil de Satan*. A long passage from the former novel illustrates this point. Its analysis will also serve as a starting point in accounting for the way the supernatural is evoked within this work.

The passage begins significantly with the characteristic device of the negative formulation serving to define the fictive referent by spelling out what it is not: '[Cénabre] attendait, *mais non pas comme on pourrait croire*, l'un de ces événements imprévus qui rétablissent tout à coup l'équilibre d'une vie bouleversée, mettent d'accord les apparences et la réalité ...' (445). By naming what it is not, the author calls upon the reader to evoke an absence, the absence of the fictive referent that is named; it is within the space at one and the same time marked out by the latter and emptied by the negative turn of phrase that the

---

10 Through the character of Chantal in particular. We do not learn of the fate of the hero of *L'Imposture*, l'abbé Cénabre, until towards the end of *La Joie* when we witness his death.

reader is free to conjure up *for himself* the phenomenon constituting the intended, unnamed fictive referent. The passage goes on to point out the difficulties involved in defining the fictive referent, the inadequacies of all language to the task of expressing man's inner experience in particular, let alone the supernatural: 'Ce qu'il attendait ne se définit pas aisément,' adding a curious *non sequitur* whereby the novelist appears deliberately to avoid having to tackle such a task thanks to a verbal sleight of hand: 'ou du moins il était bien loin d'imaginer que l'entreprise était à peine commencée ...' When an identifiable and identifying linguistic label is finally encountered – the term *mépris* – it turns out that it once again defines what it is that is *not* involved: 'Il commençait de sentir que le mépris ne se suffit pas à lui-même, qu'il doit se retremper, se renouveler dans un sentiment plus absolu – *mais lequel?*' It is characteristic of *L'Imposture* to resort to a question at the precise point where the reader could normally anticipate being provided with a definition in the form of a noun. And it is no less characteristic for the question to be left hanging, unanswered – although in the present instance the reader's suspense is at least sustained until the end of the following sentence: 'De ce sentiment, il n'était pas loin de deviner la nature, bien qu'*il usât de ruses misérables pour ne pas prononcer son nom*, car il sentait que le nouveau monstre, né en lui, ne voulait qu'être vu et caressé une fois pour croître affreusement, et rester seul, dans l'âme détruite, *comme un chancre se moule parfaitement sur le membre qu'il a dissous, et en perpétue la forme hideuse*' (446). Not only is Cénabre said to be merely quite close to guessing the nature of the feeling in question without, in fact, so doing, but we, for our part, are left wholly in the dark as to what exactly the character is on the point of surmising. Moreover, Cénabre is no less loath than is his creator to name that feeling. The final comparison with an ugly growth that has eaten away part of the human body has recourse to the imagery associated with physical disease that one encounters time and again in Bernanos's writings.

Not until the very end of the two-page paragraph is the phenomenon Cénabre is involved with finally given a name, and the task of naming it could hardly be undertaken in a more self-conscious manner: 'Etrange erreur d'un homme qui ne savait point encore que l'orgueil n'a rien en propre, n'est que le nom donné à l'âme qui se dévore elle-même. Lorsque cette dégoûtante perversion de l'amour a donné son fruit, elle porte désormais un autre nom, plus riche de sens, substantiel: la haine' (446). But the significant point here is that up until these final two sentences, we have been left to our own devices with the problem of identifying the precise nature of the character's inner experience. We have been obliged to conjure up that experience for ourselves essentially on the basis of learning what it is *not* and of being told how difficult it is to define. We inevitably experience the need to 'fill in' in some way the blank left by the text, since this is necessary in order to have the impression of understanding, without which it would not be possible to continue our reading. Thus we are led to attempt to (re)create the experience in all its apparent complexity without immediately simplifying and schematizing it in the form of one of those linguistic labels that serve to classify human emotions. By the same token, the nature of the experience resulting from the exercising of our imagination will be that much closer to the experience of the character himself, inasmuch as feelings are always experienced before they can be identified and hence named.

The following paragraph displays analogous devices at work. It opens with another comparison, this time involving not corporal disease but human sexuality; but then the connotations of both types of imagery are equally pejorative within the Bernanosian universe: 'Comme un amant s'avise tout à coup, avec épouvante, au creux même de *ce qu'il appelle son extase*, que le corps qu'il presse n'a plus rien à lui livrer de précieux, qu'il est vide et déjà délaissé, ainsi l'abbé Cénabre sentait parfois, et pour un instant, la précarité de son triomphe, l'inanité de sa possession' (447). It is interesting to note, in light of the remarks above concerning the empty space left by what is named by means of a negative formulation, that the predominant image here is also that of a void (i.e., 'creux ... rien ... vide') or of an emptiness that by definition cannot be described verbally in any detail since it is characterized precisely by a lack of any specific, definable features. This means that given no help or effective guidance in the task of concretizing the fictive referent – here, Cénabre's feeling that his hold on the situation is precarious – the reader is not only able but obliged to give free rein to the evocative powers of his imagination. The latter could not, in fact, be more forcefully solicited.

We learn that the ease and rapidity with which Cénabre has adopted a kind of hypocritical double life leaves him uneasy: 'A de tels moments, le calme où il était tombé ne le rassurait pas assez ... il sentait *non pas le remords, mais la méfiance*, et qu'une dissimulation si facile pouvait cacher un piège ...' Here then, the negative naming of what it is not is, however, immediately followed up by the naming of what the feeling involved actually is: 'la méfiance.' It is nonetheless soon qualified thus: 'Ce *bizarre scrupule* n'était d'ailleurs généralement qu'*une forme d'inquiétude vague*, mais parfois aussi il jaillissait à la surface de la conscience ...' The semantic clarity of the noun *méfiance* is thereby attenuated, and although the occasional coming into actual consciousness of this 'inquiétude vague' might have been expected to clarify the precise nature of the feeling concerned, the character's awareness of the latter is not in fact translated into the form of verbal expression for the benefit of the reader, for whom it retains its vagueness.

One such occasion occurs during Cénabre's celebration of the Mass: 'Et soudain ce point de souffrance aiguë l'arrêtait net, le clouait sur place pour une longue minute, parfois dans l'attitude la plus incommode, les bras levés présentant l'hostie à la Croix, ou la main dressée pour bénir. Il sortait alors de lui comme on sort d'un songe, se regardait faire, *non pas avec terreur mais seulement une immense curiosité*' (447). Once the feeling is named, however, the naming process itself reveals its limitations. More precisely, the author calls once again on the powers and the finesse of the reader's imagination to compensate for the inadequacy of language to describe and thus evoke what is involved: 'Curiosité impossible à définir, d'une nuance pathétique à la fois et si délicate qu'on désespère d'en donner une analyse qui ne la trahisse point.' Whereupon he resorts yet again to saying what it is not: '*Rien qui ressemblât moins à quelque repentir, même informe, à un mouvement de la grâce, ou simplement à la crainte.* Bien au contraire il lui semblait alors que ce qui pouvait subsister en lui de douloureux ou de sensible se refermait brusquement et, dans la suspension d'une extraordinaire àttente, il se sentait pétrifié.' All we learn is that it is a painful and sensitive feeling that is suddenly dulled by another feeling: an extraordinary feeling of expectation. But the latter is itself immediately qualified: 'Attente est certes ici le mot qui convient, *pourvu qu'on lui donne un sens absolu.*' In other words – and this is the important point here – it is unlike any feeling of expectation known to the reader and hence of little help to him in concretizing the phenomenon. Moreover, the character himself is quite unaware of the object of his expectation, and needless to say, we are obliged to share his ignorance of what is referred to as 'ce phénomène étrange': 'A la fois acteur et témoin de ce phénomène étrange, il attendait quelque chose, *il ne savait quoi*, quelque chose qui allait peut-être naître de son orgueil exalté jusqu'au paroxysm, crispé *ainsi qu'un muscle à la limite de son effort*' (448). In this case, however, the physiological comparison is without any apparent pejorative connotation – that is, within its immediate context at least.

'Ainsi le prêtre révolté, face à son Dieu trahi, le regard fixe, attendait une nouvelle et imminente révélation, mais venue de lui-même, et non pas de cette figure de bronze, froide et muette ...' which is, of course, the crucifix. The narrative's evocation is again interrupted by a series of questions that remain unanswered: 'Quelle révélation? Pourquoi détestait-il à ce moment le calme inouï, l'indifférence lucide, dont il était ordinairement si fier, pourquoi s'emportait-il contre sa volonté, et que désirait-il enfin?...' And another more obvious narrative sleight of hand suffices to confound the reader once and for all: 'Quiconque eût alors observé attentivement son visage eût sans doute répondu' (448). This final device could not be more ingenious, nor, by the same token, more frustrating for the reader: for *if only* someone else – another character – had been present to witness the scene, he could doubtless have read the nature of the expected revelation on Cénabre's very face. But nobody else was there – 'and whose fault is that?' the sophisticated contemporary novel reader might well retort. Only the narrator himself can enlighten us and he has neatly side-stepped the task.

From the analysis of these four pages of the novel, we observe the novelist's reluctance to *name* the fictive referent in any explicit, precise manner. Abstract nouns, which would be those most appropriate for referring to the mental phenomena concerned, are handled with the utmost caution and circumspection. The novelist consistently avoids pinning down the identity of what is being evoked with linguistic labels that, given the arbitrary relation between signifer and signified, are at best only approximations and that would run the risk of cutting short the reader's efforts to concretize the fictive referent in any detail. At the same time the author resorts to negative formulations specifying what it is that is *not* being evoked and the unanswered questions. The result is the creation of what might be called a pregnant space of potential meaning. The emptiness of that space is judiciously maintained, held in readiness for the reader himself to fill through the efforts of his continuously solicited imagination. In other words, the novelist's strategy is wholly employed to this one end: to incite and stimulate the reader's active co-operation and collaboration in bringing into being in the form of mental images the world of the novel, a world in which the supernatural has pride of place.

In a sense, the comparisons, although providing what at first sight would appear to be a more direct form of evocation, nonetheless contribute to an analogous effect, for while they establish what the fictive referent is *like*, by the same token they also state what it is *not*.

Before going on to the other strategies the author employs in this novel in his evocation of supernatural phenomena, let us examine more systematically the use of the aforementioned devices in the rest of the novel.

The void is in fact what characterizes certain aspects of the supernatural and, in particular, the inner being of Cénabre once he finds himself 'vidé de toute croyance' (458):

'Je ne crois plus,' s'écria-t-il d'une voix sinistre.

La tentation nous exerce, le doute est un supplice sagace, mais l'abbé Cénabre *ne* doutait *point*, et il *n*'était *pas* tenté. De ces épreuves à la morne évidence exprimée par son dernier cri, il y avait justement ce qui distingue l'absence du *néant*. La place n'est pas vide, il n'y a pas de place du tout, il n'y a *rien*.' (333–4)

It goes without saying that language is singularly ill-equipped to evoke a void or utter emptiness, for how can a featureless entity be characterized? There is little to be done with nothingness beyond naming it as such. This particular form of void, contrary to the space left empty by negative turns of phrase and the naming of what it is that is not involved, constitutes a vehicle of direct evocation. Here the reader is not called upon to fill in the space with the referents created by his own imagination, but on the contrary, to maintain its emptiness in order to appreciate and partake of the experience in question.

There exists another aspect of the supernatural analogous to the void: that is, a particular kind of silence. Hell itself is characterized by 'son silence absolu' (376), which means that silence is one of the manifestations of the presence of evil: 'Rien ne pourrait mieux exprimer la violence aveugle et le désordre de sa pensée qu'un cri sauvage, et pourtant le silence est solennel. De seconde en seconde, ce silence se fait plus compact, plus immobile autour de son désespoir' (371). The supernatural import of this silence is spelled out when we read that 'le silence *surnaturel* semblé scellé sur lui, pour toujours' (335). The absence of sound of any kind is yet another kind of emptiness, aural rather than spatial, even less susceptible to linguistic expression than the void, since any language whatsoever would by definition break the silence. Emptiness and silence do not pose a problem as far as their evocation by the writer and their concretization by the reader are concerned, notwithstanding the paradox of a concretized nothingness, precisely because the only conceivable way in which they can be referred to is by being named. It is only to be expected that once named, they should go undescribed and be passed over in silence. In this particular case, the text's failing to describe and falling silent constitute in themselves a process of characterization of the supernatural phenomena concerned.

Just as the novelist deliberately eschews the process of naming, as we have seen, there are numerous occasions when the Bernanosian character himself proves incapable of putting a name to what exactly he is experiencing: 'Bien qu'il s'abandonnât désormais, cet abandon ne lui apportait aucun soulagement certain: une issue semblait ouverte, au contraire, aux eaux dormantes et pourries de l'âme. Des sentiments nouveaux, et pourtant familiers à sa nature profonde, impossibles à renier, bien qu'il fût *encore incapable de leur donner un nom*, sourdaient ensemble d'un sol saturé. À sa grande surprise, le plus fort d'entre eux ressemblait singulièrement à la haine' (335). Although in this last passage, Cénabre does finally manage to identify if not all the feelings involved, at least the dominant one, it is significant first that the identification is only approximate ('ressemblait ... à') and second that he is the first to be surprised by the name, 'la haine,' that has come to mind, thereby reinforcing the suggestion that there remains much that distinguishes the feeling concerned from that of hatred. Sometimes it is through the evolution of the mental phenomenon experienced that the latter escapes nomination by the character: 'La raison gagna de vitesse; l'angoisse se fondit en un moment; le rêve hideux s'ouvrit ainsi qu'une nuée, découvrant cette part stérile de l'âme que l'ironie avait dès longtemps consumée. Le sens critique, si vanté, de l'éminent écrivain l'emporta. *Quelque chose, qu'il ne nommait déjà plus*, s'écarta de lui, d'une fuite oblique' (349). In this last sentence, the recourse to a negative verbal form has joined with the problematizing of the process of nomination itself. It should be noted, however, that the device of naming what the fictive referent is *not* does not necessarily involve a negative formulation, as in the following passage: '... *c'est l'illusion de beaucoup de naïfs qu'*un Satan seulement logicien. Tel vieillard sournois l'imagine assez sous les traits d'un contradicteur académique, mais c'est que l'observateur s'arrête aux jeux et bagatelles' (374). Here the Devil is nonetheless evoked by his absence, in that the reader is once again left to imagine the intended fictive referent in place of and within the empty space left by this caricature that is dismissed in advance by the narrator as a misleading illusion.

It would be untrue, however, to maintain that Bernanos *never* names the supernatural referent. He continually refers to the soul, for example, in the form of a direct evocation, that is to say, without merely spelling out what it is not: '... il fut donné à l'homme extraordinaire qu'on voit à ce moment chanceler pour la première fois, d'opposer une résistance victorieuse, pendant des années, à toutes les révoltes de l'âme' (362). More strikingly, Cénabre actually glimpses the soul of the wretched beggar during his epileptic fit as he looks into his eyes: 'Et, à sa grande stupeur, le prêtre y vit paraître et disparaître, ainsi que dans un remous de l'eau profonde, l'âme traquée, forcée enfin' (478). The following passage is illustrative of the more detailed type of such evocations:

... il fixa la glace à la hauteur de ses yeux, chercha son regard.
     Il le vit ... Le regard, dans le visage convulsé, demeurait clair, attentif, et même – il l'eût juré – railleur. 'Tu mens, disait-il, tu mens, tu mens!' Il ne disait que cela, mais *l'âme soulevée, comme tirée hors d'elle-même* (ainsi que l'orchestre, un moment suspendu à la première note répétée du thème, plonge tout à coup sur elle dans le déchaînement de ses cuivres), *l'âme reprenait avec une force accrue:* 'Il a raison: tu mens! Tu te joues une comédie sacrilège.' (334–5).

The evocation of the soul is not dependent solely on its being named as such but is aided by the striking and unexpected comparison with the auditory image of the evolution of an orchestral piece. The exact nature of the potential concretization thus effected by the reader is, however, far from obvious. The Devil is also named directly, although the name used to refer to him varies. It can be, for example, 'l'ange obscur': 'Car si étroitement qu'il nous presse, *l'ange obscur*, maître de la volonté, sent tressaillir sous lui, au moment suprême, la chair qu'il a trompée – la chair qui flaire la mort' (348), whose evocation is here reinforced by the additional image of 'maître de la volonté' or 'le monstre': '... vous avez introduit le péché dans l'épaisseur de votre chair, et le *monstre* n'y meurt pas, car sa nature est double. Il engraissera merveilleusement de votre sang, profitera *comme un cancer*, tenace, assidu, vous laissant vivre à votre guise, aller et venir, aussi sain en apparence, inquiet seulement' (329). This latter description of what is essentially, thanks to the Devil's dual nature, a physiological phenomenon is reinforced by the characteristic comparison with bodily disease, cancer, and the supernatural referent thus becomes that much easier to concretize in this incarnate form. Naming is, however, rarely considered sufficient in itself to conjure up the referent: 'Pour donner idée d'une âme ainsi désertée, rendue stérile, *il faut penser à l'enfer où le désespoir même est étale, où l'océan sans rivages n'a ni flux ni reflux'* (443). In fact, it is no less common to find the Devil evoked as indirectly as other supernatural phenomena, as in the following example where the negative formulation in its most absolute form, as an image of nothingness, is followed by a comparison: 'Ce qui se formait en lui échappait à toute prise de l'intelligence, *ne ressemblait à rien*, restait distinct de sa vie, bien que sa vie en fût ébranlée à une profondeur inouïe. *C'était comme* la jubilation d'un autre être, son *accomplissement*[11] mystérieux' (348). The Devil's abode, hell, is also named as such, although this does not mean that other devices such as metaphor are dispensed with: 'C'était la minute effrayante où l'enfer n'est qu'une haine, *une flamme unique sur l'âme en péril*, perce tout, consumerait l'ange même, ne rebrousse qu'au pied de la Croix' (372). For, as the text itself points out so pertinently, '... aucune expérience ici-bas ne saurait nous donner une idée satisfaisante de l'enfer' (368–9).

It is therein precisely that lies the crux of the problem posed by the evocation of the supernatural in any of its forms: the fact that not only is the supernatural wholly absent from the *Weltanschauung* of so many if not the majority of readers,[12] but also it can hardly be claimed that the nature or precise character of the supernatural can be deduced from the sum total of our experience of the world around us. Faced with the problem of actualizing the referent, the average reader therefore has in all likelihood no resources to draw upon from within personal experience to help in concretizing the world of the work. What Lefebve refers to as the kind of reservoir containing the totality of the experiences we have of the object is, in this case, probably empty and the ground in which the signified takes root and from which it draws its meaning is barren.[13] Highly pertinent here is Ingarden's remark, concerning the varying character of schematized aspects from one work to another, that 'in one work the aspects that are predominantly or even exclusively held in readiness are, so to speak, the common property of us all ... in that they are not only generally known but are an everyday and average mode of appearance [of objects], while in another work, appear aspects of a kind that we

---

11 In the original text, 'accomplissement' is italicized.
12 Need I add that while every Christian, by definition, *believes in the existence* of the supernatural, it by no means follows that every Christian has experience of the supernatural?
13 Maurice-Jean Lefebve, *Structure du discours*, 109–10

have only rarely and under extraordinary circumstances perceived.'[14] This is obviously the case with the evocation of the supernatural in whatever form.

It is hardly an exaggeration to say that the evocation of Cénabre's inner life is punctuated at crucial points by the voids created by questions left in suspense, wholly unanswered: 'Depuis longtemps d'ailleurs, il connaissait d'expérience cette difficulté singulière à suivre le rythme de la vie d'autrui, retardant toujours sur le geste fait, la parole dite, traînant derrière lui un fardeau invisible, un poids mort, l'obsession d'un acte inachevé – lequel?' (711). Just like the suspension marks with which that other novelist Céline left his sentences hanging in mid-air, these echoing voids are examples of those gaps of indetermination, defined by Ingarden[15] and analysed by Iser,[16] that we as readers are called upon to fill in for ourselves: 'Fut-il vraiment, dès lors, possédé? ... Qui le saura jamais?' (364). They call for our collaboration, even our complicity, inciting us to bring to the horizon proffered by the work our own horizon, for to begin to imagine possible answers to the questions we are obliged to draw upon our own experience, our own *Weltanschauung*, however tangentially it may relate to what the work is seeking to evoke: '... Sa pensée choppait à ce seul obstacle. Il n'était attentif qu'à la recherche de ce qui l'avait porté en avant contre un ennemi désormais disparu, effacé, anéanti, et avec une telle haine au cœur toute vive... Contre qui? Contre quoi?' (359).

It is at this point that Cénabre, not for the first time, is surprised by his own laugh – 'Alors, il entendit de nouveau son rire, et sursauta' – both because he was not expecting it and also because he doesn't recognize it:

C'était *moins un rire qu'un ricanement convulsif, involontaire, déclenché bizarrement, méconnaissable*. Depuis quelque temps déjà il accompagnait sa réflexion, ainsi qu'une ponctuation mystérieuse, et il ne s'en serait pas avisé, tant cette *chose inconnue* se liait étroitement aux plus intimes, aux moins avouées ou avouables, de ses pensées. Ce qui avait soudain retenu son attention était une *certaine disproportion essentielle* de ce rire, non pas à la rumination intérieure, mais à l'attitude, à la tenue, à chacun de ses gestes, toujours graves et mesurés, enfin à tout ce qui paraissait de lui au-dehors ... Mot à mot il guettait, il épiait le retour de *ce témoin étranger* ... (359–60)

14 *The Literary Work of Art*, 280
15 See ibid.
16 See *The Act of Reading*.

The first thing to be noted is the negative formulation, or rather an equivalent of the latter – 'moins ... que' – which in this instance, however, is followed by a positive identification. The manifestation of this shocking laugh completely alien to Cénabre introduces us to a further device that the author resorts to in the evocation of the supernatural and that we have not previously encountered: the depiction of human events and actions that escape the control of the person ostensibly responsible for them:

[Cénabre] ... se découvrait un rire ignoble.
   ... Cette espèce de ricanement sortait de lui, à n'en pouvoir douter, et *il ne le reconnaissait pas; ou, du moins, il n'avait sur lui aucun contrôle*. Il l'avait écouté avec dégoût, pris sur le fait, *ainsi qu'une soudaine clarté découvre à nos pieds une bête immonde, et tout de suite elle est replongée dans la nuit.* Il ne le reconnaissait pas, et il lui était pourtant impossible de l'attribuer à une cause purement physique, de le séparer d'une part secrète et réservée de sa pensée, peut-être, de toute autre manière, *inexprimable.* Ce claquement gras de l'air dans la gorge, si surprenant qu'il fût, *n'avait pas d'existence propre*, était dans une dépendance étroite... *De quoi?* Non pas un bruit seulement, mais un écho... *Quel écho?*' (361)

In addition to the final question, which marks the culminating point of the passage, one should also note the image of the 'bête immonde' – clearly pejorative in character – evoked by the comparison; it features the play of light and dark that often characterizes depictions of the consciousness in relation to the subconscious.

Let us now move on from the devices already encountered in the long passage analysed at the beginning of this section. The phenomenon of human actions not subject to the control of human consciousness and hence involuntary is omnipresent in the depiction of Cénabre's existence. He is, in fact, constantly surprised by his own acts, which take him completely unawares, as in the case of the strange laughter we have just cited: 'Il savait déjà que ce rire humiliant manifestait simplement au-dehors une réalité certaine, copieuse, une vie concrète, à laquelle il avait toujours souhaité rester étranger' (361). This is a way in which the supernatural becomes incarnate in an impersonal form, so to speak, detached from any psychological motivation on the part of the person through whose body it manifests itself and inaccessible to any process of self-reflection or introspection. And in this form it is much easier for the reader to concretize it: he has no difficulty whatsoever in sharing the character's astonishment when faced by such an extraordinary event, and through his identification with Cénabre the occasion for that astonishment becomes that much more real to him. What is more, the actual character of the event is not, in itself, in any way improbable or incredible – except for the fact of its manifesting itself out of the blue, without any forewarning. Indeed, the only feature that identifies it as constituting a vehicle for the supernatural is its lack of conscious human motivation: it resembles nothing so much as Lafcadio's gratuitous act as depicted by Gide in *Les Caves du Vatican*. While the event can feature the dramatic action of throwing something to the ground, as Cénabre throws his lamp, it is more often the involuntary articulation of a sound, like the laugh, or a statement:

– En êtes-vous sûr?' s'écria furieusement l'abbé Cénabre: '*J'ai songé sérieusement à me tuer cette nuit.'*
Comment cette parole vint-elle? D'où vint-elle? Lui-même n'eût su le dire. (345)

Sometimes initially the words are not even articulated, but merely erupt, as it were, within the character's consciousness before he actually mouths them: 'Il en était à ce point de la rêverie où certains mots se formulent parfois d'eux-mêmes, rompent violemment le cours de la pensée, *comme issus des profondeurs de l'être...* Renégat fut un de ces mots. Et le choc en fut si rude que les lèvres de l'abbé Cénabre le prononcèrent à son insu' (332).

As is explicitly explained in the following passage, it is because the supernatural takes on tangible form that it becomes much easier to concretize: 'Hélas! que de fois, dans les débats de l'âme, éclate au-dedans cette joie atroce! Mais nous ne l'entendons pas. Et sans doute faut-il de ces circonstances rares et singulières *pour que le mal force ainsi les frontières de son solennel empire, et se livre à nos sens, tel quel, dans un regard ou dans une voix'* (368). The evocation of the phenomenon could not be more detailed, thus establishing without any shadow of a doubt for the reader the supernatural origin of the event:

Quelque chose, dont *l'enfer* est ordinairement jaloux, se donnait ici sans réserves, avec une brutalité, une insolence inouïes. Etait-ce là le cynisme d'une âme déjà perdue? N'était-ce point plutôt, pour une dernière et miséricordieuse tentative, *l'écluse levée aux secrets hideux de l'âme, aux pensées venimeuses étouffées vingt ans, trente ans,* l'aveu forcé, involontaire, matériel, pourtant encore libérateur, *la miraculeuse déviation vers l'extérieur par*

le geste et la voix d'une hypocrisie parvenue au dernier point de concentra-
tion, au dernier degré de la malfaisance, désormais incompatible avec la vie,
comme le ventre se délivre parfois lui-même d'un poison dont il est, d'un seul
coup, saturé? (368)

The closing comparison with its by now familiar medical image suggests the running over of the cup of the supernatural, which thereby
spills over into the world of material reality, whereas the previous
metaphor of 'l'écluse levée aux secrets hideux de l'âme' suggests the
imagery commonly associated with the subconscious, which we shall
come back to later.

Finally, it should be noted that not only does the character only
become conscious of such disturbing events once they have taken
place – after he himself has uttered the word, committed the act, or
shed the tears – but the events prove no more explicable upon reflection than they were the moment they occurred:

Une fois de plus, d'ailleurs, l'abbé Cénabre ne retenait de l'angoisse qui l'avait
à trois reprises si dangereusement assailli qu'*un souvenir limité aux actes et
aux gestes, désormais difficilement explicables.* Le revolver sur le drap du
bureau, ou ces larmes dont il ne pouvait encore tarir la source, étaient pareille-
ment témoins de sa folie, mais quelle folie? Le bouleversement soudain d'une
vie si ordonnée, si bien close, le fléchissement, plus encore la disparition,
l'évanouissement total, pour un moment, de ce sens critique justement célèbre
dans le monde, *pouvaient-ils avoir d'autre cause qu'un mal physique, encore
ignoré?* (376)

The apparently rhetorical question evoking a purely physical source
for Cénabre's unsettling experiences introduces a further important
device that plays a major part in the concretization of the supernatural. But before we move on to study this, attention should first of all
be drawn to the importance in another of Bernanos's novels of these
particular involuntary acts.

In the *Journal d'un curé de campagne*, the first-person narrative
makes the evocation of the supernatural wholly dependent upon its
involuntary manifestation in the life of the narrator-hero, the Curé
d'Ambricourt. Since the supernatural forms no part of the narrator's
inner experience – in spite of his priestly function in life, he feels
himself, for example, unable to pray – and since the reader's viewpoint
on the events narrated and the world of the work in general is, of
necessity, that of the priest himself as he is writing his diary, it is

solely in material events that the supernatural finds expression within the text as a latent object of concretization for the reader. In this the most famous of Bernanos's novels, the supernatural constantly bypasses, so to speak, the consciousness of the character of the priest through whose very person God exercises his powers on the other characters, without the priest being in the least aware of his supernatural influence on his fellows – except, of course, after the event. This means that at the very heart of the novel, structurally speaking, lies a void corresponding to the consciousness of the Curé d'Ambricourt as hero in the past or narrator in the present, a void from which any manifestation of the supernatural is absent, and it is this void that we are called upon to espouse while reading the novel; we are required to concretize the supernatural happenings solely in the form of actual, albeit inexplicable events seen from the outside and hence at a distance. Elsewhere I have analysed in detail this aspect of the *Journal d'un curé de campagne*[17] and since the evocation of the supernatural in that novel is almost wholly attributable to this one device, it can now be left aside.

Let me now return to the question that ended the last quotation from *L'Imposture*: '... pouvaient-ils avoir d'autre cause qu'un mal physique, encore ignoré?' As was stated above, it is only *apparently* rhetorical. Although the formulation of the question implies a negative answer – in other words, it suggests that there could indeed be no other cause than a physical ailment of some kind – the reader has by this point in the story been led to believe that it is more than likely that there are other, supernatural forces at work. This paradoxical strategy is to be found throughout Bernanos's fiction: it consists in proposing in all seriousness perfectly natural explanations for what are, in fact, *super*natural phenomena. Since the majority of readers are far more ready to subscribe to the former than to the latter as being a priori more plausible, it is as though the author were consciously setting himself a challenge, a challenge to his very powers as a novelist: to prove that he can persuade the reader to fly in the face of all the laws of probability and reject the proposed credible, scientifically valid explanation in favor of the less readily acceptable spiritual one, which he does not even deign to articulate but passes over in silence:

Ainsi accomplissait-il ponctuellement chacun de ses devoirs, apportant à l'œuvre de sa perte une puissance de volonté inouïe. Fut-il vraiment, dès lors,

17 Fitch, *Dimensions et structures*, 139–52

possédé? Faut-il chercher dans son enfance la plus secrète une de ces fautes mères dont le germination est si lente, mais tenace, capable de pourrir une race? Qui le saura jamais? Peut-être aussi une autre hypothèse sera-t-elle mieux acceptée. Tel acteur entre assez dans son jeu pour mener un temps une existence bizarrement calquée sur celle de son personnage imaginaire, poussant ce scrupule de la ressemblance jusque dans la vie quotidienne. (364)

Here the reader is given not one wholly plausible hypothesis but two, the first one, like so many other such 'explanations' elsewhere in Bernanos's novels, having recourse to the influence of heredity and the second to elementary human psychology. What they share is their 'scientific' validity, which makes them eminently reasonable and hence believable. Allied to the idea of an intrinsic cause, heredity, is that of an *extrinsic* one in the form of social and family background:[18] 'Le goût, l'ardeur, la frénésie du mensonge, et son exercice perpétuel, aboutissant à un véritable dédoublement, à un dédoublement véritablement monstrueux, de l'être. L'origine de ce mal affreux doit être recherchée très loin, sans doute jusqu'à la première enfance, alors que le petit paysan, rongé d'orgueil, jouait presque innocemment, d'instinct, au foyer familial, la lugubre comédie de la vocation' (362).

Paradoxically, in the end this device makes the story of Cénabre's moral crisis much more credible for many readers and consequently much more readily imaginable. The novelist is, moreover, in spite of the preceding analysis of this particular strategy, not oblivious to the need to convince: 'Cette dissimulation peut surprendre d'un garçon à peine sorti de l'enfance. *À ne vouloir rien dramatiser, il est permis de croire* que le malheureux ne connut qu'à la longue la perfide et pleine possession de son mensonge' (365). To move from a technical interpretation of the present device to a more general one, the novelist could thereby be seen to come to meet the non-Christian reader halfway.

---

18 In fact, Cénabre's origins lend themselves to both a natural and supernatural explanation of his evolution: 'Le petit orphelin abandonné de tous (un de ses grand-pères compromis dans l'affaire des chauffeurs de Metz, et mourant au bagne, son père alcoolique, sa mère tôt veuve, lavant et ravaudant le linge des comères dans sa pauvre chaumine de Sarselat, puis décédée à l'hospice de Bar-le-Duc) *n'était point de ceux qui peuvent choisir*: ambitieux de s'élever, affamé de réputation, réduit à grandir sur place, risquant de tout perdre par une imprudence, et non seulement condamné au sacerdoce, mais encore à s'y distinguer de ses rivaux plus heureux, plus favorisés' (364; my emphasis). What the social scientist would attribute to a combination of social conditioning and hereditary influences, the Christian Bernanos would see as predestined.

There is, however, not the slightest doubt that he considers the natural, reasonable explanation of the experiences he is evoking to be inadequate: 'Car si désireux qu'on soit de trouver une cause naturelle à ces tragiques aberrations, comment justifier leur raffinement, ce je ne sais quoi d'inutile, de superflu, qui révèle un goût lucide, une lucide délectation?' (365). Nor, to my mind, is there any doubt that in the final analysis he manages to persuade the reader, believer and non-believer alike, to opt for the extraordinary, unnatural explanation of events and to convince him of the reality of the supernatural through the sheer impact and vividness that its evocation takes on within the imagination.

Having studied in detail the many devices contributing to the indirect evocation of the supernatural in *L'Imposture*, we have yet to consider the more direct descriptions of supernatural life. These are remarkable for their detail, given the intangible nature of the phenomena in question. I shall take the term *direct* first of all in the sense of *visual*, where what is evoked takes the form of visual images in the imagination of the reader. We have already observed the novelist's frequent recourse to comparisons. Now these comparisons are often extended to such an extent that they take on all the detail of a painting on an artist's canvas:

Des forces obscures dont il osait à peine supputer la puissance et le nombre, après s'être confrontées dans un chaos effrayant où il avait senti sombrer son âme, s'étaient non pas seulement apaisées, mais confondues, semblaient avoir contracté entre elles une monstrueuse alliance. *Ainsi que la pauvre humanité dresse sa tente misérable entre des collines autrefois jaillis du sol dans un cataclysme inouï et gratte, pour manger, la pellicule refroidie d'un astre où mugit toujours l'abîme souterrain,* il s'était installé comme au centre même de ses propres contradictions. (441)

The evocative power of these comparisons and the imaginative inventiveness to which they testify mean that they exert an extraordinary fascination on the mind's eye and take on a truly visionary quality. They are as unexpected as they are unforgettable, lingering on long after one has put down the novel.

One of the most remarkable of such passages inevitably calls to mind the works of Bernanos's favourite painter, Bosch: 'Ainsi qu'un soir d'émeute on voit surgir de toutes parts des hommes oubliés que les caves et les prisons dégorgent tout à coup sur la ville, éblouis par la lumière, prudents, furtifs, se hâtant vers la clameur et l'incendie d'un pas silencieux, ainsi l'abbé Cénabre eût pu reconnaître et nombrer, un par un, les mille visages de son enfance' (462–3). At this point, although the comparison is abandoned, the images are not:

Dans cette âme entre toutes prédestinée, l'orgueil et l'ambition avaient établi trop tôt leur empire, la volonté infléchissable avait moins vaincu que refoulé, rejeté dans l'ombre, les fantômes. Tous les coins obscurs grouillaient d'une vie féroce, embryonnaire – pensées, désirs, convoitises à peine évoluées, réduites à l'essentiel, au germe endormi mais vivant. Et ce petit peuple monstrueux, soudain tiré des limbes de la mémoire, s'avançait en chancelant au bord de la conscience, aussi difficile à reconnaître et à nommer que ces nains quinquagénaires, sans âge et sans sexe, obsession de peintres hantés. (463)

It is difficult to conceive of a more powerful, more vivid representation of the subconscious dimensions of the human mind. Even if we did not know that Bernanos was familiar with the writings of Freud,[19] such a passage would suggest as much. By the end of it the evocation has become still more direct in that it is no longer dependent upon a comparison, simile having given way to metaphor. Is it possible, in fact, to conceive of an evocation of the supernatural that is not metaphorical? No doubt only when the supernatural and the natural coincide completely and the whole of reality is seen as God's creation, each parcel of it thereby bearing eternal witness to His existence and indeed presence. Such is the case in another of the author's works, the short story *Nouvelle Histoire de Mouchette*, which until its very last page resembles nothing so much as a nineteenth-century realistic or naturalistic novel.[20]

What is most striking in the account given of Cénabre's spiritual drama is without doubt the struggle within him between the competing forces of good and evil: 'Il semblait que les forces ennemies qui se le disputaient ainsi qu'une proie cessassent dans le moment toute feinte, s'étreignissent à travers lui comme deux combattants qui se prennent à la gorge au-dessus d'un cadavre' (374). Not only are two conflicting forces, the divine and the diabolical, not named as such, but they are not identified, either, so that it is by no means clear to the reader which is which. This means first that the reader is led to concretize the experience in a form identical, or more precisely analogous (unless Cénabre's experience also be the product of his

19 See Max Milner, *George Bernanos*, 66, 97–8.
20 See Fitch, *Dimensions et structures*, 153–74.

imagination) to that which the character himself is experiencing, and second that the experience itself takes on a complexity and a subtlety it would lack if the two adversaries were identified from the outset, for one can only gradually begin to make out precisely what is at stake here:

Il se sentait vaguement non plus témoin, mais sujet passif d'on ne sait quelle cruelle et *double expérience*, enjeu d'une lutte inexpiable. La haine en crevant dans son cœur l'avait d'abord investi d'une si douloureuse brûlure qu'il n'avait porté attention qu'à elle seule, mais cela ne s'attachait à rien: c'était une haine impersonnelle, un jet de haine pure, essentielle. Il en ignorait encore l'objet. Le mépris immense qui le tenait ainsi la face écrasée sur le sol ne procédait pas de cette haine, mais d'une autre force en lui beaucoup plus mystérieuse, éclipsée un moment par le spasme fulgurant, bien qu'il sentît confusément que, cessant d'être contenue, l'expansion de cette force eût tout emporté, jusqu'à faire éclater l'armure de l'âme. *Oui, les deux forces avaient paru se confondre un instant, mais il devenait clair qu'elles agissaient à contresens. La haine, si cruelle qu'elle fût, le mettait en état de défense, le roidissait. L'humiliation déliait cette résistance, la réduisait lentement, obstinément, avec une sagacité terrible. Si l'une des forces avait retardé, puis empêché le meurtre, c'était celle-ci.* (375)

Although Bernanos has been taxed with a definite tendency towards Manicheism in his portrayal of the supernatural in *Sous le soleil de Satan*, the grounds for which we are, in light of the foregoing examination of that text, in a position to appreciate, there is no clear-cut, stark contrast between good and evil, nothing caricatural in the depiction just quoted. The supernatural is shown to be just as difficult to interpret as any other aspect of human life and reality.

The continuation of the passage does shed some further light on the identity of the two forces confronting each other: 'L'abbé Cénabre en eut conscience. Il comprit qu'elle exigeait, en retour de la vie qu'elle avait sauvée au moment suprême, un bien plus précieux que la vie, son orgueil. Elle attaquait du dedans cet orgueil, elle le dissociait.' We encounter yet again the naming of what this second force, 'l'humiliation,' is not – 'Ce n'était pas le rire ou l'insulte: l'un ou l'autre eussent plutôt redressé le misérable' – before its nature is further clarified:

C'était une tristesse pleine d'amertume, mais aussi d'une douceur inconnue, à laquelle on ne saurait rien comparer qu'une espèce de plainte tendre et déchirante, un appel venu de très loin, mais dont à travers l'espace l'oreille devine la puissance et l'ampleur, au seul accent. Et certes, il retentissait dans le cœur, il eût ébranlé le cœur le plus dur. La chair même y répondait par une sorte d'alanguissement, qui ressemblait à l'amour, qui était comme l'ombre de l'amour. Les larmes vinrent aux yeux de l'abbé Cénabre, ainsi qu'une eau qui perce à travers la pierre, et il en sentait l'humidité sur son visage, avec une extraordinaire angoisse. Il ne voulait pas de ces larmes, elles n'avaient pour lui aucun sens. Elles étaient le signe purement sensible, indéchiffrable, d'une présence contre laquelle il se sentait soulevé d'horreur ... (375–6)

Although these tears come to Cénabre's eyes in spite of himself and, like the involuntary acts and utterances examined earlier, are clearly manifestations of the supernatural, many readers will still be unsure whether the tears originate in the divine or the diabolical, and hence will continue to respect and maintain ambiguity in their concretization of them. Not until the opening of the following paragraph is this ambiguity finally resolved: 'A ce mépris de lui-même, il se rattachait comme au seul point fixe dans l'universel naufrage. L'orgueil, dont la stratégie ténébreuse est la plus subtile et la plus forte, un moment menacé, faisait ainsi la part du feu, semblait abandonner quelque chose de lui-même, *alors qu'il n'offrait à la misérable âme à l'agonie qu'une fausse et sacrilège image de la divine humilité*' (376). Only at this point do we finally come to understand that what Cénabre has been experiencing through the workings of our imagination, the onset of these strange, ostensibly unmotivated and inexplicable tears, is divine in origin.

As we have seen, the depiction of the supernatural in Bernanos's novels poses a definite and particular problem, first for the writer and subsequently for the reader. Given the context of the present study, it has naturally been the reader's perspective that has been my prime concern throughout the preceding discussion, although the reader's response to the text is of course related to the novelistic techniques and devices employed by the author.

No fictive referent can prove as problematic for the reader as one that refers to a phenomenon that lies wholly outside the realm of his own experience.[21] And here the problematization of reference is

---

21 As is clear from the preceding analysis, this chapter is written from the perspective

situated on its very first level, that of its concretization by the reader's imagination, for the reader is quite likely to resist espousing the reality of what is being evoked or, at the very least, to experience considerable difficulty in picturing within his mind the extraordinary events.

There is, however, a fine distinction that has yet to be made: that is the difference between what we have actually experienced and what we have not experienced but are able nonetheless to conceive of. If such a distinction were not operative, how could one account for the aesthetic effectiveness of science fiction or indeed Utopian literature in general? What we can conceive of is based not only upon our immediate experience but also upon our second-hand knowledge, whether this be obtained from our reading, including, of course, our reading of *other novels*, from our acquaintance with the various forms of artistic creation, or simply from what we have learned from those around us. All of these factors play their part in our ability to concretize the literary referents we encounter in our reading of novels. They circumscribe the powers of the imagination, which in this respect are never the same for any two individuals.

But here again, there is perhaps a further distinction to be made. For the suspension of disbelief to enter into play during the course of our reading of a given novel, we must be able not just to *picture* what is being described. We must also be willing and able to *subscribe to* the reality of the latter. This is where our prejudices, preconceptions, and opinions – those elements that go to make up what Gadamer would call our 'horizon' – bring themselves to bear on the outcome. A fictive universe that is wholly informed in its depiction by an ideology that is not only alien but also repulsive and hence totally unacceptable to us – such as the explicit and virulent anti-semitism of Céline's later novels, for example – is likely to be rejected out of hand and the novel that portrays it is likely to prove unreadable. This may well be the case with the Manicheism of Bernanos's first novel. At all events, the uncompromising manner in which he presents his particular *Weltanschauung* is certainly one reason why his novels, in spite

---

of a reader who, unlike the novelist, possesses no experience of the supernatural, and it is therefore subject to that limitation. This was also explicitly the case in my previous study of Bernanos's novels, which began: 'Ceci n'est pas le livre d'un chrétien qui croit se retrouver dans l'œuvre de Bernanos' (*Dimensions et structures*), claiming moreover that the resulting critical situation possessed distinct methodological advantages. The reception afforded that study appeared to validate that claim.

of their remarkable power and the visionary quality of their imagery, have not reached a wider audience.

5

A Fictive Referent
Unlike Any Other:
Blanchot's *Au Moment voulu*

Une figure? mais privée de nom, sans biographie, que refuse la mémoire, qui
ne désire pas être racontée, qui ne veut pas survivre; présente, mais elle n'est
pas là; absente, et cependant nullement ailleurs, ici; vraie? tout à fait en
dehors du véritable.[1]

There can be few novels or *récits*[2] in the history of French literature
that are characterized by a greater degree of abstraction than those of
Maurice Blanchot. Their first reading leaves us completely nonplussed
and feeling that something, somewhere must have escaped us for us
to have failed so completely to understand the text. We have little
idea of what the book is 'about,' for we are not even sure that we
know the exact nature of the events constituting the story. Once we
reflect upon our dilemma, we have the disconcerting impression that
we have had nothing to come to grips with or, more precisely, that
our imagination has had nothing to work on. It is not that our imagination has not been allowed to dwell on the ramifications and implications of what we have been reading, taking the fiction as a starting-
point for reflection, but rather that it has not been occupied by any-

---

1 Maurice Blanchot, *Au Moment voulu*, 151–2
2 *Au Moment voulu* belongs, with Camus' *La Chute*, to that peculiarly French
genre of the *récit*. In fact, of all Blanchot's fiction, only the first three works –
Thomas l'obscur (1941), *Aminadab*, and *Le Très-Haut* – were designated as
romans, and the whole evolution of his work is characterized by the gradual
shift from the novel form to the *récit* form, a shift already in evidence in the
'nouvelle version' of *Thomas l'obscur* (1950). It is generally agreed that the
récits represent the height of Blanchot's achievement as a creative writer. Moreover, the status of the fictive referent poses no problem to the reader of the
earlier *romans*. Hence the choice of the present text for this study.

thing concrete whose (fictional) existence we could be certain of. In its attempt to conjure up the world of the fiction, our imagination has been frustrated at every turn and from the outset. What is at stake then is the very possibility of concretizing the work. It is the apparent thwarting of the process of concretization that we shall now study in the *récit* entitled *Au Moment voulu*.

Significantly enough, the story opens with the mention of an absence: 'En l'absence de l'amie qui vivait avec elle, la porte fut ouverte par Judith' (7). Just so, demonstrating the same process of self-reflexivity, it will close 159 pages later with the words 'Maintenant la fin' (166). This 'absence,' it goes without saying, mirrors that other absence that arises in the mind of the reader who picks up the book and looks forward to the fictive universe that will gradually take shape with the turning of its pages, like that 'travail de tapisserie' that, as the narrator recounts later, the characters were 'en train de composer fil à fil avec [leurs] gestes – tapisserie bien faite pour le décor d'un musée' (61-2). This absence will be at the centre of our attention throughout the whole of this *récit*, which is characterized, before all else, by the absence of anything tangible for the reader to seize hold of.

'Ma surprise fut extrême, inextricable, beaucoup plus grande, assurément, que si je l'avais rencontrée par hasard,' continues the narrator. 'L'étonnnement était tel qu'il s'exprimait en moi par ces mots: "Mon Dieu! encore une figure de connaissance!"' (7). It should be noted that the words in question, not being pronounced aloud, are not addressed to anybody else, unless that somebody else be the reader, for whom they serve to make more explicit the nature of his 'étonnement.' Next comes a sentence placed between parentheses: '(Peut-être ma décision de marcher droit sur cette figure avait-elle été si forte qu'elle la rendait impossible)' (7-8). And the only problem with this latter observation is that nowhere up to this point in the text has there been any mention of walking straight up to this figure, or up to anything else for that matter – unless it were the decision itself that had been made impossible and that he had therefore not acted upon ... We certainly find ourselves *in medias res*, – of that there is no doubt.

'Mais il y avait aussi la gêne d'être venu vérifier sur place la conti-nuité des choses' (8), an embarrassment that is then added to his astonishment. And this 'continuité' is now commented upon in the form of a paradoxical statement that is the first in a whole series woven into the tapestry of the text: 'Le temps avait passé, et pourtant il n'était pas passé; c'était là une vérité que je n'aurais pas dû avoir le désir de mettre en ma présence' (8). We shall come back to the paradox later. So ends the first paragraph of the tale.

The 'absence' evoked in the very first sentence has nonetheless given way to a presence. It is as though the paragraph's role had been to mime the function and the very *raison d'être* of every novel text: the putting in place of an imaginary universe. Note that my use of the term *mime* is by no means a mere rhetorical flourish. To mime is to pretend to be doing something – and here the text is merely going through the motions of creating without in fact creating anything. For the *signifier* 'présence' does not translate into its *signified:* the only *presence* there is, literally, is that of the word *presence*, given the fact that the narrator merely expresses the desire to see himself confronted by this continuity marking the passage of time that itself appears to be an illusion.

In other words, it is as certain that as we read this first paragraph we find ourselves thrust into the middle of things as that the nature of the things in question is uncertain. It will be our task in the rest of this chapter to try to identify these 'things,' that is to say to analyse those textual indices that enable them to take shape in the reader's imagination in the form of fictive referents.

Among the 'things' represented by the fictive referents is first of all the place in which many of the events of the story occur. The bare outlines of the story – which are all that can be discerned on first reading – are as follows: a first-person narrative recounts the relationships linking three people – the narrator and two women, Judith and Claudia – living together, at least during the time span of the story, in a house. The windows of the house open onto a garden that is sometimes mentioned. It is clear that the relations between the narrator and Judith antedate his relations with Claudia. The characters' movements are confined to the bedrooms, the kitchen and the corridors of the house. Some events take place that have dramatic effects on the characters, but the exact nature of these events and, even more, their causes and significance are far from clear. Nothing further can be deduced with any degree of certainty.

The place in question at the outset is the bedroom, a room that seems remarkable precisely for its unremarkable character; it is just like any other bedroom, nondescript. This is no doubt why it is never described.[3] '... si j'étais un peu dépaysé dans cette chambre,' says the

---

3 This is true of most of the material objects actually designated as such. One is struck by the absence of adjectives when each is introduced: 'la porte' (7), 'un

narrator, 'ce dépaysement avait le naturel d'une visite quelconque auprès d'une personne quelconque, *dans une des mille chambres où j'aurais pu entrer* ... Pour tout dire, je n'avais pas l'idée que quelqu'un habitât la chambre, ni aucune autre chambre au monde, s'il y en avait, ce qui ne me venait pas non plus à l'esprit' (18).[4] It may be noted, in passing, that this last sentence – which reads uncannily like many passages of Beckett's trilogy with its series of qualifications, themselves negations, leaving the reader empty-handed, so to speak – gives us no idea of what it was exactly that didn't come to mind. The unremarkableness is expressed by 'le naturel' and nothing could be more vague than a 'visite *quelconque*' paid to a 'personne *quelconque*' and nothing less precise, less specific than 'une des mille chambres où j'*aurais pu* entrer,' which makes the room merely one of many hypothetical bedrooms. Any precise and particular fictive referent is here replaced by an evocation of the general category of things to which it belongs and thereby shades off into the vaguest of generalities – not to mention the hypothetical note on which it ends.

What is to be made of all this? The answer is, nothing in particular – in other words, nothing capable of taking shape in the mind's eye of the reader, which is unable to focus satisfactorily on a generality; one cannot make something from nothing, that is, where nothing is specified. A passage encountered a few pages farther on is much too enigmatic to clarify the character of the bedroom so that we may better imagine it: 'Bien sûr, c'était une chambre, mais tout de même si peu une chambre; et la certitude ne pouvait pas résider entre quatre murs; quelle certitude? [Judith] ne savait pas, quelque chose qui ressemblait à elle-même et qui la faisait ressembler au froid et à la tranquillité de la transparence' (23). And so it is simply a bedroom – any old bedroom, as was stated previously – while barely being one ... Now its very generic identity, which at least allowed it to be classified as a bedroom, if only any bedroom, is in turn put in question so that its existence is no more certain than the certainty that, for the young woman, was unable to reside within its four walls. Needless to say, no further clarification is provided with regard to the nature or content of this 'certitude.'

What do we find when we consider the protagonists themselves?

---

piano' (9), 'la fenêtre,' 'la rue' (11), 'la cuisine,' 'le couloir,' 'la salle de bains,' 'la seconde chambre' (13).

4 My emphasis, as in all subsequent quotations from this text, unless otherwise indicated

Judith is apparently beautiful, and yet when the narrator comes to speak of her facial features, he gives not the slightest detail: 'Parce que nous vivions ensemble, je ne regardais pas moins le visage de Judith. L'habitude ne l'usait nullement. Beau? Je pense qu'il l'était, mais le regarder, ce n'est pas le décrire.' We expect him to take this opportunity to describe her face for us; but no, any such description seems quite beyond his capabilities, or at least foreign to his inclination, as he follows up his latter remark with words whose irony can hardly escape the reader: 'Pour en dire cependant quelque chose: je la trouvais extraordinairement visible; elle apparaissait, plaisir fascinant, inépuisable' (75–6). One might add that merely to name something isn't the same as describing it any more than looking at it is. And the fact that the narrator finds the person herself to be extraordinarily visible[5] doesn't make her any more visible to the reader, who is quite unable to form a clear image of her. She is so inexhaustible, no doubt also in the sense that it is impossible to give an exhaustive account of her, that the narrator makes no attempt to give any such account, and she remains for the reader a kind of infinite potential, a fictive referent that never actually materializes.

The other young woman, Claudia, fares no better when he turns his attention to her:

Ce qui surprenait, ce n'étaient pas ces façons libres, mais la discrétion avec laquelle tout cela avait lieu, s'approchait, s'éloignait, devenait une image voilée, dévoilée, et toujours voilée par un certain air impersonnel; imperceptiblement, elle avait placé entre nous un sentiment de réserve qui la laissait et me laissait libre beaucoup plus que n'importe quel mur, car derrière un écran mon regard aurait toujours pu la chercher, mais à présent, quand il la trouvait en train de réfléchir sur ses chiffons, il ne trouvait rien qu'un 'C'est elle,' qui naturellement ne pouvait pas être aux trois quarts déshabillé. (72–3)

The most remarkable aspect of this passage can easily slip by unnoticed: it is the masculine form of the past participle 'déshabillé,' which therefore refers not to the young woman but to the actual statement 'C'est elle.' Its opening phrase once again reveals the centripetal movement of the text; it appears to provide a commentary on the status of the world it evokes ever so dimly with its fleeting forms shimmering like mirages, barely glimpsed before evaporating into thin air, imper-

---

5 Note, however, that later on the narrator, speaking of Judith's face, remarks that 'un pareil visage était peu fait pour être vu ...' (86).

sonal[6] for lack of any specificity. But then, this is also true of the last part of the passage, for it is not only the narrator's look that has to pass through a screen or filter only to encounter, instead of the woman herself, the statement 'C'est elle,' but also the reader's. For some reason or another, the act of merely *naming* the object or the person must, it appears, suffice, so that it takes on an importance that is no less than that it possesses for the poet. In this instance, however, it is not exactly a matter of naming but rather of *designating*,[7] as though the reader has only to follow the direction in which the narrator's finger is pointing to be able to see the figure of Claudia. Here, at this precise moment, the narrative perspective recalls that encountered earlier in Malraux's revolutionary novels; the novelistic universe is posited as a given without calling for any direct evocation of it for its own sake.

While one does not automatically expect to be able to picture the narrator of a tale in any detail, since he does not necessarily have the opportunity to draw his own portrait, this particular narrator has the greatest difficulty in existing as a physical presence even for the other characters, as at the beginning of the story when, having been let into the house by Judith, he is in the same room with her and yet she is initially unaware of his presence. His commentary on the situation is as singular as the situation being commented upon: '... je vis aussitôt que, si je lui avais en quelque sorte échappé – et c'était peut-être singulier –, je n'avais pas fait non plus tout ce qu'il fallait pour lui tomber réellement sous les yeux, et c'était beaucoup moins singulier qu'attristant' (11). Once again, to resort to the self-reflexive mode to which literary texts are given, one might add: nor has he as a narrator done 'tout ce qu'il fallait pour ... tomber réellement sous les yeux' of the reader.[8]

The continuation of this passage reveals that the presence of Judith will be the next to evaporate: 'Pour une raison ou pour une autre, mais peut-être parce que j'avais été moi-même trop occupé à la regarder tout à mon aise, quelque chose d'essentiel qui ne pouvait intervenir qu'à ma demande avait été oublié, et pour le moment j'ignorais quoi, mais

6 Interestingly, speaking of herself, Claudia says: 'elle est fragile; elle n'est presque personne' (112).

7 The frequency of demonstrative adjectives in this text is indicative of a tendency merely to designate the fictive referents as givens, as though any detailed evocation were unnecessary.

8 Later Claudia says to him: 'Certainement ... vous êtes là! Enfin, *plus ou moins*' (42; my emphasis).

l'oubli était aussi présent que possible, au point, maintenant surtout que la chambre était fermée, de me laisser soupçonner qu'*en dehors de lui il n'y avait pas grand'chose ici*' (11–12). The bedroom is now all that remains, and we have already seen how precarious *its* existence is for the reader. Indeed, even the narrator himself is doomed to disappear, as the rest of the passage reveals: 'Ce fut, je dois le dire, une découverte physiquement si ruineuse qu'elle me manœuvra tout à fait. En pensant cela, je fus fasciné, *effacé par ma pensée*. Eh bien, c'était une idée! et non pas quelconque, mais à ma mesure, exactement égale à moi, et si elle se laissait penser, *je ne pouvais que disparaître*.' The manner in which an abstract phenomenon such as an idea can overcome material reality in the form of the narrator's own person provides an exemplary illustration of the power of abstraction in this work and does much to account for the difficulty encountered by its reader in concretizing it, as indeed Ingarden's very term suggests. The most dramatic proof of this power is demonstrated in the remarkable scene where a door opens without the intervention of any physical human agent as though at the whim of a poltergeist: '... pour l'un et pour l'autre, en ce moment, ce qui se mettait à bouger, à ouvrir la porte dans un tel silence, n'était rien de moins terrible qu'*une pensée* ...' (48).[9] Such an event is more in keeping with the Gothic novel, or at least with the supernatural world of a novelist like Bernanos.

Judith's presence, her very existence for the narrator, appears to be intermittent, for at one point he doesn't see her in the bedroom with him any more than she was aware of his presence previously. 'Je voyais très bien certains aspects de la chambre,' he says, 'et celle-ci avait déjà renoué son alliance avec moi, mais, elle [Judith], je ne la voyais pas' (17). Within the world of this work then, existence appears, by definition, to be precarious and to enjoy an ontologically privileged status, the key to which seems to lie in a certain truthfulness:[10] 'De cette jeune femme qui m'avait ouvert la porte, à qui j'avais parlé, qui du passé au présent, pendant un temps inappréciable, *avait été assez vraie pour demeurer constamment visible à mes yeux* ...' (16–17). This

---

9 Blanchot's emphasis
10 See also, for example: 'Non, elle ne s'étonnait pas de me voir si peu attentif à sa présence – parce qu'elle non plus, à un tel moment, ne se souciait nullement de savoir si elle était présente, parce qu'en plus, bien que le fait d'être rejetée dans l'ombre comporte des sacrifices, elle trouvait une satisfaction infinie à me regarder dans ma vérité, moi qui, ne la voyant pas et ne voyant personne, me montrais dans la sincérité d'un homme seul' (20).

quality of somehow being true, however, did not make her visible to the reader.

At this point there is a danger of embarking upon a full-fledged interpretation of *Au Moment voulu* rather than focusing exclusively on the central concern of the present study – the problems posed by the novel's concretization. What should be stressed here is the fact that it is hardly surprising that a fictional world in which existence is so precarious should have great difficulty in taking on form and substance in the imagination of the reader.

That there be an absence of material reality in a French *récit* need not in itself be cause for wonderment. This particular literary genre, in comparison with the novel, has always been characterized first by its relative brevity and simplicity of plot structure and second by the stress it places on psychological[11] as opposed to physical reality, recounting as it most often does the story of a relationship between two main characters rather than depicting a social milieu. It is consequently the inner life of the protagonists rather than their life in society that is its primary concern. Certain of the features of *Au Moment voulu* noted so far are indeed also to be found in one of the classics of the genre, Benjamin Constant's *Adolphe*, such as the generality of the evocation of the characters' surroundings and the details of their respective backgrounds and past lives.[12] In *Adolphe*, too, there is a lack of specificity in what the reader is given to visualize, one cause of which is a profusion of superlative adjectives and adverbs. In short, such a tale is often distinguished by abstraction. However, contrary to what was implied earlier, abstraction does not entail an absence of concretization, but merely the possible elimination of one aspect of concretization, albeit the predominant one – that is, concretization in the form of mental images of a *visual* nature. And this distinction between visual and non-visual mental imagery within the

---

11 A passage such as the following clearly reveals the affinities between the psychological *récit* and *Au Moment voulu*: '... elle avait de grands yeux bombés, d'une grande intensité et d'une grande sécheresse de regard; sous le voile de la préoccupation, ils s'étaient encore agrandis, mais adoucis, et cette douceur était menaçante' (107). By virtue of its ready comprehensibility and the facility with which one concretizes the fictive referents concerned, it is, however, wholly atypical of this work.

12 The following passage calls to mind the opening pages of Constant's novel in this respect: 'De toutes manières, il y avait manifestement entre nous une telle accumulation d'événements, de réalités démesurées, de tourments, de pensées incroyables et aussi une telle profondeur d'oubli heureux qu'elle n'avait aucune peine à ne pas s'étonner de moi' (8).

process of concretization is crucial to the present discussion. The imagination of the reader of *Adolphe* (re)creates and dwells on the psychological realities involved in the relationship between Adolphe and Ellénore and finds there more than enough to work on and to occupy itself with.[13] Now, then, we need to examine the depiction of inner reality in Blanchot's work to see whether there is any real distinction to be made between it and the literary genre of the *récit* in general – although, as we shall discover, once again 'depiction' is hardly the apposite term.

At one point, the narrator asks his female companion what is wrong: '[Ce "Qu'avez-vous?"] était un cri faux, une interrogation lourde que pénétrait un soupçon, une pensée froide, déconcertante.' And his description of this suspicion does have its superlative: 'Soupçon étrange, je m'en rendais compte, illusion des plus confuses, et cette confusion ne reflétait pas la vision à l'infini de perspectives ouvertes les unes sur les autres, mais la tristesse stérile du chaos, l'incertitude affligée qui se referme et se retire en s'agitant' (32-3). His attempt to define the feeling in question is so complex that it offers little purchase to our powers of comprehension and we are hard put indeed to be able to attribute any precise content to this suspicion. Later on, two of the protagonists seem to be in a state of anticipation: '... chacun s'appuyait sur l'imminence du dénouement – imminence qui n'avait rien à voir avec la durée –, mais s'y appuyait si fortement que la construction d'un instant, fondée sur rien, pouvait aussi apparaître des plus solides' (57),[14] except that there can be no anticipation without an impression of temporal duration, and the state of mind of both characters thereby takes on the perplexing character of the paradoxical.

In this last quotation, we also encounter a phenomenon central to the problem of concretization in this text. Just as we saw above that the normal solidity of material reality tends to dissipate into the generality of abstraction, the corollary is true here: an abstract or at least non-tangible phenomenon solidifies through the image of the protagonists' being able to lean on the 'construction d'un instant,' much in the manner in which a thought was able to generate the

13 Interestingly enough, the same is true of a seventeenth century novel such as *La Princesse de Clèves*, also characterized by a degree of abstraction resulting from a predilection for superlatives, except that in its case this stylistic trait is in the first instance attributable to the *idealized* character of the relationships depicted.
14 Note again the superlative.

energy to open a door. Such a *transposition* of the material in terms of the abstract and vice versa inevitably calls to mind the functioning of metaphor, which we shall come back to at length in a moment.

Inner reality is not, however, reducible to feelings, thoughts, and states of mind, for it also comprises the physiological awareness of one's own body and its functions. The attempted evocation of that awareness is no less problematic. Let us look at the long passage concerning the shuddering that afflicts the narrator as he awakes: 'Je m'étais éveillé en ressentant un frisson terrible, tous les réveils sont liés plus ou moins à un frisson' (76). The adjectives he uses to describe the latter are, to say the least, curious: 'Mais que celui-ci fût une force plus grande, farouche et facétieuse, je ne l'avais pas méconnu.' One can well imagine that the shudder felt wild and uncontrollable ('farouche') but how is such a physiological phenomenon to be conceived of as being in any way facetious – an epithet that can only apply to a psychological attitude? The further evocation of this experience is hardly less disconcerting and certainly no more illuminating for the reader: '... le frémissement – le frisson n'était plus que ce frémissement – s'étendit en moi avec une lenteur assez étrange, comme une nappe lourde, pas tellement glacée, un ton au-dessous du mien, ce qui rendait l'envahissement peu désagréable. Je chavirai cependant. Je dus revenir dans la pièce, je n'avais pas l'impression de marcher, je buvais l'espace, je le rendais en eau; ivre? gorgé de vide' (77). What can this tone be that is one tone below his? Is the choice of such a term simply attributable to the stylistic device of synesthesia or is it to be taken more literally? We shall shortly come back to the problem of where literary figures begin and where they end in this text, a problem that is crucial to the concretization of the work.

Having fainted or simply fallen asleep, the narrator subsequently decides to put himself in the hands of this 'frisson,' to adopt a Blanchotian turn of phrase: 'La suite? ... Peut-être, par impatience, excès de patience, avais-je, en me découvrant lié à ce jour avide, espéré de lui qu'il conduirait désormais les choses. "Que le frisson décide," c'est là ce que le goût du repos nous porte à dire.' One notes the contradiction whereby 'impatience' and 'excès de patience' cancel each other out leaving us empty-handed once again, unless we decide to evoke and sustain within our imagination the tension of the paradoxical. Just as problematic for the concretization of this passage is the blurring of the intangible (or abstract) and the tangible in the expression 'lié à ce jour avide' with the accompanying personification of the day (or could it be daylight?). Finally, the element of truth or truthfulness encountered earlier is again evoked: 'Mais j'avais une excuse: le caprice, l'étrangeté de sa force. Il ne me donnait sûrement aucun ordre, il ne m'interdisait rien, ni de frayer avec l'espace, ni d'agir à ma guise, mais, le moment venu, il m'éparpillait à travers des abîmes et des abîmes, – ce qui, toutefois, c'était là l'étrange, ne dépassait pas pour moi la vérité d'un frisson' (78). And what weight exactly is to be attributed to this 'vérité d'un frisson'? To say that something 'ne dépassait pas la vérité d'un frisson' can certainly reveal a penchant for the cliché that would tend to confer on the narrator's experience of shuddering a certain banality[15] and thus militate against the apparently *extra*ordinary nature of what has previously been described. Once again the status of the literary figure – in this case the cliché – or more precisely its presence or absence is as unclear as was the suggestion of synesthesia above.

Let us look at a final example of a bodily sensation. It is the sensation of one person, Judith, brushing against another, the narrator:

La vie, c'était maintenant une sorte de pari s'ébauchant à l'alentour avec le souvenir de ce frôlement, – avait-il eu lieu? – avec cette sensation stupéfiante, – persisterait-elle? – qui non seulement ne s'effaçait pas, mais s'affirmait, elle aussi, à la manière sauvage de ce qui ne peut avoir de fin, qui toujours réclamerait, exigerait, qui déjà s'était mise en branle, errait et errait comme une chose aveugle, sans but et pourtant toujours plus avide, incapable de chercher, mais tournant toujours plus vite dans le vertige furieux, sans voix, murée, désir, frisson changé en pierre. (24)

The sensation is like 'une chose aveugle,' mobile like a trapped animal seeking to escape its confinement, animated if not personified by being 'sans voix,' before being transformed into the emotion of desire and finally materializing through a process of petrification. The reader's imagination is again put to the test as it attempts to follow as best it can this giddy series of transformations through the different dimensions of reality: sensation, animal or human movement and impetus, emotion, and inanimate matter. And at the end of this trajectory, what is the outcome? Far from being able better to grasp the nature of this sensation of brushing against someone else, the reader finds himself confronted by an unrecognizable phenomenon that is veritably inconceivable.

15 Later on, we read: 'ce n'était qu'une idée, la vérité d'une sensation,' (93) which could possibly throw some light on the present passage.

The passage continues thus: 'Que je l'aie pressentie, il se peut ... Qu'elle se soit dressée alors devant moi, non pas comme une irréalité vaine, mais comme l'imminence d'une rafale monumentale, comme l'épaisseur, à l'infini, d'un souffle de granit précipité contre mon front, oui, mais ce choc n'était pas non plus une vérité nouvelle ...' (24–5). Here the status of the evocations is clear although with the renewed comparison of the sensation to stone ('granit') already foreshadowed by the ambiguity of the adjective 'monumentale' (with its literal and figurative sense) and the thoroughly perplexing simile 'comme l'épaisseur, à l'infini, d'un souffle de granit,' they can hardly be said to facilitate the reader's task in grasping what is involved here.

Before exploring in more detail the crucial problem posed by the status of metaphor in this text, we should return briefly to a stylistic feature already encountered in the preceding pages: the significant role played by paradox. It is hardly an exaggeration to say that the text is punctuated by paradoxical turns of phrase. The narrator is 'occupé par une chute stationnaire' (15) and speaks of 'tous les bruits silencieux' (56), 'les pas de l'immobilité' (15), 'une allusion permise à un événement qui, lui, ne souffrait pas d'allusion' (93), and of a 'figure' that is 'présente, mais elle n'est pas là; absente, et cependant nullement ailleurs' (152). These last examples are paradoxes in their most condensed form, not to say oxymorons. Apparently contradictory statements abound on the level of individual sentences: 'J'imagine qu'au début Judith lui avait parlé de moi: *fort peu, mais néanmoins infiniment* ... ' (26). In some cases, however, once due allowance is made for poetic licence, these *can* make sense, as when the narrator observes: '... quand le temps parle, ce n'est déjà plus le temps qui parle' (103). Other passages such as the following, where the phrase after the semicolon seems to run counter to that preceding it, are more complex and tend to stop the reader dead in his tracks: 'J'ai souvent un désir infini d'abréger, désir qui ne peut rien, parce que le satisfaire me serait trop facile; si vif qu'il soit, il est trop faible pour la puissance qui est en moi sans borne de l'accomplir' (16). Others constitute veritable logical conundrums: 'Il est difficile de revenir sur une impossibilité quand elle a été surmontée, plus difficile encore, quand il n'est pas sûr que l'impossible ne demeure' (20–1). After all that, the question is whether or not the impossibility concerned has in fact been overcome. At the very least such paradoxical formulations constitute troublesome knots in the text as the reader attempts to unravel its meaning and inevitably hinder its ready concretization: '... je savais tout, et à présent j'avais peut-être tout oublié, sauf cette terrible certitude que je savais tout' (94). At worst and particularly in their most succinct form, what any reader of a literary text has initially to take to be an *apparent* contradiction – that is, a paradox – resists resolution and becomes to all intents and purposes an *actual* contradiction, the opposed elements cancelling each other out to leave nothing in their stead: ' – Mais, dis-je, ce que j'ai, je ne l'ai pas' (113). At that point then, a tear appears in the weave of the text and, to resort to Ingarden's terminology, this spot of definitive and unresolvable indeterminacy opens up a gap or a hiatus in the Gestalt the reader is in the process of forming.

Interestingly, this last formulation – 'ce que j'ai, je ne l'ai pas' – brings us back to the phenomenon of metaphor in that it recalls the opening words of folk-tales such as those of the Majorca story-tellers: 'It was and it was not,'[16] – in other words, the status of any fiction.

Contrary to what we have seen so far, there are explicit metaphors in *Au Moment voulu* that are clearly delimitated and that function in a conventional manner: '... la terreur que [Judith] avait bien dû éprouver à se perdre et à toujours recommencer à se perdre dans l'évidence sans limites, n'avait pas été apparemment plus loin que *la simple peur d'une petite fille rencontrant soudain le noir, une fin d'après-midi, dans un jardin*' (23–4). The evocation of the little girl coming upon the darkness of a summer garden is, of course, not integrated by the reader into the Gestalt he forms of the world of the book. The image in question barely, if at all, comes into focus in his mind's eye: he merely makes use of the proposed analogy between such a child's feelings and those of the protagonist Judith in order to (re)create the latter for the purposes of concretization. The same is true of the following example, where there is no question of a card-player manifesting herself within the fiction: '... son chuchotement me laissa un malaise; elle avait eu peur, elle avait approché en tâtonnant de quelque chose que, si intrépide qu'elle fût, elle avait eu peur de saisir: oui, elle avait poussé sa mise, lentement, sans me quitter des yeux, comme pour être en mesure de la retirer si le risque devenait trop grand' (35–6). The fleeting image, no sooner visualized than set aside, does however succeed in capturing a certain psychological attitude. Where the images evoked by such metaphors are actually pictured within the reader's imagination they are, as it were, always and immediately placed between parentheses, bracketed off from the world of the characters. They are there as an aid to the concretization

16 Cited by Paul Ricoeur in *The Rule of Metaphor*, 224

of something else that has called them forth. Other examples of explicit metaphors are less banal or at least come as more of a surprise when encountered: 'Ce fut en vérité notre premier contact; jusque-là, ce qui avait eu lieu ressemblait à des coups d'épée dans le ciel' (33). Here it is the addition of the closing adverbial phrase 'dans le ciel' that may well prove disconcerting and detract from the efficacy of the simile. This latter example is, in fact, the rule rather than the exception, in that it is not unusual in this text for the metaphors and similes to be more of a hindrance than a help in giving form and substance to the fictive universe. This is well illustrated by the following simile: '... [Judith] était là, comme une sorte d'image, rendue présente par le cours des choses et la bonne volonté de l'ordre quotidien ...' (31). Does this really help us to imagine the actual presence of the young woman, particularly since her physical being is reduced to an image? Does it help any more than the disconcerting metaphor that personifies a moment in time with the features of a human being: '... je crois que l'instant, lui aussi, *dans sa sincérité joyeuse et sous le visage ravissant qui était le sien*, se troublait devant sa propre apparition' (104)? Here the yawning gap separating the metaphoric image from the fictive referent that occasioned it clearly militates against our being able to concretize the 'instant'[17] in question, in spite of the fact that there can be no confusion in the reader's mind as to where the metaphor begins and where it ends.

All too often, however, the line separating the fictive referent from its metaphoric evocation is blurred to the point of disappearing, as could already be seen in so many passages cited before this discussion of *explicit* metaphors and similes. Often this is because the character of the fictive referent, its very identity, is unclear, as is the case with what the narrator refers to as a 'mouvement étrange,' which could be either a physical or a purely mental phenomenon: '... maintenant que je pouvais la regarder du fond de mon souvenir, j'étais soulevé, ramené vers une autre vie. Oui, un mouvement étrange venait à moi, *une possibilité inoubliée, qui se moquait des jours, qui rayonnait à travers la nuit la plus sombre, une puissance sans regard, contre laquelle l'étonnement, la détresse ne pouvaient rien*' (10–11). A more precise

---

17 The same is true of the following passage: 'Et ce qui rendait folle mon impatience, c'est que le bel instant voulait être retenu, éternisé, qu'il était un instant gai, et ignorant ou soupçonnant seulement qu'à s'attarder auprès de moi, il se condamnait à devenir une belle apparition, un retour à jamais beau, mais séparé de lui et de moi par la plus grande cruauté' (105).

ambiguity is found in the subject of the following sentence, where 'l'air' likewise could refer either to appearance or to the climatic atmosphere, a fact that results in the fictive referent and metaphoric image becoming so bound up with each other that they can no longer be differentiated: 'L'air, frileux et fureteur, courait sans cesse derrière elles [les deux femmes], affairé, désœuvré, sans autre rôle que d'envelopper leurs allées et venues d'une frange d'étoffe' (73). Once again, what is the reader to make of this? There *is* nothing, literally, to be made of it as far as the reader's attempt at concretization is concerned – except perhaps a surrealistic painting, which would certainly have no place in the world of *Au Moment voulu*. And yet, as suggested in the previous reference to the supernatural apropos of the door opening without anyone laying a hand on it, there is something surreal[18] – in the sense of being beyond the normal range of human experience – about this *récit*, if only because of the oft noted disappearance into thin air, so to speak, of solid bodies, human and otherwise, and the reverse process: the materialization of the intangible, whereby thoughts, feelings, and moods[19] take on a physical life of their own.

The result of these extraordinary goings-on is that the reader not only experiences great difficulty in concretizing the fictive referents that would normally make up the world proposed by the work, but also has the distinct impression that the fictive referents have receded beyond the reach of the imagination. For what is at stake here goes beyond the problem of *grasping* the fictive referent to that of being able even to *identify* it or indeed to locate it within the text: '... le jour s'était refermé en vain sur l'illimité du jour. Quelque chose lui avait échappé, sa propre transparence, cette blancheur fascinée devenue la stupeur d'un cri, figure lisse, glaciale, farouche et effarouchée, que le vent éparpillait au hasard et rattrapait au hasard' (101). What reader would have the temerity to claim to be able to identify this 'quelque chose'? How can one relate to one's own experience a kind of personified whiteness that is ephemeral and diaphanous enough to be dissipated by the wind while being tangible enough to bear facial features and be subsequently gathered up again by that same wind? And how can a single phenomenon belong at one

18 This is not the place to go into all the strange events and singular phenomena that appear to take place within this *récit*.
19 Not to mention a pure abstraction such as 'le divertissement,' which 'n'apparaît pas à un endroit ou à un autre, il rend seulement les apparences plus brillantes, plus manifestes et aussi plus étendues, de telle sorte que les confins eux-mêmes ont la belle tranquillité de la surface' (153).

and the same time to the domain of the emotions ('stupeur') and of the aurally perceptible ('cri')? Just as the narrator comments on an expression used by Claudia: '... bien que "les autres" ne fût pas une expression des mieux circonscrites' (110), the same might well be said of so many expressions encountered in this text.

The situation is virtually the same as that confronted by the reader of Sartre's *La Nausée*. To shift for a moment from a reading perspective to a writing one, in such a passage Blanchot appears to be up against the very limits of language, attempting to give expression to the inexpressible. The 'chose,' as again in the following passage, is none other than Roquentin's 'ça,' with the important proviso that the fictive referent for Sartre's narrator is a material object, a tree trunk, whereas for Blanchot's it is 'something' even less definable, imperceptible to any of the five senses:[20] ' ... une étonnante rage me souleva, j'empoignai à bras-le-corps, à défaut de moi que j'aurais voulu précipiter contre la porte, *une misérable chose, vaguement blanche,* qui n'avait cessé d'être présente pendant toute cette scène et que la puissance de l'ébranlement volatilisa. Cela fut soufflé comme une lumière. L'impression, effet de la stupeur, fut qu'il y avait par là une lacune, mais aussi, ce qui était très déprimant, que quelque chose était pris au piège: entre ciel et terre, comme on dit, je pensais ces mots en allemand, *zwischen Himmel und Erde*' (79).[21] One hesitates, however, to go so far as to claim that Blanchot, like Sartre before him, is building on the very collapse of language itself. At all events, the fictive referent here becomes the Beckettian 'indicible impensable' and the Sartrean, as well as Beckettian, 'innommable.'[22]

To turn back from the production to the reception of the text, the place occupied by the fictive referent is marked out by a void, analogous to but not the same as that other void resulting from the self-cancellation of contradictions and collapsed or imploded paradoxes noted above. In Ingardenian terminology, the spot of indeterminacy here takes on its most extreme form in that the reader's attention is

---

20 It should be made clear here that I am referring not to the language occasioned by the fictive referent, which certainly evokes sensually perceptible phenomena, but to the fictive referent itself.
21 The German is italicized in the text.
22 At one point, the protagonist of the events related, as distinct from his later persona, the narrator, experiences the same difficulty as the latter: 'je remarquai en angle près de la fenêtre une petite table, ... mais le mot pour désigner ce meuble ne me vint pas' (17).

directly focused upon it to the exclusion of all that *is* determined by the text around it and that can therefore be made out by the reader.

In the case of this text of Blanchot, it is then the first level of reference that is problematic, given the elusiveness of the fictive referent. This necessarily has an effect on the extent to which the work can be concretized by its reader or at least on the *manner* in which it is concretized. As we have seen, it is very doubtful whether it is possible to untangle the metaphorical from the literal (that is, what is directly designated by the text as an element of the fiction or, in Todorov's terminology, signified rather than symbolized[23]) in this particular novelistic discourse where language appears at times to be reduced to metaphor to the virtual exclusion of all else. Now, it is my contention that the individual metaphors and similes that possess the formal properties of those literary figures represent, in Ricoeur's terminology, a *doubly suspended reference*, in that their literal reference has to be suspended (or, as we put it earlier, bracketed) in order to allow the fictive universe to emerge as a coherent construct through the coming into play of the reference of the surrounding text, which will then, in its turn, be suspended. In less technical parlance, the images called forth by the metaphors and similes are doubly fictional, or fictional to the second degree, since, as Nathalie Sarraute's works illustrate so tellingly,[24] they are fictions within a fiction.[25]

There are, then, two levels on which the literal reference is suspended. Just as 'the literary work through the structure proper to it displays a world only under the condition that the reference of descriptive discourse is suspended'[26] – a 'being-in-the-world' corresponding to 'the world-propositions opened up by the reference of the

23 See chapter 1, pp. 15–16 above.
24 An example from Sarraute's *Le Planétarium*: ' "Eh bien quoi? Qu'est-ce que vous avez à vous exciter? C'est une maniaque, voilà tout ..." Une maniaque. Voilà tout ... La forêt luxuriante où il les conduisait, la forêt vierge où ils avançaient, étonnés, vers il ne sait quelles étranges contrées, quelles faunes inconnues, quels rites secrets, va se changer en un instant en une route sillonnée d'autos, bordée de postes d'essence, de poteaux indicateurs et de panneaux-réclame ...' (27). Needless to say, none of this scene forms any part of the world of the fiction.
25 This is not to say, however, that they have no place in the world of the fiction. Although that is indeed the case for any novel narrated in the third person, it is not so for the first-person narrative where the choice of metaphors and comparisons being directly attributable to the narrator, serve therefore to characterize him. Need I add that this would be a further complicating factor in any overall interpretation of *Au Moment voulu*?
26 Ricoeur, *The Rule of Metaphor*, 221

text'[27] – the fictional world in which the novel's characters move and have their being can only come into existence as a coherent Gestalt on condition that the literal reference of metaphor is suspended. This is the reason why the status of the fictional universe made up of the network of relations existing between the fictive referents is so problematic in Blanchot's *récit* and why its concretization is so daunting a task. For once it becomes virtually impossible to sort out what is to be taken literally as far as the evocation of the world of the fiction is concerned from what is, on the contrary, 'only' to be taken metaphorically, then by the same token it becomes doubtful in the extreme whether the reader can form a satisfactory Gestalt in his imagination as he attempts to concretize the work – that is, satisfactory in the sense that it be coherent, cohesive, and consistent within itself. For all these conditions have to be met for concretization to be successfully achieved.

Once we move beyond the first stage of reference as defined in chapter 1 or the second level of suspended reference as defined above, that is the level corresponding to the fictional universe, having noted the problematic status of the latter, we have then to ask ourselves what exactly is the nature of the 'proposed world' that 'is not *behind* the text, as a hidden intention would be, but *in front of* it, as that which the work unfolds, discovers, reveals.'[28] In fact, this is the point where the concretization, however difficult its realization has been, becomes an object for and of interpretation. For, to cite Ricoeur again, 'to interpret is to explicate the type of being-in-the-world unfolded *in front of* the text.'[29] By the same token, it is also the point at which we begin to make the world in question our own world and the work thereby becomes an object of appropriation for its reader: 'What is to be interpreted is a proposed world which I could inhabit and in which I could project my ownmost possibilities.'[30] What exactly, in Ricoeur's terms, are the 'new possibilities of being-in-the-world [that] are opened up within everyday reality'[31] by this *récit?* Formulated thus, however, such a question is too ambitious, reaching as it does beyond the confines of present concerns; it would call for a comprehensive critical study, in short an interpretation of this work. It would be more perti-

27 Ricoeur, *Interpretation Theory*, 87
28 Ricoeur, 'The Hermeneutical Function of Distanciation,' 143; Ricoeur's emphasis
29 Ibid, 141; Ricoeur's emphasis
30 Ricoeur, 'Phenomenology and Hermeneutics,' 112
31 'The Hermeneutical Function of Distanciation,' 142

nent to ask ourselves what effect the particular character of the fictive world concretized might have on the manner of the work's appropriation.

It is crucial at this point to realize that there is no distinction to be made between the status of the actual (as opposed to the literal)[32] reference of explicit metaphors and that of the rest of the language of the text; for what is to be taken literally, rather than figuratively (like the images evoked by the metaphors), with regard to the task of constituting the world of the fiction is itself nonetheless figurative or metaphorical inasmuch as it belongs to the realm of literary and not everyday discourse. What was, as we observed, a definite problem for the reader seeking to concretize the work in his imagination – the merging or blurring of the metaphorical and the literal – is no longer one as far as his actual appropriation of the work is concerned, since on this level of the process of reference the whole text functions in the same manner.

Paul Ricoeur, in his study *The Rule of Metaphor*, has made the most convincing case for a metaphorical reference:

Can one not say that, by drawing a new semantic pertinence out of the ruins of a literal meaning, the metaphoric interpretation *also* sustains a new referential design, through those same means of abolition of the reference corresponding to the literal interpretation of the statement? A proportional argument therefore: the other reference, the object of our search, would be to the new semantic pertinence what the abolished reference is to the literal meaning destroyed by the semantic impertinence. A metaphorical reference would correspond to the metaphorical meaning, just as an impossible literal reference corresponds to the impossible literal meaning.[33]

It is of course the whole text of Blanchot's *récit*, as poetic discourse, that 'faces reality by putting into play [an] *heuristic fiction* whose constitutive value is proportional to [its] power of denial' (239),[34] for there is no disputing the power of its denial of any literal, familiar reality: as will undoubtably have emerged from the foregoing analyses of passages of *Au Moment voulu*, it would in fact be difficult to conceive of a world more disconcertingly unfamiliar to the reader.

32 In other words, the reference realized by the reader through his appropriation of the work
33 *The Rule of Metaphor*, 230
34 Ricoeur's emphasis

Few texts better illustrate the way that, as Ricoeur puts it, 'everyday reality is ... metamorphised [sic] by what could be called the imaginative variations which literature carries out on the real.'[35] The imaginative power, suggestiveness, and creative innovativeness of its metaphorical discourse bears striking witness to the fact that 'language not only has organized reality in a different way, but also made manifest a way of being of things, which is brought to language by semantic innovation,' thus demonstrating what Ricoeur calls 'the enigma of metaphorical discourse,' which is 'that it "invents" in both senses of the word: what it creates, it discovers; and what it finds, it invents' (239). The parallel that the theoretician establishes between the writer's use of metaphor and the scientist's recourse to the model is here most pertinent: '... with respect to the relation to reality, metaphor is to poetic language what the model is to scientific language.' He sees the model as 'an instrument of redescription' – an expression the meaning of which he takes 'in its primitive epistemological usage' – belonging 'not to the logic of justification or proof, but to the logic of discovery' (240). What is important in light of our preceding discussion of Blanchot's *récit* is that the analogy between the scientific model and the metaphoric language of literature does not lie on the level of individual metaphors but on that of the work as a whole: '... what on the poetic side corresponds exactly to the model is not precisely what we have called the "metaphorical statement," that is, a short bit of discourse reduced most often to a sentence. Rather, as the model consists in a complex network of statements, its exact analogue would be the extended metaphor – tale, allegory' (243).

There is no question of the potential of the 'heuristic fiction' proposed by *Au Moment voulu*, and it is important to remind ourselves that the being it intends, like that of all fiction and poetry, is 'under the modality of power-to-be.'[36] However, for this hypothetical model of reality to exercise its influence on the reader, an exceptional effort is required from the latter; he must dispossess himself of himself in order to achieve the disappropriation of self that has to precede appropriation. For 'it is not a question of imposing on the text our finite capacity of understanding, but of exposing ourselves to the text and receiving from it an enlarged self, which would be the proposed existence corresponding in the most suitable way to the world proposed.'[37]

35 'The Hermeneutical Function of Distanciation,' 142
36 Ibid.
37 Ibid., 143

Whether the reader of Blanchot's *récit* is prepared to accept this 'enlarged self' is another question, and in this regard, his situation is not unlike that of the non-believer reading Bernanos.

Ricoeur's reference above to the literary genre known as the allegory brings us back to the question of the interpretation of *Au Moment voulu*. It is hardly surprising that so many of the critics writing on Blanchot have opted for a clearly allegorical reading of this text.[38] One of the few clear conclusions that emerge from the preceding pages is that it does tend to take on, for the reader, all the appearance of an elaborate extended metaphor.

And there is good reason to believe that in this respect at least, appearances are not, for once, deceptive. For what this *récit* is in fact concerned with is, as has been demonstrated elsewhere,[39] none other than language itself. The reason why the reader experiences such difficulty in identifying the nature of the fictive referent in this text is that the (only) fictive referent proposed is the very space of language itself.[40] It is little wonder that the reader has difficulty in seeing the forest for the trees. It should be stressed once again that it is on this very first level of reference, the constitution of the fictive universe, that the reader's dilemma lies. When the actual *location* within the text of the evocation of the fictive referents – let alone the *identity* of the latter – proves to be problematic, then one is hard put even to pursue one's reading, for one has not the faintest idea of what is going on. Reading of any kind has to be concomitant with understanding just as understanding is concomitant with interpreting.

38 In 'Un Référent fictif pas comme les autres: *Au Moment voulu* de Maurice Blanchot,' I taxed such allegorical interpretations as being perhaps too hastily arrived at. The hermeneutic problem posed by this work was also addressed therein and deliberately set aside for present purposes, for I maintain that the hermeneutic process is curiously displaced since it coincides with that other process that normally precedes it: concretization.

39 See Fitch, 'Temps du récit et temps de l'écriture dans *Au Moment voulu* de Blanchot.'

40 Blanchot's remarks in a footnote to *L'Espace littéraire*, which are subsequently developed in an appendix under the title 'Les Deux Versions de l'imaginaire' (341–55), would appear to concur with my reading of this text: '...est-ce que, dans le poème, dans la littérature, le langage ne serait pas, par rapport au langage courant, ce qu'est l'image par rapport à la chose? ... est-ce que le langage lui-même ne devient pas, dans la littérature, tout entier image, non pas un langage qui contiendrait des images ou qui mettrait la réalité en figures, mais qui serait sa propre image, image de langage – et non pas un langage imagé...' (31–2, n. 1; my emphasis).

The problems posed by this work, however, are by no means exhausted once the nature of the fictive referent has been recognized for what it is. For the concretization of a phenomenon as abstract in character and as absent from the awareness of the majority of readers as is the space delimited by the ontological dimension of language represents a considerable challenge. At the very least, it makes exceptional demands on the imagination. It is precisely the nature of the abstraction that is at the root of the problem here. When the abstraction takes the form of human emotions, thoughts, or states of mind, as in so many French *récits*, where it is merely a question of concretizing a represented psychic space as opposed to the represented real space pre-eminent in the novels of French realism, the fictive referent can be readily imagined by the reader since it corresponds to analogous elements of one's own experience. The space of language, on the other hand, is an *ideal* space with no human content whatsoever. Consequently, there is no question of the reader's empathizing or identifying with what is being depicted. Moreover, any linguistic representation of an abstraction that lends itself to visualization is therefore, by definition, metaphorical. And this brings us back to our point of departure: the difficulty the reader of *Au Moment voulu* experiences in attempting to determine where metaphor begins in the text and where it ends.

Ultimately, Ricoeur's concept of an 'enlarged self' may prove to be inoperative here. Since to appropriate the space of language, to take up one's abode therein, is to become dispossessed of one's very selfhood; it is a process of alienation, which is, moreover, not exercised in favour of any other human being or indeed of any human attribute whatsoever. The reader is thereby following in the footsteps of the writer before him, for, as Blanchot states at length, 'l'écrivain appartient à un language que personne ne parle, qui ne s'adresse à personne, qui n'a pas de centre, qui ne révèle rien' and although 'il peut croire qu'il s'affirme en ce langage ... ce qu'il affirme est tout à fait *privé de soi*':[41] 'Ce qui parle en lui, c'est ce fait que, d'une manière ou d'une autre, il n'est plus lui-même, *il n'est déjà plus personne.*'[42] Like the reader of Simon's novel *Histoire*, as will be seen, although for very different reasons, Blanchot's reader is in the same position as the author in relation to the language of the text.

41 *L'Espace littéraire*, 21; my emphasis
42 Ibid., 23; my emphasis

6

The Empty Referent:
Camus' *La Chute*

Camus' last novel, *La Chute*, like Beckett's *L'Innommable*, is a work
to which one constantly returns. It is without a doubt the most intriguing of his novels and its original publication in 1956 threw a whole
new light on his works, causing considerable consternation among his
critics. Over the years, I have proposed a number of different readings
of this text, the first being centred on the image of falling,[1] the second
on its theatrical attributes,[2] the third analysing it in terms of speech-
act concepts,[3] and most recently viewing it as a paradigm for the
hermeneutic process in light of the writings of Paul Ricoeur and Hans-
Georg Gadamer.[4] The topic of the present study calls for an examination of the status of the fictive referent and the manner in which
referentiality functions in general within this work.

It has always appeared to me that the totality of Camus' production
as a novelist posed certain problems in terms of the fictional referentiality of *L'Étranger*, *La Peste*, and *La Chute*.[5] The fictive universes of
his first two novels are held at a distance from the reader, viewed
as though through a distancing filter. The filter in question is the
consciousness of the narrator, to which it is difficult indeed to attribute
any precise content that would serve to individualize him as a character. This narrative/narrating consciousness that interposes itself
between the reader and the characters living out past events is very

---

1 'Clamence en chute libre: La cohérence imaginaire de *La Chute*'
2 'Une Voix qui se parle, qui nous parle, que nous parlons, ou l'espace théâtral de
  La Chute'
3 'Locuteur, délocuteur et allocutaire dans *La Chute* de Camus'
4 'The Interpreter Interpreted: *La Chute*,' in *The Narcissistic Text: A Reading of
  Camus' Fiction*
5 See Fitch, 'Le Statut précaire du personnage et de l'univers romanesques chez
  Camus.'

much an unknown quantity, whether it bear the name of Meursault or Rieux, and remains so even when one has finished reading the novel. If we know who Meursault is *not* – that is, the person whose portrait emerges from his own trial – that does not mean that we know who he really is, any more than we can feel we know Rieux – even after Rieux has revealed his role as narrator of the chronicle just read. And given the detached manner in which the narrators speak of their own past, it is no easier for the reader to come to grips with them as protagonists in the stories they tell, for each speaks of himself as though of another. Clamence, the narrator-protagonist of *La Chute*, is just as elusive, although for rather different reasons. In his case, while we may well think we are gradually getting to know Clamence as his story unfolds, evoked by his own words, this impression is dramatically dispelled by his final revelation of the role he has been playing from the beginning. He ends up by revealing himself to be even more an unknown quantity for the reader than his two precursors.

The situation in *La Chute* is nonetheless very different from that in Camus' two preceding novels. From the moment it appeared, its readers were struck by the formal originality of this work, situated as it clearly was somewhere between the novel and the theatre. Unlike Meursault and Rieux, the narrator of *La Chute* exists as a character in his own right independent of his function as the main protagonist of the story he has to tell. The evocation of Clamence by the text in the present is no less vivid and immediate than the evocation of his past life through his own words. What results from this state of affairs is the coming into being of not one fictive universe but two, corresponding to the past and the present, but it is clearly the creation of the latter to which the work owes its originality.

Not surprisingly, those particular parts of speech that the linguists call deictics or shifters play as significant a role here as they will be seen to play in Beckett's *L'Innommable*. Any fictive universe situated in the present tends quite naturally to draw upon the evocative powers of shifters, for such a universe nearly always features the person of the narrator himself and it is precisely the function of the shifter to evoke the situation and circumstances in which the discourse is being articulated: 'Puis-*je*, monsieur,[6] *vous* proposer mes services, sans risquer d'être importun?' begins the text:

---

6 It should be noted here that there is no doubt about the gender of Clamence's companion. The significance of that fact will become apparent later in this chapter (see n. 25 below).

Je crains que *vous* ne sachiez *vous* faire entendre de l'estimable gorille qui préside aux destinées de *cet* établissement. Il ne parle, en effet, que le hollandais. A moins que *vous* ne *m'*autorisiez à plaider *votre* cause, il ne devinera pas que *vous* désirez du genièvre. *Voilà*, *j'*ose espérer qu'il m'a compris; *ce* hochement de tête doit signifier qu'il se rend à *mes* arguments. Il y va, en effet, il se hâte, avec une sage lenteur. *Vous* avez de la chance, il n'a pas grogné. Quand il refuse de servir, un grognement suffit: personne n'insiste. Être roi de ses humeurs, c'est le privilège des grands animaux. Mais *je* me *retire*, monsieur, heureux de *vous* avoir obligé. *Je vous* remercie et *j'*accepterais si *j'*étais sûr de ne pas jouer les fâcheux. *Vous* êtes trop bon. *J'*installerai donc *mon* verre auprès du *vôtre*. (1475)[7]

The very first sentence of this initial paragraph reveals another distinguishing feature of *La Chute:* the presence of an explicit interlocutor or, to resort once again to the linguist's terminology, the presence of an addressee within the fictive universe. Now, the nature of linguistic shifters entails that their existence be interdependent: the presence of one implies that of all the others. Such is, therefore, the case of the personal pronouns *I* and *you*, for as Benveniste points out: '... *je* pose une autre personne, celle qui, tout extérieure qu'elle est à "moi," devient mon écho auquel je dis *tu* et qui me dit *tu*. La polarité des personnes, telle est dans le langage la condition fondamentale, dont le procès de communciation ... n'est qu'une conséquence toute pragmatique ... aucun des deux termes ne se conçoit sans l'autre; ils sont complémentaires ... et en même temps ils sont réversibles.'[8]

In the majority of novels narrated in the first person the existence of a second person, grammatically speaking, remains implicit, whether the person in question be thought of in terms of an 'implied reader' (Iser[9]) or as a 'narratee' (Prince[10]). It is, above all else, the presence of an actual addressee and the resulting dialogic situation that is so reminiscent of the theatre and so atypical of the novel genre. However, if the presence of the addressee is here *explicit*, his actual contribution to the conversation between Clamence and himself remains *implicit* insofar as the actual words he utters are concerned, as when Clamence says: 'Je vous remercie et j'accepterais si j'étais sûr

---

7 *La Chute* in *Théâtre, récits, nouvelles*. The shifters have, of course, been italicized by me.
8 *Problèmes de linguistique générale, 1,* 260
9 *The Implied Reader*
10 'Introduction to the Study of the Narratee'

de ne pas jouer les fâcheux.' And once again, when he adds or rather responds to his interlocutor's invitation: 'Vous êtes trop bon. J'installerai donc mon verre auprès du vôtre.' The latter then, like the proverbial good child, is seen but not heard.

The first chapter of *La Chute* is devoted initially to the evocation of the bar in Amsterdam in which Clamence and his companion are conversing, *Mexico-City*, and its proprietor, referred to by Clamence as 'l'homme de Cro-Magnon' (1475). Their surroundings are sketched in: 'Voyez, par exemple, au-dessus de sa tête [the proprietor's], sur le mur de fond, ce rectangle vide qui marque la place d'un tableau décroché. Il y avait là, en effet, un tableau, et particulièrement intéressant, un vrai chef-d'œuvre' (1476). Before the drinks arrive Clamence proceeds to speak of the city of Amsterdam and of its inhabitants the Dutch: 'On nous apporte enfin notre genièvre. A votre prospérité. Oui, le gorille a ouvert la bouche pour m'appeler docteur ... Au demeurant, je ne suis pas médecin. Si vous voulez le savoir, j'étais avocat avant de venir ici. Maintenant, je suis juge-pénitent' (1477). Thereupon, Clamence turns his attention to his companion:

Vous êtes sans doute dans les affaires? A peu près? Excellente réponse! Judicieuse aussi; nous ne sommes qu'à peu près en toutes choses ... Vous avez à peu près mon âge, l'œil renseigné des quadragénaires qui ont à peu près fait le tour des choses, vous êtes à peu près bien habillé, c'est-à-dire comme on l'est chez nous, et vous avez les mains lisses. Donc, un bourgeois, à peu près! Mais un bourgeois raffiné! Broncher sur les imparfaits du subjonctif, en effet, prouve deux fois votre culture puisque vous les reconnaissez d'abord et qu'ils vous agacent ensuite. Enfin, je vous amuse, ce qui, sans vanité, suppose chez vous une certaine ouverture d'esprit. (1478)

He then adds to his own portrait: 'Par la taille, les épaules, et ce visage dont on m'a souvent dit qu'il était farouche, j'aurais plutôt l'air d'un joueur de rugby, n'est-ce pas? Mais si l'on en juge par la conversation, il faut me consentir un peu de raffinement ... Enfin, malgré mes bonnes manières et mon beau langage, je suis un habitué des bars à matelots du Zeedijk' (1478). After a further evocation of the city and its inhabitants, Clamence bids his drinking companion good night: 'A demain donc, monsieur et cher compatriote. Non, vous trouverez maintenant votre chemin; je vous quitte près de ce pont' (1481).

The second chapter opens with Clamence immediately referring again to his profession before beginning the detailed account of his past: 'Qu'est-ce qu'un juge-pénitent? Ah! je vous ai intrigué avec cette histoire. Je n'y mettais aucune malice, croyez-le, et je peux m'expliquer plus clairement. Dans un sens, cela fait même partie de mes fonctions. Mais il me faut d'abord vous exposer un certain nombre de faits qui vous aideront à mieux comprendre mon récit' (1482). It is now the story-teller proper who takes over, and the world of Clamence's past life begins to take on form and substance at the expense of the surroundings in the bar *Mexico-City*, which recede into the background of the reader's imagination – that is, until the return to them at the end of the chapter: 'Non, non, je ne puis rester. D'ailleurs, je suis appelé en consultation par l'ours brun que vous voyez là-bas ... Vous estimez qu'il a une tête de tueur? Soyez sûr que c'est la tête de l'emploi.' We learn that the person in question deals in stolen paintings, and Clamence explains: 'En Hollande, tout le monde est spécialiste en peintures et en tulipes. Celui-ci, avec ses airs modestes, est l'auteur du plus célèbre des vols de tableau' (1493–4). Clamence's hobby, he says, is helping such people by giving them legal advice.

The next chapter begins with Clamence's response to his companion's question: 'Vraiment, mon cher compatriote, je vous suis reconnaissant de votre curiosité' (1495). It is not until they have finally left the bar to return home on foot ('Tiens, la pluie a cessé! Ayez la bonté de me raccompagner chez moi' [1509]) that their surroundings are once again commented upon and hence evoked for the reader: 'Mais nous sommes arrivés, voici ma maison, mon abri! Demain? Oui, comme vous voudrez. Je vous mènerai volontiers à l'île de Marken, vous verrez le Zuyderzee' (1509).

Naturally, the following chapter opens with the island setting: 'Un village de poupée, ne trouvez-vous pas? Le pittoresque ne lui a pas été épargné! Mais je ne vous ai pas conduit dans cette île pour le pittoresque, cher ami. Tout le monde peut vous faire admirer des coiffes, des sabots, et des maisons décorées où les pêcheurs fument du tabac fin dans l'odeur de l'encaustique' (1510). A detailed evocation of the island's landscape follows, 'le plus beau des paysages négatifs' (1510), as Clamence calls it. Once again we finally come back to the immediate situation after he has recounted further details from his past: 'Mais la mer monte, il me semble. Notre bateau ne va pas tarder à partir, le jour s'achève. Voyez, les colombes se rassemblent là-haut. Elles se pressent les unes contre les autres, elles remuent à peine, et la lumière baisse' (1522).

The next chapter finds Clamence and his companions still on the boat on the way back to Amsterdam: 'Vous vous trompez, cher, le bateau file à bonne allure. Mais le Zuyderzee est une mer morte, ou presque. Avec ses bords plats, perdus dans la brume, on ne sait où elle commence, où elle finit. Alors, nous marchons sans aucun repère, nous ne pouvons évaluer notre vitesse. Nous avançons, et rien ne change' (1523). It concludes with Clamence's invitation to his interlocutor to visit him the next day at his home but without any evocation of their immediate surroundings.

To recapitulate: chapters 2 to 5, while devoted almost exclusively to the recounting of Clamence's past life, begin by evoking the material surroundings in which this one-sided conversation is pursued and finally – with the exception, as we have seen, of chapter 5 – return to that same setting. Even during the course of the narration, although the world of the past clearly and continually occupies the forefront of the reader's imagination, the text is regularly punctuated by expressions the function of which is phatic, the speaker thereby reassuring himself that he still has his interlocutor's undivided attention. An obvious example is the expression 'n'est-ce pas?': 'On ne peut pas nier que, pour le moment, du moins, il faille des juges, n'est-ce pas?' (1482); 'N'était-ce pas cela, en effet, l'Eden, cher monsieur: la vie en prise directe?' (1487). Such linguistic features of the text ensure that the reader is never permitted to lose sight of the presence of Clamence's interlocutor: 'Je vois que cette déclaration vous étonne' (1489). In fact, the latter is often addressed directly: 'A la fin, son tort lui devint insupportable. Que croyez-vous qu'il fît alors? Il cessa de la [his wife] tromper? Non. Il la tua' (1483); 'Vous admettrez alors que je puisse parler, en toute modestie, d'une vie réussie' (1487). Many of Clamence's questions, however, are rhetorical ones: 'N'avez-vous jamais eu subitement besoin de sympathie, de secours, d'amitié? Oui, bien sûr' (1489). Exclamations are also frequent and fulfil an analogous function; they, too, serve to evoke the physical presence not so much of the addressee but rather of the speaker himself: 'Il me suffisait cependant de renifler sur un accusé la plus légère odeur de victime pour que mes manches entrassent en action. Et quelle action!' (1482); 'Combien de crimes commis simplement parce que leur auteur ne pouvait supporter d'être en faute!' (1483). They ensure that an oral discourse never runs any risk of being perceived as a written text.[11] In other words, the dialogic situation that is the occasion for the recounting of Clamence's biography is continually being brought to the reader's attention. And the setting in which the conversation is

11 The dialectic relationship between the oral and the written is analysed within a hermeneutic perspective in 'The Interpreter Interpreted' in *The Narcissistic Text*.

taking place is returned to through the evocations at the beginning and end of each chapter.

However, we should not lose sight of the fact that this is a decidedly one-sided conversation; quite naturally, critics have been inclined to speak of what they call Clamence's 'monologue.' Moreover, as far as the reader is concerned, a monologue is indeed what he is confronted with, since the text does not contain a single word spoken by the interlocutor. The result is that it is Clamence, whether as the protagonist in his past existence or as story-teller, who occupies the reader's imagination to the total exclusion of his unheard companion.

I have used the term *story-teller* advisedly, for in the final chapter we suddenly discover to our dismay that the story of Clamence's past life to which we have been listening from the second chapter onwards is no doubt more of a fictive 'story' than a real 'life.'

The final chapter begins with Clamence receiving his visitor while lying ill in bed: 'Je suis confus de vous recevoir couché. Ce n'est rien, un peu de fièvre que je soigne au genièvre' (1535). His first words are disquieting, to say the least: 'Je sais ce que vous pensez: il est bien difficile de démêler le vrai du faux dans ce que je raconte. Je confesse que vous avez raison. Moi-même... Voyez-vous, une personne de mon entourage divisait les êtres en trois catégories: ceux qui préfèrent n'avoir rien à cacher plutôt que d'être obligés de mentir, ceux qui préfèrent mentir plutôt que de n'avoir rien à cacher, et ceux enfin qui aiment en même temps le mensonge et le secret. Je vous laisse choisir la case qui me convient le mieux.' The possibility we are now confronted with is that there is not a word of truth in what he has been telling us: 'Qu'importe, après tout? Les mensonges ne mettent-ils pas finalement sur la voie de la vérité? Et mes histoires, vraies ou fausses, ne tendent-elles pas toutes à la même fin, n'ont-elles pas le même sens? Alors, qu'importe qu'elles soient vraies ou fausses si, dans les deux cas, elles sont significatives de ce que j'ai été et de ce que je suis' (1535). (We shall later have occasion to clarify the nature of the 'truth' in question.)

Clamence then evokes the surroundings once again, as we have been led to expect by now: 'Vous regardez cette pièce. Nue, c'est vrai, mais propre. Un Vermeer, sans meubles ni casseroles. Sans livres, non plus, j'ai cessé de lire depuis longtemps.' Thereupon he adds a remark that is hardly reassuring to the reader: 'D'ailleurs, je n'aime plus que les confessions, et les auteurs de confession écrivent surtout pour ne pas se confesser, pour ne rien dire de ce qu'ils savent.' For what has the reader been reading up to this point if not an apparent confession?

'Quand ils prétendent passer aux aveux,' he adds, 'c'est le moment de se méfier, on va maquiller le cadavre. Croyez-moi, je suis orfèvre' (1536). Nothing could be clearer. Without being aware of the fact, the reader has been involved all this time with that peculiar and unusual literary phenomenon identified by Wayne Booth many years ago as the 'unreliable narrator.'

This does not prevent Clamence from imperturbably returning to the 'story' of his life in the form of what he calls his 'aventures pontificales' (1536). But the damage has been done as far as the reader is concerned. The reality of the world of Clamence's past life with which the reader's imagination has been primarily occupied throughout the preceding chapters – not only because the majority of the fictive referents had contributed to the evocation of that reality but also because the events and experiences of the Parisian lawyer as he practised his profession far from the mists of Amsterdam had quite naturally been thought to constitute the *raison d'être* of the narrator's tale – has suddenly become, at the very least, problematic, particularly when the reader recalls certain of the narrator's previous remarks to which he paid little attention at the time – 'Je m'arrête: trop de symétrie nuirait à ma démonstration' (1517) – but which now take on added significance. The fictional referentiality of the text on the level of the past tense has suddenly revealed itself to be doubly fictional in that Clamence's story-telling is without any referent whatsoever, since its content is itself a work of fiction, a creation of the speaker's imagination.

In more technical terms, this means that the actualization of the fictive referents corresponding to his past Parisian existence has been further suspended or deferred in relation to those other referents evoking the presence of the narrator. It has acquired a third level of reference; the first level, corresponding to the fiction, has split in two or doubled up upon itself, thus causing the real reference of the second level that is only actualized by the reader's final appropriation of the work, to recede farther into the background and hence become that much more inaccessible. Having actualized, that is concretized, the fictive referent in the form of the Parisian lawyer and his clients, we cannot then proceed to move beyond this level on which reference is suspended to the real referent that involves our own existential situation. For before we can do so, having lifted, as it were, the suspension of reference relating to the past, we have to draw back to the first level and reinstate the suspension of reference once again on the level of the evocation of the Amsterdam bar that we began by actualizing.[12] Only once this first level has been reactivated, can the fictive referents finally be left behind us and the suspension of reference be effaced (referentially speaking) once and for all. Needless to say, the concretization of all this calls for some imaginative dexterity on the part of the reader. To shift to Ingardenian terminology, it poses the problem of effecting a concretization within a first, initial concretization; in this respect it bears some similarity, in terms of reader reception, to the situation we shall find in Simon's novel *Histoire*, which involves the concretization of a work of art within the concretization of the world of the novel.

Two things are significant here: first, immediately after the story of Clamence's pontifical adventures, we return to the evocation of the room in which the conversation is taking place ('A propos, voulez-vous ouvrir ce placard, s'il vous plaît? Ce tableau, oui, regardez-le. Ne le reconnaissez-vous pas? Ce sont *les Juges intègres*' [1540]); second, from now on the world of the present replaces that of the past. With the putting in question of the reality of Clamence's past life, all that remains is the presence of the loquacious story-teller. But do we really *know* who this person is to whom we have been listening all this time? What exactly do we know of the Amsterdam *juge-pénitent* now that we realize that he is not necessarily the Parisian lawyer we had taken him to be?

The person confronting us as he revels in his adopted function of *juge-pénitent* is the only remaining fictive referent, and he alone, surrounded by the decor of his bedroom, is all that is left for the reader's imagination to dwell upon and for the reader to conjure up in the mind's eye. Can we even be sure that 'Clamence' exists other than as a role the speaker has chosen to adopt for his own purposes? Didn't his visiting card suggest as much: 'Sur mes cartes: "Jean-Baptiste Clamence, *comédien*" ' (1498)?[13] After all, wasn't his self-attributed role of Parisian lawyer indistinguishable from that of any actor: 'Donc, je jouais le jeu ... Je n'étais pas en peine de discours, étant

---

12 Which level is to be designated as the first level of suspended reference and which as the second is a moot point here. The fact is that the reader had not at the time of listening to the story of Clamence's past life been aware of having shifted onto another level of suspended reference. At that time, his life in Paris was the most immediate level of reference and in that sense the first level. Only subsequently does the reader become aware of its receding to a further removed level of fictivity.

13 My emphasis

avocat ... Je changeais souvent de rôle; mais il s'agissait toujours de la même pièce' (1504)? He said himself that he had never stopped playing a role in life: '... je continuais seulement de jouer mon rôle ... j'étais comme mes Hollandais qui sont là sans y être: absent au moment où je tenais le plus de place' (1518). Indeed, the more he speaks, the more elusive he turns out to be. All that we can be certain of – as soon becomes clear – is that he is not the person we had thought him to be: 'Ne croyez pas en effet que, pendant cinq jours, je vous aie fait de si longs discours pour le seul plaisir. ... mon discours est orienté' (1541). His motivation is not, as we had believed, the need to confess and confide but, on the contrary, the desire to judge and condemn: 'Il est orienté par l'idée ... de faire taire les rires, d'éviter personnellement le jugement ... Le grand empêchement à y échapper n'est-il pas que nous sommes les premiers à nous condamner? Il faut donc commencer par étendre la condamnation à tous ... Pas d'excuses, jamais, pour personne, voilà mon principe, au départ' (1541).

Since the narrator does not seek to confess but, on the contrary, to accuse, there is no longer any reason to believe that he has revealed himself to us at all. Indeed, all we actually know of him is his physical appearance, the portrait, quoted earlier, that he drew for us in the first chapter. His whole discourse, in fact, rather than serving in any way as a means of self-expression, has, to resort once again to the linguist's terminology, a solely *perlocutionary* function, seeking to solicit from his listener, as it does, a certain response:

J'exerce donc à *Mexico-City*, depuis quelque temps, mon utile profession. Elle consiste d'abord ... à pratiquer la confession publique aussi souvent que possible. Je m'accuse, en long et en large. ... Mais attention, je ne m'accuse pas grossièrement ... Non, je navigue souplement, je multiplie les nuances, les digressions aussi, j'adapte enfin mon discours à l'auditeur, j'amène ce dernier à renchérir. Je mêle ce qui me concerne et ce qui regarde les autres ... je fabrique un portrait qui est celui de tous et de personne. Un masque en somme ... Quand le portrait est terminé, comme ce soir, je le montre, plein de désolation: 'Voilà, hélas! ce que je suis.' Le réquisitoire est achevé. Mais, du même coup, le portrait que je tends à mes contemporains devient un miroir. (1545)

The perlocutionary character of 'Clamence''s discourse was moreover evident long before this point: 'Oui, l'enfer doit être ainsi: des rues à enseignes et pas moyen de s'expliquer ... *Vous, par exemple, mon cher compatriote, pensez un peu à ce que serait votre enseigne. Vous vous taisez? Allons, vous me répondrez plus tard'* (1497).[14] Even the earliest critics writing on *La Chute* had been struck by the gradual shift in 'Clamence''s discourse from 'moi' to 'nous,' thus preparing the ground for the final accusatory 'vous' as he little by little appealed first to his listener's intelligence and sense of humour and then to his understanding and finally empathizing with him to the point of being able to picture himself in his interlocutor's shoes. What he has been attempting to solicit from his interlocutor all along is the latter's own personal confession, which the speaker's pseudo-confession has been devised to summon up: 'Ne vous fiez pas trop d'ailleurs à mes attendrissements, ni à mes délires. Ils sont dirigés. Tenez, *maintenant que vous allez me parler de vous, je vais savoir si l'un des buts de ma passionante confession est atteint'* (1548).

The spotlight is now clearly focused on the character of the unheard interlocutor, who quite appropriately has been passed over in silence by my commentary up to this point. While there is nothing unreal about the world of the Amsterdam bar *Mexico-City*, contrary to that of 'Clamence''s past, its only inhabitant in the reader's imagination is a perfect stranger who has succeeded in buttonholing his every listener as effectively as Coleridge's ancient mariner. The presence of this one and only human referent to be evoked directly by the speaker ('Clamence') is as certain as his identity is uncertain. In terms of fictional referentiality, the protagonist is a referent whose outline we were encouraged gradually to fill in by using our imagination during our reading, only to discover to our dismay and consternation that his words, instead of progressively characterizing him, have in fact emptied him of any substance in a process of linguistic haemorrhage. In fact, the real subject or, in linguistic terms, the *délocuteur*[15] of 'Clamence''s discourse is, and has been all along, his interlocutor. Through his every word, in spite of the apparently autobiographical nature of his comments, 'Clamence' has been referring not to himself but to his addressee, whose portrait, as we have seen, he has been concerned with sketching in. With the reader's realization that 'Clamence' is a wholly unknown quantity, able to be visualized to a certain extent but only in the form of a complete stranger, the only referent that remains for the reader's imagination to work on and

---

14 My emphasis, as for all other emphasis within quotations from *La Chute* except where otherwise indicated.
15 See 'Locuteur, délocuteur et allocutaire.'

with has to be 'Clamence''s interlocutor. Let us finally then turn our attention to him.

The very fact that it has been possible to omit any mention of the interlocutor for his own sake up to this point speaks for itself. The only existence he enjoys is an *implicit* one, in the sense that while his presence is implied by the narrator's words (particularly when the latter take the form of what is obviously a response to a question or observation of some kind), with the sole exception of the narrator's already quoted portrait of him in the first chapter he is never directly evoked by the text. Apart from that brief portrait – the fact that he is more or less a bourgeois, with some education, cultural pretensions, and a sense of humour – there is little in the text that characterizes him. It is moreover significant that whatever he is, he is only 'more or less.' It is true that the whole of Clamence's discourse serves, as was just pointed out, to draw his portrait. However, the portrait in question is precisely that of Everyman[16] – a portrait 'qui est celui de tous et de personne': 'Je prends les traits communs, les expériences que nous avons ensemble souffertes, les faiblesses que nous partageons, le bon ton, l'homme du jour enfin, tel qu'il sévit en moi et chez les autres' (1545). In other words, it is all too easy to lose sight of this character – which is, needless to say, precisely what was intended. And if there is one form of literature in which, even today, authorial as well as textual intention has its place, it is surely polemical literature, a category to which *La Chute* clearly belongs, given the circumstances of its genesis: Camus' bitter quarrel with Sartre.[17]

Let me pause here for a moment in the development of my argument in order to establish the polemical character of *La Chute*. Related to this aspect of the text are the autobiographical resonances of many of its passages, such as the following portrait of Clamence:

Je n'était pas mal fait de ma personne, je me montrais à la fois danseur infatigable et discret érudit, j'arrivais à aimer en même temps, ce qui n'est

16 As is suggested by the quotation from Lermentov that the novelist chose as the epigraph for one of the versions of his manuscript: ' "Un héros de notre temps" est effectivement un portrait, mais ce n'est pas celui d'un homme. C'est l'assemblage des défauts de notre génération dans toute la plénitude de leur développement' (Quoted by Roger Quilliot (ed.) in *Théâtre, récits, nouvelles*, 2007).

17 Critical documentation for this aspect of *La Chute* is found in the following articles: Roger Quilliot, 'Un Monde ambigu'; Adèle King, 'Structure and Meaning in *La Chute*'; Barbara J. Royce, '*La Chute*, and *Saint Genet*: The Question of Guilt'; and Warren Tucker, '*La Chute*, voie du salut terrestre.'

guère facile, les femmes et la justice, je pratiquais les sports et les beaux-arts ... peu d'êtres ont été plus naturels que moi. Mon accord avec la vie était total, j'adhérais à ce qu'elle était, du haut en bas, sans rien refuser de ses ironies, de sa grandeur, ni de ses servitudes. En particulier, la chair, la matière, le physique en un mot, qui déconcerte ou décourage tant d'hommes dans l'amour ou dans la solitude, m'apportait, sans m'asservir, des joies égales. J'étais fait pour avoir un corps. (1487–8)

What reader would fail to be reminded of the author himself while reading these lines? Particularly since a little farther on, the reader encounters this observation: '... à force d'être comblé, je me sentais, j'hésite à l'avouer, désigné. Designé personnellement, entre tous, pour cette longue et constante réussite' (1488). This cannot fail to bring to mind Camus' remark, in a questionnaire filled out for an American scholar in 1958, that he had had 'le sentiment d'une "étoile," '[18] a star that, eight years earlier in his *Carnets*, he had claimed to have 'toujours suivi[e] d'instinct.'[19] Similarly, Clamence's remark: 'Hors du désir, les femmes m'ennuyèrent au-delà de toute attente ...' (1525) echoes that found in the *Carnets*: 'La femme, hors de l'amour, est ennuyeuse.'[20] This is not to maintain, of course, that Clamence is Camus' self-portrait. It is, however, my contention that the person portrayed represents Camus *as seen through the eyes of Jean-Paul Sartre and his friends*. And evidence to support this contention is also found within the text.

Few readers can fail to have been struck by the existentialist themes that emerge from so many of Clamence's formulations; for example, he remarks: 'Au bout de toute liberté, il y a une sentence; voilà pourquoi la liberté est trop lourde à porter ... Ah! mon cher, pour qui est seul, sans dieu et sans maître, le poids des jours est terrible' (1542). It is clear that Clamence shares with his existentialist kindred spirits the belief that existence precedes essence: 'Les hommes ne sont convaincus de vos raisons, de votre sincérité ... que par votre mort. Tant que vous êtes en vie, votre cas est douteux' (1511). Is this not the core of Sartre's *Huis clos*? Indeed, the existentialism of *La Chute* – and this is less obvious – smacks more of Sartre's writings than of *Le Mythe de Sisyphe*: 'Dieu n'est pas nécessaire pour créer la culpabilité, ni punir. Nos semblables y suffisent ... j'ai connu ce qu'il y a de pire, qui est le

18 In Carl A. Viggiani, 'Notes pour le futur biographe d'Albert Camus,' 206
19 *Carnets, janvier 1942–mars 1951,* 303
20 Ibid., 58

jugement des hommes' (1530). Hell lies in being reduced to what we are for others: '... si tout le monde ... affichait ... son identité ... ! Imaginez des cartes de visite: Dupont, philosophe froussard, ou propriétaire chrétien, ou humaniste adultère ... Mais ce serait l'enfer! Oui, l'enfer doit être ainsi ... On est classé une fois pour toutes' (1497). Was it not the author of *L'Etre et le néant* who held that it is our feeling of shame that proves to us the existence of other people: '... je ne sais comment nommer le curieux sentiment qui me vient. Ne serait-ce pas la honte?' (1508)? Moreover, Sartre is explicitly designated in his capacity as director of the journal *Les Temps modernes* when Clamence refers to the prostitute who 'a consenti ... à écrire ses souvenirs pour un journal confessionnel très ouvert aux idées modernes' (1527). It is, above all, the *irony* characterizing so many of the evocations of existentialist themes that first alerts the reader to the book's polemical intent as when the theme of *engagement* takes the following form: 'J'ai vécu ma vie entière sous un double signe et mes actions les plus graves ont été souvent celles où j'étais le moins engagé' (1518). Or when human freedom is spoken of in these terms: 'Autrefois, je n'avais que la liberté à la bouche. Je l'étendais au petit déjeuner sur mes tartines, je la mastiquais toute la journée ... J'assénais ce maître mot à quiconque me contredisait ...' (1541). Finally, we may note actual textual references to Camus' polemical exchange with Sartre and Sartre's collaborator, Francis Jeanson, in the pages of *Les Temps modernes*, as when Clamence observes: 'Sans doute, je faisais mine, parfois, de prendre la vie au sérieux. Mais, bien vite, la frivolité du sérieux lui-même m'apparaissait ...' (1518), echoing Sartre's reproach: 'Mon Dieu Camus, que vous êtes *sérieux* et, pour employer un de vos mots, que vous êtes frivole!'[21] Or when he claims: 'Chacun exige d'être innocent, à tout prix, même si, pour cela, il faut accuser le genre humain et le ciel' (1515), as though confirming Sartre's accusation: 'Pour vous garder la conscience bonne, vous avez besoin de condamner, il faut un coupable: si ce n'est pas vous, ce sera donc l'univers.'[22] As for Francis Jeanson, he saw Camus as 'cette grande voix planant au-dessus des factions.'[23] just like Clamence, 'planant par la pensée au-dessus de tout ce continent qui [lui] est soumis sans le savoir ...' (1547).

No, there is no doubt that Camus' bitter quarrel with Sartre and his

21 'Réponse à Albert Camus,' 370; Sartre's emphasis
22 Ibid., 345
23 'Pour tout vous dire,' 383

friends was responsible for the genesis of *La Chute*. Clamence's own remarks suggest as much when he says: 'J'avais vécu longtemps dans l'illusion d'un accord général, alors que, de toutes parts, les jugements, les flèches et les railleries fondaient sur moi, distrait et souriant' (1514). It was very much in the novelist's own interest to enable Sartre to slip into the shoes of Clamence's interlocuter and thus feel the full force of Clamence's accusations at the end of the tale. Paradoxically, this does not, however, confer on Camus' work a purely topical and polemic interest whereby it would soon have become classified under what the French refer to as *une littérature de circonstance*; for while undoubtedly taking aim at Sartre, at the same time *La Chute* manages to put every reader on the spot, so to speak.[24] We are now in a position to appreciate that Camus had more than one reason for leaving Clamence's precise features as vague as possible.

The reason it is all too easy to lose sight of the presence of the interlocutor in spite of all the textual indications pointing to the latter that I referred to earlier, is that his fictional existence is no more substantial in terms of what the reader is able to conjure up in his mind's eye than is that of Clamence itself. In fact, it is *less* substantial, in that not only is it just as difficult to *characterize* him in any detail, but even his actual *presence* goes unevoked, for the main part, by the text, whereas Clamence's very words, constituting an unquestionably *oral* utterance, cannot fail to evoke the presence of their speaker.

What then remains in the end as far as fictive referents are concerned? What is there finally to be 'concretized' by the reader? With the impossibility of picturing the interlocutor and faced by the implacably accusatory finger pointed at him by the stranger who was 'Clamence,' the way is thus open for us to make the uncomfortable discovery that we alone can fill the interlocutor's shoes,[25] as we have been gradually led to do with each new stage in the protagonist's narration by his

24 How the novelist realizes this feat is shown in 'Locuteur, délocuteur et allocutaire.'

25 Given the male identity of the interlocutor, it could well be maintained that any female reader might not feel able, or be as willing as a male reader, to step into his shoes. Be that as it may, it has to be recognized that the empty slot programmed into the text by the author in the place of the fictive referent corresponding to Clamence's unheard companion is explicitly designated as a male. If my reading of this text is correct and the novelist intended us to identify with Clamence's interlocutor, then given the fact that the French language distinguishes between genders, he had little choice but to opt for a specific gender for the character of the interlocutor, which, in that case, is tantamount to his having thereby opted for a *male* reader.

appeal, mentioned earlier, to his listener's understanding, intelligence, sense of humour, and so on. Indeed, the way is not only open for us to do so but we have no alternative but to duly take up our position in the *malconfort* which the *juge-pénitent* has been preparing for us from the very beginning of his tale. We have had every possibility to empathize so completely with the fictive 'Clamence' that we can well see ourselves in the very skin of the Parisian lawyer: 'Mais, bien entendu, vous n'êtes pas policier, ce serait trop simple. Comment? Ah! je m'en doutais, voyez-vous. Cette étrange affection que je sentais pour vous avait donc du sens. Vous exercez à Paris la belle profession d'avocat!' (1549). The text's reference points in one direction and one direction alone and that is indisputably and disconcertingly outside of itself towards the reader: 'Alors, racontez-moi, je vous prie, ce qui vous est arrivé un soir sur les quais de la Seine et comment vous avez réussi à ne jamais risquer votre vie. Prononcez vous-même les mots qui, depuis des années, n'ont cessé de retentir dans mes nuits, et que je dirai enfin par votre bouche:[26] "O jeune fille, jette-toi encore dans l'eau pour que j'aie une seconde fois la chance de nous sauver tous les deux!" ' (1549). This whole text is in a very real sense perlocutionary.

In terms of fictional universes, we have seen at work in this text of Camus a process by which its level of fictional referentiality corresponding to what Ricoeur refers to as a literary work's 'suspended' reference and constituting what is traditionally known as the fictive heterocosm – the universe in which its characters move and have their being – becomes further suspended or 'bracketed.' It has proved to be 'fictive' in that other, everyday sense of the term, that is to say, a figment not of the author's imagination, in the first instance, but of the narrator-protagonist's imagination. Fictional reality is thus *displaced* and brought closer to the reader as it is now seen to occupy the territory of the narrator himself, who is transformed from being the *narrator* of his own autobiography to being a *narrating character* so to speak – that is, a narrator existing in his own right as a character. However, 'Clamence' is as elusive as a character as he was unreliable as a narrator: the fictive referent designated by the proper noun 'Cla-

---

26 It could be pointed out that 'Clamence''s wish has already been exorcised by the very fact of the reader's having read, and hence internalized, the narrator's monologue up to this point. Here, the emphasis that Ricoeur places on the self-referential character of all discourse is particularly pertinent: '... discourse refers back to its speaker by means of a complex set of indicators, such as personal pronouns. We can say, in this sense, that the instance of discourse is self-referential' ('The Hermeneutical Function of Distanciation,' 133).

mence' is no less unsatisfactory as far as the reader is concerned since even – or, rather, especially – at the end of the book, he remains a complete stranger.[27] The world of Amsterdam, of the *Mexico-City* bar and the concentric canals recalling Dante's masterpiece, is, however, real enough. It is on this setting that the reader's attention is now forced to dwell, together with its other main occupant, Clamence's interlocutor. They are the only fictive referents, the only 'reality,' – apart, it must not be forgotten, from Clamence's physical presence – actually evoked, implicitly or explicitly, by the latter's discourse comprising the whole of this text.

We now come to the key transition in the referential process, the moment when or the point where the text opens onto the real world of the reader as a person in his own right, for, in Ricoeur's terms, '... it is precisely insofar as fictional discourse "suspends" its first order referential function that it releases a second order reference, where the world is manifested no longer as the totality of manipulable objects but as the horizon of our life and our project, in short as *Lebenswelt* [life-world], as being-in-the-world,'[28] since, as the same theoretician puts it elsewhere, '... there is no discourse so fictional that it does not connect up with reality. But such discourse refers to another level, more fundamental than that attained by the descriptive, constative, didactic discourse which we call ordinary language.'[29] In the present context, however, it is essential to realize how the suspension of this first level of reference is achieved: it is through the *ostensive* reference yielding to a kind of *non-ostensive* reference.

Such a distinction is fundamental to Ricoeur's whole argument, for it comes about through the very transformation of oral discourse into written text, by which the dialogic situation is itself provisionally 'suspended' (only to be subsequently reinstated through the act of reading):

... the referential function of written texts is deeply affected by the lack of a situation common to both reader and writer. It exceeds the mere extensive designation of the horizon of reality surrounding the dialogical situation. *Of*

27 All that we can be sure of is that he may well be an inveterate liar and that, if indeed he is a lawyer by profession, as well as an amateur actor, then he has clearly been 'pleading a case' as we have been listening to him, though whether the 'case' in question has really been his own rather than the one he has been attributing to his listener remains a moot point.
28 'Phenomenology and Hermeneutics,' 118
29 'The Hermeneutical Function of Distanciation,' 141

course written sentences keep using ostensive devices, but these ostensive terms can no longer hold for ways of showing what is referred to. This alteration of the ostensive designation ... implies an extension of the referred to reality. Language has a world now and not just a situation. But, to the extent that this world, for most of its parts, has not been shown, but merely designated, a complete abstraction of the surrounding reality becomes possible. This is what happens with some works of discourse, in fact with most literary works, in which the referential intention is suspended ...[30]

Now, it is obvious that shifters constitute one of the main 'ostensive devices' in any piece of writing. What is remarkable and particular to *La Chute* is that it is the ostensive devices themselves that, through a kind of 'reprogramming' of their habitual functioning, serve to designate what is, in Ricoeur's terms, the *non-ostensive* reference of the text. Here we do not witness 'the effacement of the ostensive and descriptive reference' but it is the latter itself that 'liberates a power of reference to aspects of our being in the world which cannot be said in a direct descriptive way.'[31] Contrary to the majority of literary texts that 'point to a possible world thanks to the non-ostensive reference of the text,'[32] this text does so through its ostensive reference.

Moreover, here, as with Beckett's novel *L'Innommable*, the text does not have to 'decontextualise' itself 'in such a way that it can be "recontextualised" in a new situation ... by the act of reading,'[33] because the very process of contextualization itself encompasses the world of the reader and his being in the world. There is, however, an important difference between Camus' text and Beckett's; it lies both in the precise manner in which the second level of reference is realized and in the nature of the latter. This second level of 'real' reference is of course actualized, in both cases, by the act of reading. However, whereas in *L'Innommable*, as I shall be at pains to stress, the 'real' reference remains deliberately *potential* since it concerns the possibilities offered by man's relationship to language, *La Chute* actually *opens onto* the world of the reader, articulating, as it does, the very passage between the world of the book and the real world of the reader. It gives a new, fuller meaning to Ricoeur's statement that 'the sense of a text is not behind the text, but in front of it,' that it is 'not something

30 *Interpretation Theory*, 80; my emphasis
31 Ricoeur, 'Writing as a Problem,' 10
32 *Interpretation Theory*, 87
33 'The Hermeneutical Function of Distanciation,' 139

hidden, but something disclosed'[34] so that '... to interpret is to explicate the type of being-in-the-world unfolded *in front of* the text.'[35] Thanks in large measure to the important role played by the shifters and to the oral nature of a discourse addressed to a silent addressee, a world does indeed unfurl in front of this text. It advances progressively to meet its reader and with Clamence's revelation at the end of the book finally encompasses its hapless victim in one fell swoop, making of him the centre of that world. Hence the reader's realization of being not only 'dans le malconfort' but more precisely *sur la sellette* or on the spot, like a prisoner undergoing interrogation and blinded by a relentless light that prevents him from making out the shadowy form of his persecutor.

What exactly takes place to produce this remarkable and unsettling effect can best be illuminated on the level of its reception by certain distinctions made by Roman Ingarden between the different categories of space involved.[36] The space unfolded or projected by the work itself is what Ingarden refers to as 'represented space,' which he describes as 'a unique space which essentially belongs to the represented "real" world' and 'exhibits a structure that allows us to call it "space" even though its possession of this structure is only a simulated, make-believe possession' (223). Then there is the space that is an integral part of the fictional universe in the form in which it is concretized in the act of reading, which he calls 'imagined space.' Now, the reading of fiction always entails the merging of these two types of space, or, more precisely, the actualization of the first in the second. However, 'represented space does not allow itself to be incorporated either into real space or into the various kinds of perceptible orientational space, even when the represented objects are expressly represented as "finding" themselves in a specific location in real space, e.g. Munich' (224) – or, for that matter Amsterdam. ('Orientational space' is, incidentally, defined as that which 'necessarily belongs to the perceptible primary giveness of things and that forms a constitutive substratum of the appearance of unique real space and, as such, shows in itself an existential relativity with respect to the perceiving subject' [222–3].)

---

34 *Interpretation Theory*, 87
35 'The Hermeneutical Function of Distanciation,' 141; Ricoeur's emphasis
36 See 'Represented Space and "Imaginational Space," ' in *The Literary Work of Art*, 222–33. All page references within parentheses in the present paragraph refer to this work.

Now, in addition to represented, imagined, and real space, Ingarden identifies a fourth kind of space that he calls 'imaginational space,' which, as he puts it, 'essentially belongs to every intuitive *imagining* of extensive objects' (223) and which, he insists, 'must be sharply distinguished from *imagined* space and, even more, from *represented* space in a literary work' (227). Now, there is no question but that imaginational space 'can never coincide nor become one with real space' (223), and the reference to the reader in the previous discussion of *La Chute* does not concern the real space in which the bound volume of the book and the hands that are holding that book are situated: what *is* involved here is the imaginational space of the reader.

In the account he gives of these various forms of space, Ingarden makes an observation that is highly pertinent to the present discussion of *La Chute* when he says: 'Of special interest is ... the fact that, despite the dissimilarities between represented space and the "imaginational space" of a particular imagining conscious subject, there exists the possibility that in reading the work we can see, by means of a lively intuitive imagining, *directly* into the given represented space and can thus in a way bridge the gulf between these two separate kinds of space' (225). He goes on to speak of 'the danger of confusion of the two kinds of space,' since the aforementioned possibility 'does not argue against the difference between represented and imaginational space' (225). And the reader of Camus' work runs precisely this 'danger.' However, what is important is not the possible mental *con*fusion arising from the experience of his reading but rather the actual *fusion* that characterizes the experience itself. It is my contention that there occurs a merging of represented space and imaginational space through the intermediary of imagined space so that the space of the imagined fiction (corresponding to the represented space marked out by the shifters, for example, and by the voice of Clamence the narrator) runs (over) into the imaginational space of the reader's mind. Imagined and imaginational space are experienced first of all as overlapping and then as intermingling before finally fusing into one. What needs to be stressed, however, is that their merging is not exactly the reciprocal process, the to-and-fro movement that the latter image suggests and that would produce a fusion of the two in which fiction and reality would become indistinguishable from each other. It is rather the imagined space that encroaches upon the imaginational space so that it appears to the reader to acquire all the attributes of the latter. The imagined space is thus taken for imaginational space and is wholly incorporated into it. In other words, Clamence's accusatory presence becomes part of the reader's own inner reality as he puts himself, in the fullest existential sense of the term, in question.

The process described here is, of course, remarkably analogous to the appropriation of any fictional text by its reader. It bears a mimetic relationship, in fact, to the process of appropriation[37] or at the very least it anticipates the inevitable outcome of novel reading in general. In my view, no better illustration can be found of the conception of appropriation as it is elaborated by Paul Ricoeur, which is one of the most original of his many contributions to hermeneutic theory: 'Ultimately, what I appropriate is a proposed world. The latter is not *behind* the text, as a hidden intention would be, but *in front of* it, as that which the work unfolds, discovers, reveals. Henceforth, to understand is *to understand oneself in front of the text.* It is not a question of imposing on the text our finite capacity of understanding, but of exposing ourselves to the text and receiving from it an enlarged self, which would be the proposed existence corresponding to the most suitable way to the world proposed.'[38] No one could feel more 'exposed' and vulnerable to the interrogation of the text than the reader of *La Chute.* This 'enlarged self' will be the product of our being obliged to respond sooner or later – perhaps long after having laid down the book – to Clamence's insistent and persistent questioning: 'Vous, par exemple, mon cher compatriote, pensez un peu à ce que serait votre enseigne. Vous vous taisez? *Allons, vous me répondrez plus tard'* (1497).[39] We know that our persecutor is justified in his optimism and his certainty that he has attained his ultimate objective: 'Alors, racontez-moi, je vous prie, ce qui vous êtes arrivé un soir sur les quais de la Seine et comment vous avez réussi à ne jamais risquer votre vie. Prononcez vous-même les mots qui, depuis des années, n'ont cessé de retentir dans mes nuits ...' (1549). The full realization comes home to one of how the 'proposed world' of the fiction is one 'which I could inhabit and in which I could project my ownmost possibilities'[40] – for better or for worse, one is tempted to add in this present context. There could be no more dramatic illustration of how 'through fiction

---

37 This is one of a number of reasons, including its parodying of the dialogic situation, why I maintain elsewhere that this text constitutes a paradigm of the hermeneutic process. See 'The Interpreter Interpreted: *La Chute,*' in *The Narcissistic Text,* 69–88.
38 Ibid., 144–5
39 My emphasis
40 'Phenomenology and Hermeneutics,' 112

and poetry, new possibilities of being-in-the-world are opened up within everyday reality' in that 'fiction and poetry intend being, not under the modality of being-given, but under the modality of power-to-be.'[41] Moreover, the fact that we find ourselves obliged to put ourselves into question and risk seeing our conception of ourselves and our past life undergo a radical transformation enables us to appreciate how 'relinquishment is a fundamental moment of appropriation' distinguishing it from 'any form of "taking possession."'[42] All reading, in fact, involves this 'letting go,'[43] for 'even when we read a philosophical work, it is always a question of entering into an alien work, of divesting oneself of the earlier "me" in order to receive ... the self conferred by the work itself.'[44] And it is through the giving-up of oneself to the world proposed, and here projected by the text, that 'the revelation of new modes of being ... *gives* the subject new capacities for knowing himself'[45] and 'engenders a new "*self*-understanding."'[46]

Such is the paradox presented by the reader's experience of any literary work, which is that of an 'appropriation-divestiture'[47] whereby he loses himself only to refind himself: '... just as the world of the text is real only insofar as it is imaginary, so too it must be said that the subjectivity of the reader comes to itself only insofar as it is placed in suspense, unrealised, potentialised. In other words, if fiction is a fundamental dimension of the reference of the text, it is no less a fundamental dimension of the subjectivity of the reader. As reader, I find myself only by losing myself. Reading introduces me into the imaginary variations of the *ego*.'[48] In this way, everyone who reads a literary work in the full sense of that verb puts himself at risk, for he subjects himself to 'the *power of a work* to project a world of its own and to set in motion the hermeneutical circle, which encompasses in its spiral both the apprehension of projected worlds and the advance of self-understanding in the presence of these new worlds.'[49] The dialectical relationship involved is that of the hermeneutic process, which brings about the coming together and the subsequent fusion of

41 'The Hermeneutical Function of Distanciation,' 142
42 'Appropriation,' 191
43 Ibid.
44 Ibid., 190
45 Ibid., 192
46 Ibid., 193
47 Ibid., 191
48 'The Hermeneutical Function of Distanciation,' 144
49 'Metaphor and the Problem of Hermeneutics,' 171; Ricoeur's emphasis

the horizon of the work and that of its reader as Hans-Georg Gadamer has analysed the phenomenon in *Truth and Method*. On the one hand, 'a work opens up its readers and thus creates its own subjective *vis-à-vis*,'[50] and on the other hand, '... we understand ourselves only by the long detour of the signs of humanity deposited in cultural works.'[51]

What distinguishes Camus' *La Chute* from other novels is that it makes us uncommonly aware, whether we like it or not, of the process in which we are engaged as readers. While our acute discomfort is undoubtedly made to appear to us to be moral in origin, arising as it does from the impossibility of avoiding the most searching and demanding self-scrutiny, it in fact arises from our intuitive awareness of the paradoxical interdependence that exists between ourselves as readers and the text we are reading. There is no way for us to be able to walk away from such a work unscathed, for to cite Ricoeur yet again, 'the *self* which emerges from the understanding of the text'[52] stands in contrast to 'the *ego* which claims to precede this understanding.'[53] And in the end Camus' reader comes to understand that 'it is the text, with its universal power of unveiling, which gives a *self* to the *ego*.'[54]

50 'The Hermeneutical Function of Distanciation,' 143
51 Ibid., 143
52 Of course Ricoeur, when speaking of the 'text' in this and all other quotations from his work, is not referring to any specific text but rather to the literary text in general. This does not *preclude* the possibility of a given general statement (such as those cited) being considered, by the author of *Interpretation Theory*, to be applicable to the text of *La Chute*. I contend, in fact, that *La Chute* is not only exemplary with regard to Ricoeur's theory of literary appropriation but that it functions in a self-referential manner in this respect, making the reader acutely aware of the process.
53 'Appropriation,' 192; Ricoeur's emphasis
54 Ibid., 193; Ricoeur's emphasis

7
The Referent Deferred:
Beckett's *L'Innommable*

L'Innommable is a pivotal text in the evolution of Beckett's fiction, and its central place in the Beckettian canon is hardly surprising given the harrowing and devastating experience its writing constituted for its author. From the very beginning, when he was writing short stories, such as those gathered together under the collective title of *More Pricks Than Kicks*, and novels, such as *Murphy*, solely in the English language, his fiction revealed an exceptional degree of self-consciousness that threatened to undermine the fictional world it was ostensibly depicting. With the appearance of *Watt*, his second novel, this propensity to undermine had yielded to a radical subversion of the fictive referent. It was during the evolution of the trilogy, his third novelistic work and the first written in French, that he gradually came to discard the novel form completely, for as we move from *Molloy* to *Malone meurt* and thence to *L'Innommable*, we realize that the novel is in the process of becoming unrecognizable, the mere shadow of its former self. The next prose work to appear, *Comment c'est*, resembles nothing so much as a poem in prose. And as the subsequent prose pieces become shorter and shorter, there is born a new literary genre of which the discourse of modernism has made us more and more aware: that of the 'text.' With the emergence of the 'text,' old habits that die hard have had to be set aside by reader and critic alike, the latter being threatened with obsolescence by the appearance on the literary scene of a new player, the poetician; new ways of reading, making sense of, and writing about this new genre have had to be explored.[1]

  L'Innommable marks the turning point in this development, since it displays the genre of the novel on its last legs, so to speak, on the

1 See the chapter 'The Bilingual Text' in Fitch, *Beckett and Babel*, 193–216.

point of extinction, an extinction that, paradoxically, its narrative voice seeks in vain. This work pushes to the limit the problems posed by our relationship to language both in the process of reading and in that of writing, while at the same time it puts in question the other side of the same coin, the very possibility of *any* relationship existing between language and reality – in other words the referentiality of language. As we shall see, reference is here problematized to the most radical degree possible.

'Où maintenant? Quand maintenant? Qui maintenant? Sans me le demander. Dire je. Sans le penser. Appeler ça des questions, des hypothèses. Aller de l'avant, appeler ça aller, appeler ça de l'avant.'[2] The opening lines of *L'Innommable* situate this text at the precise point of articulation between the act of writing and the act of reading, inscribing in its very warp and woof the production and reception of the literary work. The initial question is none other than the question of writing and the question of reading posed simultaneously and yet, in a sense, mutually exclusive since, in terms of traditional textual interpretation, to read here an allegory of writing is by definition to fail to perceive an allegory of reading (as is amply demonstrated by Beckettian criticism), the one interpretation tending inevitably to mask the other. To resort to metaphor, one might say that the shadow of a presence is cast over the text and that only the source or identity of the shadow is in question. For the shadow of the writer and that of the reader intermingle playing on its surface. And what could be more fitting, since it is indeed this shadowy middle ground or no man's land that the text inhabits between the moment the writer has yielded up his manuscript to the publisher and the point when the first reader takes up the book and begins to read the printed page. It is this shadowy presence that marks out the place of the fictive referent. Within the confines or silhouette of the latter lies a void so that behind the shadow there is nothing, nothing for the shadow to conceal. It is then not so much that the fictive referent is *absent* as that it is *hollow*. Its existence is characterized by its latency and is wholly analogous to those empty slots found in language that the linguists refer to as shifters and whose referential content changes every time they are used according to the situation and circumstances in which they are articulated.

The initial question is that of the beginning of a reading and that of the beginning of an act of writing. How to begin? – *commencer*, the

2 *L'Innommable*, 7

verb that will produce *Comment c'est*, the title and point of departure of Beckett's next novel. Where to begin? When to begin? Either writing or reading, or rather, logically speaking, writing *hence* reading? But we have omitted the crucial question: who is beginning? The writer, or the reader, or both? This question, once formulated, cannot fail to evoke one of the critical clichés that the French New Novel constantly calls forth. For is the latter not characterized precisely by the curious and original manner in which the reader becomes writer, giving rise to the supplanting, in Roland Barthes' by now all too familiar terminology, of the *texte lisible* by the *texte scriptible*?[3]

We are here then concerned with a question of beginning: how to begin writing/reading? And it is the beginning of the text that raises and articulates this question. In other words, in the beginning is the question of the beginning. That is to say, we are confronted with a self-reflexive process whereby the text begins by putting its beginning, and indeed the very possibility of beginning, in question. The resulting self-reflexive structure can be likened to an echoing void that rejects both writer and reader, holding them at bay, refusing them access – what Maurice Blanchot has called 'le lieu vide où parle le désœuvrement d'une parole vide,'[4] 'le lieu vide et animé où retentit l'appel de l'œuvre.'[5] It is thus the text itself that incarnates the difficulty of its own beginning, taking on flesh and linguistic substance through the very process of questioning the possibility of coming into being.[6]

This self-reflexive structure superimposes itself upon the space of the latent fictive referent and through the ceaseless reverberation it sets up, it maintains that emptiness, which hollows out the referent and ensures that its identity remains in the realm of the potential. It is, in fact, the general tendency of all textual self-reflexivity to keep the reader at a distance,[7] while at the same time seriously discouraging the normal suspension of disbelief or illusion-creating capacity of the work for the reader and, by the same token, undermining the very existence of the fictive referents. This is because, as Jean Ricardou has

3 *S/Z*, 10
4 Blanchot, 'Où maintenant? Qui maintenant?' 681
5 Ibid., 684
6 My *Dimensions, structures et textualité dans la trilogie romanesque de Beckett* traced the movement of this 'parole neutre qui se parle seule,' as Blanchot puts it ('Où maintenant? Qui maintenant?' 681).
7 This is the case, too, with the texts of Camus' novels and short stories, with the notable exception of *La Chute*, where shifters play as important a role as in *L'Innommable* (see *The Narcissistic Text*).

pointed out at considerable length, like all such self-reflexive devices, the *mise en abyme*, for example, 'conteste le récit [en] *contredi*[*sant*] *le fonctionnement global du texte qui le contient*'[8] since 'la pratique assidue de l'analogie textuelle met en cause la dimension référentielle sur laquelle ... le récit s'appuie *pour faire illusion*' (75).[9]

If we are here concerned with a question of beginning, we are also more particularly concerned with beginning as question. In other words, in the beginning is not only the question of the beginning but also the beginning's question or rather questions. What exactly happens to the reader-text relationship when a novel narrative begins with a question or, in the present case, a series of questions? The resulting situation for the reader does not appear to have attracted the attention of the proponents of *Rezeptionsesthetik* such as Wolfgang Iser, nor, curiously, have the problems it poses the reader of *L'Innommable* been addressed by the considerable body of Beckettian criticism. In the present instance, the reader does not find, as usually happens when one begins reading a novel, that he is called upon to assume through the act of reading a statement but rather that he is confronted by a question. If, as we find here, the subsequent implied answers to the initial question remain vague or indeed indeterminable, giving rise to further questioning, then the reader finds that the point at which it is possible to 'climb aboard the text,' to use Iser's delightfully evocative expression, is further delayed, and a state of anticipation fed by frustrated expectation then sets in as he waits for the narrative presence to yield to the telling of a tale that can only begin once the questioning has, as it were, been laid to rest through the provision of some kind of answer. The narrative statement, on the other hand, constitutes and activates a referent, albeit in the fictional mode, and although questions themselves necessarily imply certain

---

8 Jean Ricardou, *Le Nouveau Roman*, 73; Ricardou's emphasis
9 Ricardou's emphasis. He goes on to explain: 'Que des lieux, des événements, des personnages cessent chacun d'afficher une singularité comparable à celle qu'offre "la vie même" pour se permettre respectivement de se ressembler, l'attention du lecteur, loin de rester soumise à l'illusion de représentation, est attirée sur la manière selon laquelle ces lieux, ces événements, ces personnages sont engendrés, respectivement, les uns à partir des autres. Ce qui surgit alors c'est ... une opération génératrice.' And '*la fascination qu'exercent les aventures d'un récit est inversement proportionnelle à l'exhibition des procédures génératrices*' (75–6; Ricardou's emphasis). Chapter 8, on Simon's *Histoire*, goes some way towards addressing the complex problem of the reception of formal devices. For a different treatment of the same topic, see Lucien Dällenbach's essay 'Reflexivity and Reading.'

presuppositions in the form of a frame of reference positing thereby, implicitly and indirectly, a referent, the same cannot be said of the most general or basic questions concerning the fundamental categories of time, space, and identity with which the present text begins. For the status and the identity of the speaker, the addressee, and what is being spoken of are unclear and indeed wholly indeterminable, since, in the case of each of these questions, there are only two constitutive elements: first, uncertainty with regard to location, time, or identity; and second, a shifter *now*, what Emile Benveniste has referred to as an 'empty slot,'[10] pointing back to, without identifying, the speaker – in other words a situational rather than a semantic reference. The association, twice repeated, of an interrogative pronoun and a shifter constitutes a putting in question of what the French call the *instance d'énonciation* or the context of the speech utterance. And it is of course the latter that determines the narrative perspective proffered by the text. The initial question raises the expectation of a reply of some kind, an expectation that can only be heightened and intensified when this first question gives way to a second question that in its turn gives rise to a third question. Until this expectation is fulfilled in some form, then all there is for the reader is the presence of a voice questioning itself, which cannot be identified or situated whether spatially or temporally – and moreover, it must not be overlooked, that the voice in question is inevitably the reader's own, since it is produced by his reading of the text.

The lack of any definable context here that would enable the reader to situate himself and at the same time provide the basis for the tentative fleshing out of a fictive referent has far-reaching consequences. If, as Paul Ricoeur has maintained, 'the text[11] must be able, from the sociological as well as the psychological point of view, to "decontextualise" itself in such a way that it can be "recontextualised" in a new situation – as accomplished, precisely, by the act of reading,'[12] then the present text complies with this condition, as it were, *avant la lettre*. For, as we have just seen, the present text never does manage to contextualize itself. And there can obviously be no question of *de*contextualizing what has never been *con*textualized in

---

10 *Problèmes de linguistique générale 1*, 263
11 See chapter 6, n. 52. Here, of course, the same proviso obtains concerning the original status of Ricoeur's statement.
12 'The Hermeneutical Function of Distanciation,' 139

the first place. Any possible contextualization here remains latent, unrealized.

Unbelievable though it may seem, this is even more true of the English version, where the sequence of the three questions is changed to: 'Where now? Who now? When now?'[13] with dramatic or at least disturbing consequences. It is, in fact, the status of the third and final question that has been transformed and rendered ambiguous. For what precisely is the relationship between its two terms *when* and *now*? Is it to be understood as 'When now?' or as 'When "now"?' Is what is being questioned the temporal status of the *now*, or is what is being evoked the possibility of now uttering the question 'when?'? In the first case, precisely which *now* is being questioned? The sequence of the questions in the English text suggests that the referent of the third *now* is none other than the preceding two *nows* in 'Where now? Who now?' In other words, the three questions are not then parallel as in the French version, constituting an enumeration of questions each with an analogous status, but rather the third question, 'When now?' becomes a putting in question of the *one stable element*, the one linguistically non-interrogative part of speech featured in each of the two preceding questions. In short, the third one is not so much a question as a *questioning of a question*. This finally dissolves the latent situational frame of reference of the shifter *now* in the first two questions, since it questions the temporal identity of what is at best merely a potential point in time. And, it should be added, inasmuch as it thereby points to and underlines the lack of any precise semantic content or reference, a lack that can be attributed to *any* shifter, it can be said that we have here yet another self-reflexive process at work. As for the situation of the reader, the resulting disorientation is here even more complete than that of his counterpart reading the French version,[14] since there is even less basis for picturing any kind of fictive referent.

What the reader is, in fact, faced with is none other than the mirror reflection of the very activity of reading. For these three questions correspond precisely to any reader's expectations as he reads the opening lines of any novel: 'Où maintenant? Quand maintenant? Qui maintenant?' In other words, 'Where am I heading, where am I going to find myself as the fiction unfolds? At what point in time shall I be

13 *The Unnamable* in *Three Novels by Beckett*, 291
14 The innumerable problems posed by the differences between the French and English versions of Beckett's works are studied in my *Beckett and Babel*.

situated? Who am I going to be this time, what new characters shall I be called upon to identify with?'[15] These questions all concern the fiction awaiting one upon settling down to read any novel: that which remains to be invented by the novelist and brought to life by the reader. They delimit the threshold of fiction, the precise moment that *precedes* the tale that is expected. It is that moment when the actor is waiting for the curtain to rise as he prepares himself for the role he is to act out, and yet, curiously, here it is as though he were at the same time seated on the other side of the curtain passively awaiting, in pleasant anticipation, the spectacle that is to unfold before his eyes.[16]

'Sans me le demander. Dire je.' In order for the play to begin, for the story to unfold, I have to be prepared to let myself be transported into the world of the fiction, to suspend my normal sense of disbelief when confronted by events that clearly do not belong to the world in which I move and have my everyday being:[17] 'Dire je. Sans le penser.' I have to pretend, or as the French say, *faire comme si ...* 'Appeler ça des questions, des hypothèses. Aller de l'avant, appeler ça aller, appeler ça de l'avant.' That is the only way to start reading, that is by saying the words to myself as though they were my own. But to

15 This formulation of the process of reader-identification represents, of course, a simplification of what actually occurs in practice, for, as Michel Picard points out, 'on s'"identifie" non à un personnage, comme on le croit généralement, mais à un personnage en situation' (*Le Jeu de la lecture*, 93). This fact does not, of course, detract from the validity of my analysis of the present text, since the actual situation in which the character of the narrative voice fails to materialize remains equally undefined and undefinable. Picard, whose approach to reading is in no wise hermeneutic or phenomenological but, rather, psychoanalytical, goes on to add: 'Cette appropriation singulière à quoi pousse le besoin de lire conduit, quelle qu'en soit la base libidinale lointaine, introjection, incorporation anale, voyeurisme, à intégrer temporairement, comme pour les essayer, des *situations*, dont les héros ont seulement pour fonction de dessiner les contours' (93–4; Picard's emphasis). Here Picard appears to echo Paul Ricoeur's statement that 'the reader ... is invited to undergo an imaginative variation of his *ego*' ('Appropriation,' 189), to which we shall be returning later. See also Jauss's five, 'modalities of identification' (in 'Levels of Identification in Hero and Audience,' 298).

16 Here the reader's situation is identical to that of the spectator watching the opening scene of *En Attendant Godot*, where the situation of Godot and Estragon on the stage waiting for Godot mirrors exactly the spectators' waiting in vain for the play to begin. Of course, in a sense, the play no more begins than does Godot materialize for the two characters.

17 A first draft of the present commentary appeared under the title '*L'Innommable* and the Hermeneutic Paradigm.'

start with, I am in need of encouragement and so must egg myself on
in my reading: 'Se peut-il qu'un jour, premier pas va ...' What was
ostensibly the writer attempting to summon up his scriptorial energies
becomes the reader's efforts to get into and persevere with his reading.
'Cela a pu commencer ainsi ... Peu importe comment cela s'est produit. Cela, dire cela, sans savoir quoi.' The 'cela' appears to be referring
to the fiction to come, but one cannot be sure, and in any case any
possible fiction or tale remains for the present an unknown quantity.
And so the word *cela*, like all the other words here at the threshold of
the novel, has to be taken on trust as likely to signify something sooner
or later, and whether it will subsequently prove meaningful can only
be discovered by dint of persevering with one's reading and saying
'cela, sans savoir quoi.'

'J'ai l'air de parler, ce n'est pas moi, de moi, ce n'est pas de moi.' I
seem to speak since I am uttering or rather mouthing these words if
only to and for myself. But I am not ultimately responsible for them
since they did not originate with me but pre-existed my reading of
them. And by saying 'I,' paradoxically I do not mean 'me,' for I am
not, in fact, talking about myself at all but about some fictive persona.
As Georges Poulet puts it in his account of the experience of reading:
'Whatever I think is a part of my mental world. And yet here I am
thinking a thought which manifestly belongs to another mental world,
which is being thought in me just as though I did not exist ... Whenever I read, I mentally pronounce an *I* and yet the *I* which I pronounce
is not myself.'[18] It should be noted that although Wolfgang Iser has
strongly objected to this formulation of Poulet's, criticizing it for its
substantialism,[19] Paul Ricoeur whose theoretical and philosophical
credentials are, in my estimation, of a wholly different order from
those of the Belgian literary critic, makes essentially the same point:
'It is easy ... to generalise beyond the novel or the story: even when
we read a philosophical work, it is always a question of entering into
an alien work, of divesting oneself of the earlier "me" in order to
receive, as in play, the self conferred by the work itself.'[20] And I shall
be returning in a moment to the concept of play.

'Comment faire, comment vais-je faire, que dois-je faire, dans la
situation où je suis, comment procéder?' However, how can one do
such an unlikely thing as espousing the words of another? The diffi-

18 'Phenomenology of Reading' 56
19 In *The Implied Reader*, 293
20 'Appropriation,' 190

culty involved in pursuing such an apparently barren discourse is the same for the reader as for the writer: '... comment procéder. Par pure aporie ou bien par affirmations et négations infirmées au fur et à mesure, ou tôt ou tard?' The difficulty in proceeding lies, to begin with, in the gratuitousness of any fiction the nature or content of which is always, in a sense, arbitrary. And at the same time the reader finally has some intimation of the likely status of the fiction to come. Not only any affirmations but also any negations will, no sooner formulated, be ruled out of court or inoperative. The tantalizing tale, those fictive referents that appear to be taking so long to materialize, remains a vague 'something' on the horizon of the reader's expectations. Moreover, even within those vaguest of contours the 'something' will not, we are told, bear scrutiny. And contrary to the later formulation of the same idea – 'D'abord salir, ensuite nettoyer'[21] – it is not that the *something* will give way to *nothing*,[22] for even the latter will prove illusory. What then is left? If what awaits us is neither something nor nothing, it can only be *any*thing. Now *anything* is, as it were, open-ended, an empty slot exactly analogous to that of the aforementioned linguistic shifter, which we shall come back to later, the personal pronoun *I*. It is the germ of something: a potentiality. Out of *anything* something can arise. *En attendant Godot* has been described as a play in which 'nothing happens – twice'; this is a text where 'nothing becomes anything – ever.'

It is precisely because the 'something,' that series of fictive referents that would furnish the substance or content of a fiction, never materializes but rather constantly recedes out of reach over the text's immediate horizon, that one may speak of this text's playing *on* and *with* that process of reader-expectation that accompanies the reading of any novel. To return again to the three opening questions – 'Où maintenant? Quand maintenant? Qui maintenant?' – just as their interrogative status indicates a lack or absence calling for some form of completion in the shape of an answer that can only come in the future, a potential actualization that will only *subsequently*, if at all, be realized, the only possible situation to which they can refer is itself necessarily located at some future point in time. Their status as pointers towards the future constitutes in itself the paradigm of expectation. The point that needs to be stressed here is that *what we have is not*

21 *L'Innommable*, 25
22 *L'Innommable* contains at least 342 occurrences of the word *rien*. For their significance see my *Dimensions, structures et textualité*, 177–83.

an example of the kind of expectation aroused in the reader of any novel text but rather the model of the process itself. In other words, the text thereby becomes self-reflexive, drawing attention to the way novelistic texts, that is, *all* novelistic texts, are wont to work themselves out. It does not so much *stand for* all such literary texts but rather deconstructs and breaks down their functioning as texts through a process the Russian formalists called 'dénudation du procédé.'[23]

The concept of *parody* might well come to mind here to account for *L'Innomable*'s status, and inasmuch as parody implies intertextual activity, it would not be altogether misleading, for this text does refer to other texts. However, it does not refer to any *specific* texts: it refers to all texts and no texts in particular, and hence to the *model* of the novelistic text. If it can be said to parody something, that 'something' is the whole corpus of literature corresponding to the genre of the novel.

Let us dwell for a moment on the concept of reader-expectation. Reader-expectation is bound up with that process of the forming of illusions that is implied in the expression the 'suspension of disbelief.' In Wolfgang Iser's words, comprehension of a literary text 'is inseparable from the reader's expectations, and where we have expectations, there too we have one of the most potent weapons in the writer's armory – illusion.'[24] Thus, 'as we read, we oscillate to a greater or lesser degree between the building and the breaking of illusion.'[25] And it is this 'oscillation' between the two that is painfully accentuated and accelerated time and again by the text of *L'Innommable*, and thereby, as it were, placed beneath a magnifying glass.

It is important to realize that an analogous process operates both on the level of the macrostructure that is the whole text and on that of the microstructure constituted by the sentences the latter is made up of. The larger movement is analysed by Iser as follows: 'The text provokes certain expectations which in turn we project onto the text in such a way that we reduce the polysemantic possibilities to a single interpretation in keeping with the expectations aroused, thus extracting an individual, configurative meaning. The polysemantic nature of the text and the illusion-making of the reader are opposed factors. If the illusion were complete, the polysemantic nature would

23 See the chapter 'The Bilingual Text' in Fitch, *Beckett and Babel*, 193–216.
24 *The Implied Reader*, 284
25 Ibid., 288

vanish; if the polysemantic nature were all-powerful, the illusion would be totally destroyed.'[26] In Iser's terms, the tendency manifested by Beckett's texts throughout the evolution of the trilogy is, of course, to shift from the 'illusion' to the 'polysemantic nature' of the text. Within *L'Innommable*, however, it is the struggle between the two and the impossibility of any resolution that provides the occasion for the text. And on this level, we have a parody of the novel form as a genre. The same movement on the level of the microstructure of the individual sentences is accounted for by Iser with the help of certain concepts of Husserl's already utilized by Roman Ingarden: 'The semantic pointers of individual sentences always imply an expectation of some kind ... As this structure is inherent in *all* intentional sentence correlates, it follows that their interplay will lead not so much to the fulfillment of expectations as to their continual modification ... Each new correlate, then, will answer expectations (either positively or negatively) and, at the same time, will arouse new expectations.'[27] This account of the process enables us to understand how the self-reflexive activity of the text also operates on both levels so that what is thematized and inscribed in the text (*mis en abyme*, as the French would say) is also the actual reading of novels and indeed, the activity of reading in general.

I should now like to take the argument one decisive stage further by moving beyond the hermeneutic paradigm of the reading process to the linguistic paradigm of the acquisition of language. It is my opinion that over and above the way one reads and relates to novels, what is really at stake in *L'Innommable* is the manner in which the individual relates to language, whether it be his own in the act of writing or that of another in the act of reading.

It would be difficult to find a better illustration of Benveniste's analysis of the personal pronoun than the opening pages of the *L'Innommable*. However, 'illustration' is not the right term. For both the linguist and the novelist are dealing, each in his own fashion, with the same phenomenon: the way in which and by which each one of us is able to relate to and use for our own purposes the linguistic system. The key to this process is found in those parts of speech the linguists call *shifters*: 'C'est ... un fait à la fois original et fondamental que ces formes "pronominales" ne renvoient pas à la "réalité" ni à des positions "objectives" dans l'espace ou dans le temps, mais à

26 Ibid., 285
27 *The Act of Reading*, 111

l'énonciation, chaque fois unique, qui les contient, et réfléchissent ainsi leur propre emploi.'[28] What they are then is what Benveniste calls 'un ensemble de signes "vides," non référentiels par rapport à la "réalité," toujours disponibles, et qui deviennent "pleins" dès qu'un locuteur les assume dans chaque instance de son discours.'[29] These signs mark the interface between the linguistic system (*langue*) and speech (*langage/parole*), the individual's use of language: 'C'est cette propriété qui fonde le discours individuel.'[30] Thereby is founded the identity of the person: 'Est "ego" qui *dit* "ego." Nous trouvons là le fondement de la "subjectivité" qui se détermine par le statut linguistique de la "personne." '[31]

As Olga Bernal points out, 'le drame qui renaît dans chacun des romans de Beckett pour atteindre, dans *L'Innommable*, une portée tragique, est un drame linguistique, un drame entre le pronom et la personne.'[32] What is at stake is nothing less than the relationship man establishes with language, through writing, reading, and even thinking. Even Blanchot, whose thought could hardly be said to be lacking in audaciousness, does not perhaps go far enough when he writes: 'Peut-être ne sommes-nous pas en présence d'un livre, mais peut-être s'agit-il de bien plus qu'un livre: de l'approche pure du mouvement d'où viennent tous les livres ...'[33] If, as another critic maintains, Beckett 'dévoile le mouvement qui transforme le langage en littérature,'[34] before language can be transmuted into literature, there has to exist an individual to assume language through the performance of the speech-act, for the literary text, as Paul Ricoeur has amply demonstrated,[35] is the written form of the speech-act of oral discourse. To put this another way, the appropriation of the text by its reader has, of necessity, to be preceded by the appropriation of the linguistic system by the writer. In summary, what I am maintaining is that *L'Innommable* stands in relation to literature as the shifter stands in relation to the linguistic system.

Let us now turn once again to the concept of play, which Paul Ricoeur has taken over and developed from Gadamer's analysis of the

28 'La Nature des pronoms,' in *Problèmes de linguistique générale 1*, 254
29 Ibid.
30 Ibid.
31 'De la subjectivité dans le langage' in ibid., 260
32 *Langage et fiction dans le roman de Beckett*, 153
33 'Où maintenant? Qui maintenant?' 681
34 Gérard Durozoi, *Beckett*, 194
35 See, in particular, his *Interpretation Theory*.

aesthetic experience of play[36] in *Truth and Method*. Gadamer has shown that play is not determined by the consciousness that plays but possesses its own mode of being and that the experience of play transforms the player. In the same way the subject of the aesthetic experience is not the player but rather what happens during the process of playing. Play destroys the seriousness of utilitarian preoccupations in which the self-presence of the subject is too assured, for in play, subjectivity forgets itself. Now Ricoeur develops this concept of play in an important article entitled 'Appropriation,' in order to account for the relationship between the writer and his work. He speaks of the 'playful relation' that exists between the two in the form of the relationship the author entertains with his characters: 'The author is rendered fictitious; and the different modalities of the relation of author to narration are like so many rules of this playful relation ... while it is true to say that the narrator is never the author, nevertheless the narrator is always the one who is metamorphosed in a fictional character which is the author. Even the death of the author is a game the author plays.'[37] He sees a parallel here with the reader's situation:[38] 'It is now possible ... to treat the reader in turn as a fictive or playful figure. For the author's subjectivity, submitted to imaginative variations, becomes a model offered by the narrator to the subjectivity of his reader. The reader as well is invited to undergo an imaginative variation of his *ego*.'[39] To read a novel, as we have seen above, is to play, to play at believing in the world of the fiction, in other words to *make believe* just as children do in play. And Ricoeur concludes thus: 'In entering a game we hand ourselves over, we abandon ourselves to the space of meaning which holds sway over the reader.'[40]

The space of the literary work is thus analogous to the space in which any game is played out, and like the latter it is, of course, not the space of everyday reality. In *L'Innommable*, the outline of this space is marked out by the 'empty' referentiality of the shifters. The players of the game are, of course, two in number: the writer and the

36 See the bibliography of Picard's *Le Jeu de la lecture* for works devoted to play. Interestingly, both Ricoeur's essay, 'Appropriation,' and Gadamer's treatment of appropriation in relation to aesthetic experience are missing from Picard's list.
37 'Appropriation,' 188–9
38 For a more recent and very different treatment of the relationship between reading and play informed by psychoanalytical theory, see Picard, *Le Jeu de la lecture*.
39 'Appropriation,' 189
40 Ibid., 187

reader, or more precisely, the writer then the reader, since here the game cannot be played by both at the same time. However, to return to the metaphor evoked at the beginning of this chapter of the shadows on the text, it is indeed only the *shadows* of writer and reader that occupy the space of the work, shadows cast by their respective proximity to the space of the work into which neither in fact actually enters, remaining poised on its threshold. There is a game to be played, available and ready at hand, but it remains just that: it is not actually played by anyone. The traditional mode of fictional make-believe does not here prove to be a possibility because of the absence of any identifiable fictive referents.

There is, however, another sense of the word *play* that is no doubt even more relevant with regard to this text of Beckett and that is the play that one finds in the hinge of a door – virtually synonymous with the word *give*, as when we say that something gives ever so slightly as one puts pressure on it. Play of *that* kind is perhaps the main characteristic of this text in relation to its reader, and it is once again the shifters that are primarily responsible for the possibility of that slightest of movements that allows the reader to adjust to and thereby occupy the empty slots corresponding to the shifters and fit in, so to speak, to the world of the text – a world that, it should be stressed once again, is waiting to receive him and yet, contrary to other novelistic universes, is empty until he himself occupies it. This particular quality would be called in French the text's *ustensilité*, its capacity to serve as a tool that can be taken up and employed by the craftsman-reader, ever available to take on the role of an extension of the person's own being.

Now Ricoeur insists on the fact that the appropriation of any work by its reader has to be preceded by a dispossession of self by the latter: 'To appropriate is to make what was alien become one's own. What is appropriated is indeed the matter of the text. But the matter of the text becomes my own only if I disappropriate myself, in order to let the matter of the text be. So I exchange the *me, master* of itself, for the *self, disciple* of the text.'[41] And although Ricoeur, true to the custom of the whole hermeneutic tradition, speaks only of the reader, I believe a similar process is at work for the writer, just as, as was pointed out earlier, the reader's appropriation of the text has, of necessity, been preceded by the writer's appropriation of language: both are in fact concerned with the appropriation of language, and

41 'Phenomenology and Hermeneutics,' 113

only the medium of that appropriation differs – reading as opposed to writing. The writer, too, has to dispossess himself of himself. As Maurice Blanchot, who throughout his work addresses the situation of the writer, puts it with respect to Beckett himself, the act of writing is 'l'expérience qui l'a entraîné hors de soi, qui l'a dépossédé et dessaisi, qui l'a livré dehors, qui a fait de lui un être sans nom,' for the reader has come to occupy 'le lieu vide où parle le désœuvrement de soi.'[42] The space of the language he is called upon to occupy is no more that of everyday reality than is the space of play: '... l'écrivain appartient à un langage que personne ne parle, qui ne s'adresse à personne, qui n'a pas de centre, qui ne révèle rien,'[43] a language that 'se parle et ... s'écrit.'[44] The writer then, like the reader, leaves behind him everyday reality, and with it, his everyday self.

In the process of leaving behind the world of practical, day-to-day considerations and concerns, the player, and with him the reader – Ricoeur concurs with Gadamer – experiences 'the transformation of everything into its true being': 'Everyday reality is abolished and yet everybody becomes himself ... The player is metamorphosed [*sic*] "in the true"; in playful representation, "what is emerges." But "what is" is no longer what we call everyday reality; or rather, reality truly becomes reality, that is, something which comprises a future horizon of undecided possibilities, something to fear or to hope for, something unsettled.'[45] Thus it is that appropriation, as we saw in the previous chapter, becomes 'the process by which the revelation of new modes of being or ... new "forms of life" *gives* to the subject new capacities for knowing himself,'[46] for paradoxically, 'the most imaginary creation elicits recognition.'[47] The American philosopher Nelson Goodman made this point most tellingly in a passage, quoted earlier, from his book *Ways of Worldmaking*: 'Fiction operates in actual worlds in much the same way as nonfiction. Cervantes and Bosch and Goya, no less than Boswell and Newton and Darwin, take and unmake and remake familiar worlds, recasting them in remarkable and sometimes recondite but eventually recognizable – *re-cognizable* – ways.'[48] This final stage of the text's reception represents the realization of the

42 'Où maintenant? Qui maintenant?' 681
43 *L'Espace littéraire*, 21
44 *La Part du feu*, 48
45 'Appropriation,' 187
46 Ibid., 192
47 Ibid., 187
48 *Ways of Worldmaking*, 104–5; Goodman's emphasis

text's ultimate referentiality through the act of reading,[49] a process whereby its referentiality, which had been suspended at the level of its fictive referents, is reactivated. In other words, its referentiality has moved from the fictional mode to reality itself in the form of its reader.

However, in the case of *L'Innommable*, the question is exactly what form these 'new modes of being' might take, given the failure of the fictive referents to give rise to even a semblance of fictional reality. Indeed, I said a moment ago that the reader remains poised at the edge of the play-area without in fact entering it. More precisely, he goes through the motions of play without, for all that, 'the space of [play's make-believe] meaning,' to use Ricoeur's expression, 'hold[ing] sway' over him since this particular play *has no meaning*. It is, as it were, empty play into which the player is never able to enter completely but remains painfully self-conscious of the fact that he is 'merely' playing. In this case, the reader's situation is no different from the writer's. For contrary to the reader's normal situation, the writer's dispossession of himself through the act of writing is *never* facilitated by any revelatory power of language, since language, for him, 'ne révèle rien,' as Blanchot stresses.

The similarity of the reader's situation in *L'Innommable* to that of any writer provides the answer to our question. The new mode of being that the reader encounters and carries away with him from the reading of this text is none other than man's interface with language, the revelation of what it is to relate, or rather interrelate with language itself – a revelation that *precedes* any encounter with the literary text as such. We have now come full circle and returned to our starting point: the meeting and interplay of the shadow of both writer and reader on the surface of the text, a shadow that occupies what Jean-Paul Resweber calls 'cet espace d'écoute commun à l'auteur et à l'interprète,'[50] which, in the case of *L'Innommable*, retains all its latency, problematizing thereby the very listening that it alone makes possible rather than offering up to the listeners – that is both the reader *and* the writer – something to be heard. Its emptiness, the confines of which no echo delimitates, testifies to the confrontation of two silences, realizing thus perhaps more completely then any other of his works to date Beckett's ultimate objective.

49 See *Interpretation Theory*.
50 'Dialoguer avec un écrit, ce sera interroger cet écrit et déployer cet espace commun à l'auteur et à l'interprète' (Jean-Paul Resweber, *Qu'est-ce qu'interpréter*, 17).

8

When the Fictive Referent Is Itself
a Work of Art:
Simon's *Histoire*

In order to clarify the title of this chapter, I should begin by explaining what is meant by the term *work of art*. My main concern here is with what is undoubtedly by far the most important fictive referent of Simon's *Histoire*, a series of postcards. Now, the principal characteristic of postcards – that is, as material objects existing in space – is that they are flat or two-dimensional just like any other sheet of paper or cardboard. Their main function is to transmit messages through the postal system, but also they often reproduce a pictorial representation of reality in the form of a photograph or painting. This is the case with the postcards in *Histoire*. In this respect, postcards have much in common not only with photographs and paintings but also with posters, advertisements, and even postage stamps. Postage stamps, in fact, also exist either side by side with the photo or painting reproduced on the postcard or on its reverse side. With regard to their representational function, postcards have affinities with works of art such as statues, fresco and other forms of sculpture: they constitute visual representations of reality produced with aesthetic intent – even if photographs possess a potential rather than a necessary artistic character. This grouping of objects bearing affinities with the postcards that we shall be primarily concerned with is thus heterogeneous, in that it includes both two- and three-dimensional objects (such as sculpture) and both aesthetic and utilitarian objects (such as stamps, advertisements, and posters); the postcard belongs to both categories. It is, however, homogeneous in that all these phenomena constitute *non-linguistic representations* of reality. It is this feature that gives them their particular status as fictive referents, for once they take their place within the world of the novel, they then become representations *within* a larger representation, in a sense pictorial and sculptural representations contained within a linguistic representation. *Except*, of course, – and the proviso is a crucial one – they themselves are *re*-represented in linguistic form rather than being reproduced directly as visual images and inserted between – or as in Malraux's *Le Musée imaginaire*, for example, within – the pages of the text. All the different objects mentioned are to be found, as we shall see, within the pages of *Histoire*.

Once a situation is evoked where an object is reproduced on a smaller scale within a like object so that the two objects concerned share a common identity – in this case, a work belonging to the plastic arts being reproduced within a work of literature – then one of the key figures of contemporary poetics immediately comes to mind: that of the *mise en abyme*[1] and its poor cousin, the *enchassement*.[2] This is one of the main reasons why I adopt a dual approach in this chapter: hermeneutic, as in the rest of this book, *and*, though to a lesser extent, formalist. And although these two approaches are usually considered to be mutually exclusive, in light of Paul Ricoeur's writings on literary theory they are seen ultimately to be, on the contrary, complementary.[3] For if literary referentiality is the privileged domain of hermeneutics, auto-referentiality – an intratextual phenomenon – for its part is clearly the concern of an approach to literary studies that concentrates on the internal functioning of texts: formalism or poetics. It would be perverse to deny the *auto*-referentiality of such a text for the purposes of the present study with its focus on the more com-

1 I refer the reader to what has come to be considered as the 'classic' study of this formal device, which occupies so central a place in writings on the literature of what the French have baptized *la modernité*, Lucien Dällenbach's *Le Récit spéculaire: Essai sur la mise en abyme*.

2 The difference between the two lies in the fact that whereas they both entail that their object – that which is *mise en abyme* or *enchassé* – enjoys a relationship with its context of *contained* to *container*, only in the case of the *mise en abyme* is a *common identity* shared by the two elements. The relationship between *microcosm* and *macrocosm* constitutes an intermediary factor, since while it definitely characterizes the *mise en abyme*, it does not necessarily characterize the *enchassement*. Inasmuch as in the present chapter we shall be concerned with postcards represented within a novel, or pictorial representations of reality within other pictorial representations of reality where what is represented, the content, is not the same in both cases, it appeared most appropriate to use the term *enchassement*, i.e., 'embedding,' reserving the term *mise en abyme* for those instances where the embedded object represents the process of either the production or the reception of the pictorial representation or work of art.

3 I sought to demonstrate this in 'La Navette et l'ellipse chez Malraux,' where the same textual device was read as an illustration both of the *mise en abyme* and the hermeneutic circle.

mon or 'positive' form of referentiality. A large body of criticism and critical debate, both in literary journals and academic colloquia (notably those held at Cerisy-la-Salle devoted to Simon in particular or the French New Novel in general), testify to the self-reflexive character of a work such as *Histoire*. In fact, it would be no exaggeration to claim that we shall be passing over in silence what are the most important aesthetic characteristics of this text of Simon. As I made clear in the preface, auto-referentiality is not, in itself, my concern in the present study. However, the intricacy with which the whole process of reference functions within *Histoire* is such that it is impossible to amputate from reference certain key stages in its evolution that are marked by a distinctive mirroring effect. Once this has been said, the justification for examining the manner in which referentiality works itself out in this novel is not far to seek: indeed, the predominant role of pictorial and sculptural representations as fictive referents in *Histoire* confers upon them what could well be a unique status in the history of the novel.

In order to study the manner in which the postcards and other related objects function referentially within the novel, it is necessary to take into account the context in which they appear. We have to consider whether they are alone among all the fictive referents that make up the world of the novel in enjoying a distinctive and unusual status. As it happens, the evocations of *all* the fictive referents in this work tend to take on certain particular features, although these features are not those of the category of objects just enumerated – on the contrary. In fact, if this were not so and they were to function referentially in the same way as the postcards, and so on, then there would be no justification for singling out the latter for closer analysis.

Ever since the publication of *Le Vent* in 1957, the most distinctive stylistic trait of Claude Simon's novels has been the exceptional predominance of the present participle,[4] which far outweighs the presence of any other verbal form. Present participles have borne the brunt of the task of moving the narrative along, however paradoxical such a role for this particular form of the verb may be, as we shall see. It therefore is not surprising that they play a significant and analogous

---

4 A more detailed account of their functioning within Simon's earlier novels *Le Vent*, *L'Herbe*, and *La Route des Flandres*, is to be found in my 'Participe présent et procédés narratifs chez Claude Simon,' which is why comments here on this stylistic feature are restricted to what is essential.

role in *Histoire*, as can be seen in an examination of the narrative texture of the first paragraph of the novel. *Histoire* opens thus, with its first paragraph indented and yet at the same time in mid-sentence:

l'une d'elle touchait presque la maison et l'été quand je travaillais tard dans la nuit assis devant la fenêtre ouverte je pouvais la voir ou du moins ses derniers rameaux éclairés par la lampe avec leurs feuilles semblables à des plumes *palpitant* faiblement sur le fond de ténèbres, les folioles ovales teintées d'un vert cru irréel par la lumière électrique *remuant* par moments comme des aigrettes comme animées soudain d'un mouvement propre (et derrière on pouvait percevoir se *communiquant* de proche en proche une mystérieuse et délicate rumeur invisible se *propageant* dans l'obscur fouillis des branches), comme si l'arbre tout entier se réveillait s'ébrouait se secouait, puis tout s'apaisait et elles reprenaient leur immobilité, les premières que frappaient directement les rayons de l'ampoule se *détachant* avec précision en avant des rameaux plus lointains de plus en plus faiblement éclairés de moins en moins distincts entrevus puis seulement devinés puis complètement invisibles quoi-qu'on pût les sentir nombreux *s'entrecroisant* se *succédant* se *superposant* dans les épaisseurs d'obscurité d'où parvenaient de faibles froissements de faibles cris d'oiseaux endormis *tressaillant* *s'agitant* *gémissant* dans leur sommeil[5]

The paragraph also ends in mid-sentence. The fact that the text begins and ends *in medias res* – that is, that it neither begins nor ends[6] – already reflects the functioning of the present participles, which them-selves evoke an action or event that has already begun and whose ending remains unspecified. Just as such an action implies a point in time at which it must have begun so that its evocation is incomplete, the first words, 'l'une d'elles,' imply an antecedent that is also missing and without which the identity of the corresponding fictive referent is not only unclear but wholly indeterminable. It is only when we reach the words 'ses derniers rameaux' that we are finally able to fill in the 'blank,' or what Ingarden would call the 'spot of indeterminacy,' and concretize the referent in the form of a tree, necessarily of a certain size suggested by the initial mention of the fact that its branch

5 *Histoire*, 11–12; my emphasis, as in all subsequent quotations from this novel. Page references placed within parentheses are to the 'Folio' edition.
6 That is, of course, from a syntactical point of view and on the level of the signifieds. Formally speaking, as a *text* corresponding to a paragraph typographi-cally distinguished from the sum total of paragraphs constituting the novel, it does have a beginning and an ending.

'touchait presque la maison.' However, before the subject of the initial sentence ('l'une d'elle') is clarified, a 'je' is introduced, and with it a narrative perspective that is defined both spatially and temporally: 'quand je travaillais tard dans la nuit assis devant la fenêtre ouverte je pouvais la voir'; the following qualification by the addition of 'du moins' ('du moins ses derniers rameaux' etc.) testifies to the fact that the reader's perspective is indeed subject to the same limitations as those of the 'je.'

In complete contrast to the situation at the opening of Beckett's *L'Innommable*, this establishment of perspective readily effects a concretization of the fictional space in question, and it is the precise nature of this space that plays a paramount role in the analyses that follow. The temporal – as opposed to the spatial – situation is less closely demarcated and its character links up precisely with our initial observation above, for all three verbs up to this point are in the imperfect tense, a tense designating a *continuous* action without any specified beginning or ending. In simple terms, this is a description rather than a narrative; in French a narrative is invariably characterized by a predominance of the past definite or preterite tense. And in itself nothing could be less surprising than to find a description 'setting the scene,' as the saying goes, for the story that is to come – if it were not for the fact that the reader of *Histoire* (in spite of its title) is no less frustrated than the reader of *L'Innommable* in his expectation of a story made up of a chronological sequence of clearly delimited events. The fact is that all the paragraphs that follow this initial paragraph are characterized by the very same features that have just been noted.

Of the five senses, the sense of sight is the predominant one ('je pouvais la *voir*') with the emphasis on lighting, contrast, and colour: 'ses derniers rameaux *éclairés par la lampe* avec leurs feuilles semblables à des plumes palpitant faiblement *sur le fond de ténèbres*, les folioles ovales *teintées d'un vert* cru *irréel par la lumière électrique* remuant par moments comme des aigrettes comme animées soudain d'un mouvement propre.' Present participles have now taken over from the imperfect tense in an eminently natural, unremarkable manner whereby the continuity of the actions they evoke merges into the habitual past previously evoked by the imperfect, pursuing the description of a state of affairs, so to speak, rather than a series of events. It is true that the phrase within parentheses with its two additional present participles does appeal to the sense of hearing with its 'rumeur invisible' as well as to the sight: 'l'obscur fouillis.'

Although the indication 'animées soudain d'un mouvement propre' does evoke the beginning of a movement, an event of sorts, the temporal outline of this movement is immediately blurred by imperfect tenses in the following comparison: 'comme si l'arbre tout entier se réveillait s'ébrouait se secouait.' And if the following 'puis' that is so characteristic of the narrative form leads us to expect to learn what came next temporally speaking, in fact it merely announces the stilling of the movement in question: 'puis tout s'apaisait et elles reprenaient leur immobilité.' The present participles now take over the paragraph for good, and with the return to the visual image, for the first time a three-dimensional effect begins to emerge with respect to the fictive referent of the tree: 'les premières que frappaient directement les rayons de l'ampoule se détachant avec précision en avant des rameaux plus lointains de plus en plus faiblement éclairés de moins en moins distincts entrevus puis seulement devinés puis complètement invisibles.' This impression of spatial volume with its different 'layers' as it stretches away from the perceiver is, however, immediately counteracted by the next three present participles, which, through the blurring of outlines noted earlier, tend to flatten out once again the image evoked by the referent: 'quoiqu'on pût les sentir nombreux s'entrecroisant se succédant se superposant dans les épaisseurs d'obscurité' – before a new image is introduced, that of the birds, in which the visual (movement) is accompanied by the audible: 'd'où parvenaient de faibles froissements de faibles cris d'oiseaux endormis *tressaillant s'agitant gémissant* dans leur sommeil.' We should note, however, that the faintness of the birds' chirping blurs away into the same indistinctness that is produced by the present participles.

In the context of the reader's reception of such a passage, what needs to be stressed is the *flattening out* of the image corresponding to the fictive referent: the tree and its branches with its natural garb, the leaves, and its natural occupants, the birds. The common denominator running through the foregoing analysis is the impression of blurring – spatial, by definition, but also temporal. And it is partly because blurring is primarily a spatial phenomenon that the spatial completely overwhelms any latent temporality, time taking the form of an undifferentiated continuum as reflected in the images produced not only by the present participles but also by the verbs in the imperfect tense. The space concerned, corresponding to that occupied by the referent, is however two-dimensional, being characterized by blurred outlines. In fact, the present participle evokes nothing so much as the *photograph* of a movement that has been arrested by a camera whose shutter speed was not fast enough to produce a sharp image – as in many photographs of athletes or racing cars, where the effect is almost always deliberate. What also needs to be emphasized here is that the blurring effect applies not only to the shapes and outlines of moving objects, but also to the *relationship between* the images, corresponding to each of the present participles, so that, paradoxically, while within the individual movement there is a definite impression of *continuity*, between the movements there is a no less definite an impression of *dis*continuity: the impression of *sequentiality* conveyed by the series of preterite tenses one finds in any narration of events is here totally absent.

The two-dimensionality of the space occupied by the referent does not, however, denote the complete absence of the third dimension. For, as was noted, right from the opening of this initial paragraph, there was posited as the first identifiable referent, a 'je,' but only inasmuch as a shifter such as 'je' can be said to be identifiable; in reality, its identity, when first encountered, is no less latent than that of 'l'une d'elles.' However, the 'je' did evoke a definite narrative perspective encompassing not only the fictive referent in the form of the tree but also the space the 'je' was looking out across as he sat by the window. And there is no doubt of its three-dimensional volume since it was this space that separated the narrator from the tree. Indeed such a space is necessarily evoked by any shifter whose semantic content is defined by a certain positioning in space (and/or time).[7]

A peculiar effect is created by the juxtaposition of a three-dimensional and a two-dimensional space. The basic difference in dimension means that they cannot be of like nature; if they were, they would inevitably merge with each other, whereas in fact the space encompassing the window is felt by the reader to be somehow superimposed on that occupied by the tree. Now it is obvious that the tree must occupy a fictional space corresponding to that of material reality in which we live out our physical existence. What, then, can be the space that is, as it were, pushing up against and flattening out the material volume of the tree so as to reduce it to a flat image? It can only be a psychic or mental space of some kind, whether it be that of

---

7 To avoid any ambiguity here, it should be pointed out that this represented material space, possessing cubic volume and corresponding to that in which the fictional characters move and have their being, soon becomes effaced in favour of the represented two-dimensional space and replaced, in the reading experience, by the imaginational space evoked below.

the human imagination or that of memory, what Ingarden would call 'imaginational space.' Indeed, the lack of a third dimension that is particularly noticeable in photographs of imperfectly 'frozen' action can just as readily call to mind the kind of image that is not the product of any of our five senses but that we conjure up for ourselves within our minds, that is a mental image. The impression registered by the reader resembles a series of images flashed onto a cinema screen in the dark or, more precisely, a film run in slow motion creating the effect of a certain discontinuity in the normally smooth flow of the images from frame to frame.

It should be noted that the 'je' does, in fact, remain an implicit 'je,' never to be explicitly fleshed out, largely because the present participle does not require (although it does not exclude[8]) the naming of the subject of the verb, as is illustrated by the opening of the fourth paragraph: 'les imaginant, sombres et lugubres, perchées dans le réseaux des branches ...' (12) and the fifth paragraph: 'pouvant entendre dans le silence le pas claudiquant de la vieille bonne ...' (13). As a fictive referent, the 'je' therefore never materializes for the reader in any visible, tangible form.

If we now turn to the process of the work's reception in light of the above, what do we find? Represented space in *Histoire* would, at first sight, appear to be of two kinds: real space and imaginational space. The reader finds himself called upon to concretize a fictional real universe in the form of a two-dimensional image together with a fictional imaginational space that stretches out in front of the latter. This imaginational space begins at a point whence the narrative voice is emanating and therefore where the reader himself is situated. However, the fictional real space is in fact subordinate to the fictional imaginational space upon which it is dependent for its very existence. This means that the space of the fiction is, notwithstanding the distinction just made, homogeneous. For the tree together with all the other fictive referents of this novel with the sole exception of that corresponding to the 'je' (and only as existing in the narrative present, it should be stressed) exist within the fiction only as *mental images*. There is then one fictional space represented in this work, and one

---

8 See, for example: 'l'autre gommeux en gilet rouge pantalon gris perle et canne débitant ses fadaises ...' (61), or: 'Et la même semeuse phrygienne couleur vert amande se détachant sur un fond strié de fines raies horizontales ...' (61).

alone, and it is imaginational in character. In short, what it is that the reader is involved in concretizing is *a mind remembering*.[9]

It is important to point out at this stage that in spite of the fact that images are readily conceived of as being two-dimensional by analogy with images that have been drawn, painted, or printed, as well as photographed, they most often create a three-dimensional effect. In the same way, mental images are also commonly *experienced* as possessing a third dimension and as giving an impression not of flatness but of relief. There is no reason whatsoever to presume that this is not the case for the narrator of *Histoire* as he relives past events. The reason why the fictive referents are experienced as flat by the reader of this work is because of his awareness of the aforementioned imaginational space corresponding to the *inner*, mental world of the narrator. The concretization of the latter is made more difficult by the fact that, apart from the mental images occupying it that have been resurrected by memory, the imaginational space is never *represented directly*. This produces a distinctly paradoxical situation, in that – and here I am giving a further 'twist' to the foregoing analysis – what *is* represented, to the virtual exclusion of anything else, is the series of flat images.

To sum up the complex reading phenomena involved here, the only truly *represented* space is indeed two-dimensional since the fully 'rounded out' imaginational space concerned is only represented *by implication*. This imaginational space in fact lacks any content (that is, other than the mental images) and is therefore an empty space. We finally come to the crux of the problem posed by the concretization of the main body of this novel (for in a moment we shall consider the particular, related, but different problem posed by the postcards and analogous objects): the considerable difficulty experienced by the reader in attempting to concretize not an abstraction as in the case of Blanchot's *Au Moment voulu* but a *void*, the nature of which is quite different from that supernatural *néant* or nothingness represented intermittently in Bernanos's *L'Imposture*. The need to produce such a void for oneself, within one's mind, *at the same time as one is reading and picturing the flattened images of the fictive referents*, and even more, to maintain and sustain this space in all its emptiness, creates

---

9 This is a more plausible interpretation of the situation in *Histoire* than to maintain that the narrator is merely *imagining* all that is depicted, although the ambiguity of the title, of course, allows for both possibilities.

a mental tension that taxes the powers of the reader's imagination to the limit. The psychic space in question has no doubt, in the end, to be equated with that of self-consciousness – not in the sense of that self-consciousness that gives rise to the self-scrutiny of introspection but rather mere self-awareness that in this instance means the awareness of being in the process of remembering.[10] It should be stressed that I am not maintaining that self-consciousness is *represented* in any form within the novel; the narrator does not reveal himself to be self-conscious as he relives the past. At most, the fictional existence of the self-consciousness located in the 'je' is implied by the two-dimensionality of the fictive referents. In all likelihood, the non-represented imaginational space becomes, as it is imagined by the reader, indistinguishable from the reader's own psychic space with which it gradually merges and to which it finally yields completely under the pressure of the mental tension needed to sustain its existence.

Only now are we in a position to turn to the actual topic of the present chapter: the postcards and allied objects. For the task of their concretization has naturally to be seen in the context of the reception of the whole of *Histoire*.

The reader of *Histoire* cannot fail to be struck by the large number of descriptions of postcards that he encounters: '... prenant dans son classeur une de ces autres cartes postales dont elle semblait elle-même avoir une inépuisable réserve, représentant des sites pittoresques des Pyrénées un vieux berger en costume local ou des statues dans un jardin public ...' (34). In the following passage, the postcard is not evoked in its own right but is rather a point of comparison: '... le personnage ne paraissait pas tout à fait réel: immatériel et anachronique, extrait aurait-on dit d'une de ces cartes aux personnages désuets (peut-être cette vue des Grands Boulevards, peut-être celui qui s'éten-

---

10 This would appear to correspond to what Sartre refers to as 'conscience non-thétique': 'La conscience imageante de l'objet enveloppe ... une conscience non-thétique d'elle-même. Cette conscience, qu'on pourrait appeler transversale, n'a pas d'objet. Elle ne pose rien, ne renseigne sur rien, n'est pas une connaissance: c'est une lumière diffuse que la conscience dégage pour elle-même, ou, pour abandonner les comparaisons, c'est une qualité indéfinissable qui s'attache à chaque conscience. Une conscience perceptive s'apparaît comme passivité. Au contraire, une conscience imageante se donne à elle-même comme conscience imageante, c'est-à-dire comme une spontanéité qui produit et conserve l'objet en image. C'est une espèce de contrepartie indéfinissable du fait que l'objet se donne comme un néant' (*L'Imaginaire*, 35).

dait complaisamment sur le perdreau qu'il venait de manger et la pipe qu'il était en train de fumer) ...' (55). Not the least interesting aspect of many of the descriptions of postcards lies in their inordinate length, occupying, as they often do, several pages. In this, they recall the extended metaphors so characteristic of Nathalie Sarraute's novels,[11] metaphors that almost become novels within the novel. Needless to say, the length of such passages inevitably invites, if not incites the reader to actualize their reference; in the case of *Histoire*, it invites the reader to lose sight of the description's point of departure, and in the case of Sarraute's novels, to forget that the object of the description has no place in the fictional universe as such.

Now the process of concretization that this gives rise to naturally takes place within the reading phenomena just analysed. As the evocation of what is represented on the postcard develops, the two-dimensional space of the fictive referents gradually takes on a third dimension, so that the referents acquire within the reader's imagination the rounded-out materiality of real objects. This development is well illustrated by the following description of a photograph, where such a transition is already effected by the nature of the images evoked: 'puis le long navire plat et bas aux cheminées vomissant d'épais panaches de fumée charbonneuse, c'est-à-dire que des deux hauts tubes jumeaux noirs et luisants s'échappent ... deux nuages d'abord étroits ensuite *boursouflés crépus faits de volutes tourbillonnantes s'accumulant s'étageant se poussant s'enroulant rapidement sur elles-mêmes comme des bobines se bousculant* ...' (40). This newly created represented real space, which, contrary to the flattened images of the preceding fictive referents, is measurable in terms of cubic capacity, 'crowds out,' so to speak, the represented imaginational space of self-awareness described above. That this development is paradoxical is obvious: whereas fictive referents corresponding to real-life objects had become reduced to images, to the pale reflection of themselves in the mind's eye, here by an exact reversal of the very same process mere images or pictorial representations of reality take on all the attributes of their real-life counterparts. Imaginational space is now displaced by real space; the reader tends eventually to lose sight of the fact that he is actually reading the description of a postcard. The reason for the displacement is no doubt the extreme difficulty, if not the impossibility, of creating and sustaining within one's mind the

11 See the example cited in chap. 5, n. 24.

coexistence of imagined imaginational space and imagined real space.[12]

What are most often pictured on the postcards are photographic images:

... ces photographies maladroitement prises pâles jaunâtres où de minuscules silhouettes de belluaires costumés et d'animaux s'affrontaient dérisoires dans le dévorant soleil d'interminables après-midi, semblables à des jouets de plomb ... que la lumière corrodait peu à peu, de plus en plus diaphanes, leurs fastueux et suaves déguisements de plus en plus fanés, et pisseux à la fin ... (36)

... au-dessus de son épaule gauche je pouvais maintenant le voir lui c'est-à-dire cet énorme agrandissement qu'elle avait fait faire et placer sur le mur parallèle à son lit à droite de sorte qu'elle n'avait qu'à tourner légèrement la tête pour le regarder sa courte barbe sépia ses yeux sépia clair qu'on devinait bleus sous les sourcils touffus et ses cheveux sépia clair ... le fond sépia clair allant pâlissant en dégradé jusqu'au blanc ... (20)

But we also find posters containing pictorial representations of different kinds: 'L'affiche apposée sur le mur, représentant en trompe-l'œil un coffre fort ouvert à l'intérieur duquel on peut voir quelques piles de pièces de monnaie de différentes hauteurs ...' etc. (93);[13] advertise-

---

12 In fact, the imagined imaginational space yields completely to the imagined real space and become effaced by the latter, since what was originally 'intended' as imaginational by the reader in his production of the mental image cannot *subsequently* be transformed into something real. For modifications cannot be effected on a mental image once it has been created, given the fact that 'dans l'acte même qui me donne l'objet en image,' as Sartre puts it in *L'Imaginaire*, 'se trouve incluse la connaissance de ce qu'il est' (27). Consequently, it can only be abandoned or dispelled from consciousness and a new image with a different existential status created in its stead, as is clear from Sartre's analysis: 'Dans l'image ... une certaine conscience se donne un certain objet. L'objet est donc corrélatif d'un certain acte synthétique, qui comprend, parmi ses structures, un certain savoir et une certaine "intention." L'intention est au centre de la conscience: c'est elle qui vise l'objet [in the present case: imaginational *or* real space], c'est-à-dire qui le constitue pour ce qu'il est. Le savoir, qui est indissolublement lié à l'intention, précise que l'objet est tel ou tel, ajoute synthétiquement des déterminations' (28).

13 For reasons of space, I have deliberately truncated such descriptions to the first few lines or so where they in fact continue for a dozen lines or more and in some cases for more than a page, indicating the remainder of the relevant passage by the word 'etc.'

ments on packages for various products: 'semblable avec sa chevelure dénouée répandue en éventail sur ses épaules et son dos son long peignoir traînant sur le tapis aux guirlandes de roses à l'une de ces héroïnes de théâtre ou plutôt d'opéra druidesses ou fiancées de paladins, un peu forte comme ces cantatrices imposantes et virginales semblables elle-mêmes aux réclames pour baumes capillaires ou secrets orientaux que l'on pouvait voir à cette époque sur les empaquetages bleus d'épingles à cheveux ou dans les journaux de mode féminins ...' (34); not to mention book covers: 'sur la couverture rouge blanche et noire était représenté un marin vêtu d'un maillot rayé coiffé d'un béret plat dont les rubans retombaient sur sa nuque, armé d'un fusil, un pistolet passé dans sa ceinture, le visage maigre, hâve, tourné vers la gauche, le bras droit tendu lui aussi vers la gauche, la main grande ouverte ...' etc. (137); and illustrations reproduced in books: 'les imaginant, sombres et lugubres, perchées dans le réseau des branches, comme sur cette caricature orléaniste reproduite dans le manuel d'Histoire et qui représentait l'arbre généalogique de la famille royale dont les membres sautillaient parmi les branches sous la forme d'oiseaux à têtes humaines coiffés de couronnes endiamantées et pourvus de nez (ou plutôt de becs) bourboniens et monstrueux ...' (12–13). What is more, photographs are not the only representational images to be pictured on the postcards, for there are also, quite naturally, stamps: '... le timbre d'un gris mauve représentant une sorte de pendule de dessus de cheminée où deux personnages à demi nus la femme tenant un rameau feuillu l'homme un caducée où s'enroulent deux serpents sont appuyés symétriquement de part et d'autre du chiffre 10 ...' etc. (25).

To take this analysis one stage further by addressing the functioning of the reference, what all these passages have in common is that their fictive referent consists of an object that is itself the representation of something else. This means that while, as was seen in chapter 1, the reference is, in Ricoeur's terms, 'suspended' on the level of the individual fictive referent before subsequently being reactivated on the level of the totality of actions, situations, characters, objects, and so on, that come together to form the fictive heterocosm through the process of concretization so that the potential non-ostensive reference of the text is realized in a new situation, that of the reader, here, on the level of the individual fictive referents, the reference is in fact doubly suspended, since the fictive referents that are the postcards give rise to a further set of fictive referents in the form of the images represented on the latter. In the case of both the postcards and the posters, as was pointed out in the introduction to this chapter, the text furnishes a linguistic representation of a representation that is itself non-linguistic, that is to say pictorial. We have therefore a representation within a representation (the novel itself), thus creating an *enchassement* effect, the former being embedded within the latter.

The situation takes on a further, intriguing complexity when this representation within a representation – the fictive referent – also enjoys the status of a work of art. Such is the case with the stained-glass window, for example: 'Sur le vitrail je pouvais voir l'éternelle charge des zouaves pontificaux le drapeau brandi claquant au vent les fulgurants éclats des bombes les nuages de fumée sertis de plomb inscrits dans une rosace et dans la rosace à côté ... Du Guesclin agonisant sous son arbre Moïse enveloppé dans un péplum violet ...' etc. (47). And similarly with the various paintings: '... ce petit tableau soi-disant de l'école hollandaise où l'on ne distinguait guère dans une obscurité bitumeuse qu'une lanterne jaunâtre tenue par un personnage à demi invisible dont le visage éclairé par en dessous peint en touches grasses ocre vermillon semblait suspendu dans l'obscurité au-dessus et à droite d'une vague forme une bête (un bœuf?) couchée ...' (30–1); '... l'étang morne peint à l'huile ses eaux métalliques semées de touffes de joncs frissonnant entre lesquelles se reflétaient le ciel les lents nuages au-dessus des arbres déhanchés lugubres bordant la rive ...' (30).

It is not only the reference that is thus suspended but also the hermeneutic process as such, every artistic object being of course an object for interpretation. What this means for the reader is that he is faced with the unusual and intricate task of effecting an interpretation *within* an interpretation, since he will have to integrate the result of his interpretation – and for 'interpretation' one could as well read 'reception,' since the two are inseparable – of the work of art represented in the form of the fictive referent within his overall interpretation or reading of the novel as a whole. In other words, in theory at least, the interpretation of the given painting[14] is an essential prerequisite for the interpretation of the novel in which it takes its place.

14 In fact, it is not possible to 'scrutinize' the painting in the form in which one has concretized it in order to then interpret it, that is, form an aesthetic appreciation of it, 'car l'objet de l'image n'est jamais rien de plus que la conscience qu'on en a ... : on ne peut rien apprendre d'une image qu'on ne sache déjà' (Sartre, *L'Imaginaire*, 27). In the same way and for the same reason that one cannot look more closely at a mental image that one fails to recognize and attempt to identify it ('Dans le cas de l'image, je le sais immédiatement: c'est le gazon de tel

This is, of course, no less true of those fictive referents consisting of representations of reality that, contrary to all those mentioned so far, are composed not of two dimensions but three and that also belong to the world of art. In the first place, there are the statues:

Cour intérieure: fontaine ornée d'une statue représentant un fleuve, le dieu figuré sous les apparences d'un robuste vieillard à demi étendu son bras replié reposant sur une sorte d'urne ou de jarre renversée d'où s'échappent des flots de pierre serpentant en méandres comme la longue barbe sinueuse qui descend sur sa poitrine – Corridor: colossale statue de Minerve aux yeux aveugles sans prunelles une expression sereine absente sur le visage sculpté dans une pierre grisâtre mate au-dessus du péplum drapé fait d'un marbre rouge sang de bœuf parcouru de veinules finement ramifiées ... (126)

Then there is the stage-setting for the opera *Aida*:

... lorsque le rideau de pourpre peint en trompe-l'œil s'élève et qu'elle apparaît porteuse d'eau dans le décor stéréotypé de palmiers poussiéreux sur l'azur poussiéreux de la toile de fond, vêtue d'une comment appelle-t-on ces robes djellaba ou quoi prune à rayures les seins cachés par le foulard bayadère une main sur la hanche l'autre bras au bout duquel pend la cruche de carton le long du corps et sous les sequins de tôle dorés qui pendent à son front son regard fendu allongé de noir d'enfant prostituée calme neutre avec son nez de Sphinge sa bouche de Sphinge telle qu'elle continue à sourire au-dessus du lourd menton, énigmatique, ennuyée et impitoyable sous les mutilations tandis que l'orchestre attaque le prélude Aïda ... (63)

In these last two cases, of course, we do not encounter the paradoxical situation whereby what is represented in the form of two-dimensional pictorial reproductions of fictional reality (postcards, posters, and so on) acquires, as the content of imagined space, the volume it had been deprived of by its reproduction. As far as the reference is concerned, this means that as readers we have to 'zero in,' so to speak,

---

pré, à tel endroit. Et cette origine ne se laisse pas déchiffrer *sur* l'image: dans l'acte même qui me donne l'objet en image se trouve incluse la connaissance de ce qu'il est' [27; Sartre's emphasis]), any aesthetic appreciation of the painting concerned would have had to inform its concretization by the reader at the outset. Is this not to say quite simply that concretization and interpretation are one and the same process? Or rather that what has been 'interpreted' are the original words in the text rather than the painting that is their referent and that cannot therefore itself be an object of aesthetic appreciation for the reader?

on the work of art, picking it out from among all the other fictive referents that go to make up the novelistic universe and concretizing it in our mind's eye before subsequently drawing back to reintegrate it within its context, that of the other fictive referents that frame or surround it and in which it is embedded. Its reference in the form of what is depicted by the work of art in question has first to be fully plumbed for its own sake. Only subsequently does it become part of its context. The reference of the totality of that context has then, in its turn, to be realized by the reader. The reason for this is, in Ingardenian terms, that on the level of the meaning-units of the work, although its 'existential characterization' determines that the object (statue or stage setting, for example) is real, an 'existentially real position, however, is thoroughly lacking.'[15]

There is a further complication in those evocations where the represented work of art is incomplete and only a fragment of it remains. One might well believe such a situation to be far from common within the literature of the novel genre, and yet it, too, is to be found in this remarkable work *Histoire*. It figures in the description of the banknotes, to which we shall return later: 'devant d'allégoriques fonds de glaives, de trophées, de galions, d'épis et de balances et sur lequel la mémoire identifiant armures, hermines, perruques ou cravates victoriennes pose un de ces noms interchangeables aux creuses et poussiéreuses sonorités de plâtre César, Verrius, Charles, Laurent ... rangés sur les étagères des classes de dessin pêle-mêle avec les têtes de déesses, les écorchés et les moulages de pieds comme cette main coupée suspendue au mur à l'arrière-plan de ce portrait peint en grisaille accroché entre la vitrine et le piano ...' (94). It should be noted that whereas the 'têtes de déesses' are, within their *immediate* context, mental images conjured up from memory, the 'main coupée' constitutes an *enchassement* to the *second degree*, in that it is contained within a painting. The fact that it is only a part of a work of art and is completely detached from the missing remainder, which is by the same token wholly inaccessible to the reader and therefore not available to him for concretization, prevents the reader from realizing the reference of the sculpture in question through its reception as an aesthetic object. The only exception would be found in the case – this time a

15 Ingarden, *The Literary Work of Art*, 70. If the statue were to represent a historical person rather than a mythological character, then as in the case of the historical novel, the referent would no longer be fictional, since it would possess an 'existentially real position' (see my conclusion to this chapter).

quite hypothetical one, it should be added – where the work of which the fragment had been a part was a sculpture known to the reader, in other words a sculpture existing in the real world and enjoying some renown. What should not be lost sight of is the length of these evocations of sculptural or pictorial representations within this novel, for they can take up several pages each. This is what gives the present analysis an interest and a significance that goes beyond the purely theoretical; in the attempt to understand and interpret the text of *Histoire*, the reader cannot fail to be confronted by the complexity of the situations just described.

So far two levels of representation have been identified, the first constituted by the verbal texture of this novel in general (including those referents examined in the first section of this chapter) and the second corresponding to those passages featuring evocations of photos and works of art in particular. But there are occasions when we encounter fictive referents in the form of pictorial representations containing within themselves further representations, no less pictorial in character, thus creating an *enchassement* effect to the second degree or, if one prefers, at one remove. (It should be noted, in passing, that such a state of affairs is not possible in the case of a sculptural reproduction, since a statue cannot contain within itself another statue.[16]) The poster referred to earlier is a good example of this doubling up of the *enchassement*:

L'affiche apposée sur le mur, représentant en trompe-l'œil un coffre-fort ouvert à l'intérieur duquel on peut voir quelques piles de pièces de monnaie de différentes hauteurs, tours fragiles, branlantes, l'une d'elles abattue répandue sur la tablette, présentant cet aspect de saucisson coupé en tranches comme les rouleaux défaits et comptés par un caissier, certaines ayant roulé çà et là sur des billets éparpillés reproduits eux aussi en trompe-l'œil et où on pouvait reconnaître le cardinal à la barbiche en pointe, au regard froid, rusé, flasque, à la calotte rouge se détachant sur un ciel saumon devant des bâtiments alignant leurs toits d'ardoise en forme de triangles, de trapèzes et de pyramides tronquées ... (93)

The banknotes quite naturally bear the portrait of the cardinal standing out against a background that itself forms a miniature landscape,

16 The famous Russian dolls, however, each contained within a larger identical sister and containing in its turn a smaller version, represent precisely such a phenomenon.

or rather cityscape. But that is not the end of the matter, for subsequently we come across the one element lacking so far (in light of the preceding discussion): a real painting enjoying the status of a work of art. And it is introduced in the form of a comparison: 'le dernier billet dépassant du tiers de sa longueur environ le rebord de la tablette d'acier, la partie en porte-à-faux légèrement pendante, affaissée, le visage acéré du prince de l'Église encore aminci effilé déformé comme ces peintures qu'il faut regarder dans un miroir pour rétablir leurs vraies dimensions et découvrir ce qu'elles représentent' (93–4). This is then a pictorial representation that is contained within another pictorial representation that is, in its turn, compared to a third representation of like nature. This bears eloquent testimony to Simon's predilection for the plastic arts. Or to put the point in textual terms, this text appears to go to endless lengths to defer and hinder the transition from the fictive referent to the actualization of the real referent through the reader's appropriation of the work. In this way, the reader finds himself constantly obliged to defer to a later point in time the task of gathering together elements of reality conjured up by the fictive referents so that the latter may, in their turn, go to make up a further signifier to be deciphered. The same situation obtains, it seems to me, whenever the object of the *enchassement* takes the form of a representation of something else – the case with any work of art.[17]

At this point, let us stop for a moment to consider within an Ingardenian perspective the situation regarding the *enchassement* to the second degree. It is all the more interesting to do so given the sad lack of any meaningful dialogue to date between formalism or poetics on the one hand and phenomenology on the other. The concretization of the novel *Histoire* first of all produces a further object of/for concretization in the shape of a pictorial representation, which produces, in its turn, yet another object of/for concretization. However, as the object of/for concretization recedes farther and farther, it becomes more and more fuzzy or blurred in that one leaves the words of the actual text ever

17 This is a new element to be added to the studies – rare to date – devoted to the reception of the *mise en abyme*, initiated by Lucien Dällenbach's essay 'Reflexivity and Reading' – an element that can only come to light through an analysis of the *referential* functioning of this figure. I have difficulty in understanding how writers on Reception Theory, like Dällenbach in the aforementioned essay, have so often ignored the problem of reference for, as Paul Ricoeur points out so tellingly, 'une esthétique de la réception ne peut engager le problème de la *communication* sans engager aussi celui de la *référence*' (*Temps et récit*, 117; Ricoeur's emphasis).

farther behind one. That is to say that the reader's imagination is put to the test to an ever-increasing degree, since it is called upon to conjure up mental images *within* mental images *within* mental images, *while at the same time the reader must hold in his mind's eye each image within which each new image is evoked.*[18] The next step – which entails returning from the last image evoked to the image containing it and thence to the image containing that image, in order to integrate the concretization of each image that has been *enchassé* or embedded with the concretization of all those fictive referents surrounding it – although it may be theoretically conceivable, may well prove in practice to be impossible.

To resort yet again to Ingarden's spatial categories in order to subject this situation to more detailed scrutiny, within the represented truly two-dimensional *real* space of the pictural reproduction as a material paper object (postcard, poster, and the like) – as opposed to the really three-dimensional space of the other fictive referents (such as the initial tree) discussed at the beginning of this chapter, which were merely perceived or rather imagined as two-dimensional – the reader's imagination has to posit on the level of what is represented in the reproduction a three-dimensional *imaginational* space. He then has to posit *within* the latter a further two-dimensional *real* space corresponding to a further painted, printed, or photographed image on a sheet of paper within which the reader must imagine (that is, transform into 'imagined space') another three-dimensional imaginational space represented by the latter. The problem lies in separating all these different heterogeneous spaces from one another while at the same time ensuring their contemporaneous coexistence. Theoretically speaking – and the preceding discussion may well be deemed theoretical enough already – it seems to me that their coexistence can only

---

18 Why this should be a problem for the imagination is readily ascertained by referring to Sartre's account of the workings of the imagination. Although images with different existential status can succeed one another in a linear, chronological fashion (see n. 12 above), an image cannot be contained *within another image* since 'l'image est un acte *synthétique* qui unit à des éléments plus proprement représentatifs un savoir concret, non imaginé' (*L'Imaginaire*, 25; my emphasis). In order for an image to take its place within another image it would have to occupy only a part of the available 'space' of a given consciousness, whereas in fact it is inseparable from the consciousness as a whole being, as Sartre puts it, nothing but a 'conscience imageante': 'L'image est une conscience *sui generis* qui ne peut en aucune façon *faire partie* d'une conscience plus vaste. Il n'y a pas d'image *dans* une conscience qui renfermerait, outre la pensée, des signes, des sentiments, des sensations' (37; Sartre's emphasis).

be effected by the introduction or insertion of *psychic* (that is, non-imagined) space, no doubt analogous to Sartre's 'conscience non-thétique,' that 'lumière diffuse que la conscience dégage pour elle-même,'[19] between each different level or dimension of imagined space.

Such a possibility is at best barely conceivable. What we are witnessing in the situation described above is no doubt nothing less than the ultimate collapse of the reference, which, as it were, implodes rather than explodes, falling in upon itself. Out of the ashes of the literary *work* arises the literary *text*: an auto-referential, centripetal closed system such as was studied in *The Narcissistic Text*.

Yet a further complicating factor that enters into the concretization of this work now calls for consideration. It arises in those passages where the novel itself depicts the actual perception and potential appreciation of the work of art by evoking, for example, a character contemplating a painting. Formalistically speaking, this constitutes an example of the *mise en abyme* of the work's reception. In terms of its actual reception by the reader, we have, ideally at least, to attribute to the fictional character concerned our own concretization of the painting described.

The description of the stage setting for the opera *Aida*, quoted earlier, already furnished an example of this. In the following passage, the reception – here the perception of posters – is situated on the level of a *mise en abyme* or *enchassement* to the second degree, since the posters in question are already depicted on a postcard:

... une vue des Grands Boulevards aux bords dégradés en flou artistique, avec une colonne Morris surmontée de son dôme miniature, décoré d'un œil-de-bœuf et recouvert de fausses tuiles en zinc semblables à des écailles de poisson ...: deux chapeautés de hauts-de-forme gris clair vêtus de redingotes les mains croisées derrière le dos, en train de regarder les affiches de la colonne: JOB en très grandes lettres blanches LANGUES ETRANGERES en oblique de gauche à droite, et une autre représentant le buste opulent d'une femme coiffée en coques, aux épaules et à la gorge entourées d'une écharpe aux inflexions d'iris, deux fiacres et une charrette à bras rangés le long du trottoir ... etc. (38–9)

Note that as far as the first of the two posters is concerned, what the two gentlemen are looking at is a text made up of printed letters and not a pictorial representation of reality as in the case of the second

19 *L'Imaginaire*, 35

poster. It is obvious that when it is a text, an object constituted by language, that is *enchassé* or *mise en abyme*, we have a far more faithful reflection of the literary work *Histoire* than when it is a question of a pictorial representation, that is, a non-linguistic transposition in the form of visual images. But it should not be forgotten that the images in question are, in the first instance, rendered in a linguistic or verbal form, having been translated into language: all that is provided by the text is an *interpretation* of the fictive referents corresponding to the pictorial representations since their verbal transcription is itself a hermeneutic process. And in that sense, every occurrence of a pictorial representation within the text of the novel is necessarily accompanied by and gives textual embodiment to its own reception.

In the preceding quotation, the basic situation is the same as in the description of the banknotes: within the represented truly two-dimensional *real* space of the postcard as a material paper object, the reader has to imagine on the level of what is depicted in the reproduction a three-dimensional *imaginational* space. A further two-dimensional *real* space corresponding to the two posters within which must be imagined (that is, transformed into 'imagined space'), in the case of the second poster, another three-dimensional imaginational space has then to be concretized *within* the latter.[20] Although there is no actual *obligation* to do so, there exists for the reader, as he concretizes the scene on the postcard, the distinct temptation to step, momentarily at least – out of curiosity, for example, and because of the possibility that the scene in question could well prove subsequently to have a particular significance for the rest of the novel – into the shoes of the 'deux chapeautés de hauts-de-forme gris clair vêtus de redingotes' and attempt to imagine their reaction to the image of 'le buste opulent d'une femme coiffée en coques, aux épaules et à la gorge entourées d'une écharpe aux inflexions d'iris'; in other words, to concretize the two characters' perception of the poster. That this would call for even more mental dexterity than that already involved in the previous example is self-evident.

The continuation of the description of the poster adds yet a further dimension to the functioning of the *mise en abyme*:

l'homme rouge, le cardinal, et ce roi qui en fabriquait de la fausse rognant un peu chaque écu, et ce banquier qui possédait un bateau tellement rapide qu'il

20 In reality, these different spaces can only be evoked by the reader one after another in a linear, chronological sequence, for reasons outlined in n. 18 above.

connaissait le premier les nouvelles de victoires ou de défaites, la théorie, le défilé, la frise grisâtre des empereurs, des conquistadors et des financiers dévisageant les visiteurs de leur même regard à la fois morne et pénétrant dans leurs identiques visages creusés d'identiques sillons: comme si le même modèle au masque pensif, impitoyable et désabusé posant pour le même peintre avait revêtu chez un costumier de théâtre leurs défroques successives ...

The evocation of the possible model for the portrait on the banknote constitutes this time a *mise en abyme* of the work's production, in a manner analogous to the description (with respect to the representation of a photo) of 'toutes les têtes expectatives tournées vers l'appareil du photographe' (74).

The rest of this passage is particularly interesting in that it features a *mise en abyme* that involves at one and the same time both the production *and* the reception of the work, since it suggests the possibility that the painter is painting himself as he looks into a mirror and hence as he watches himself painting himself, while reproducing within the same painting yet another sculpture:

... cet arrière-grand-père représenté debout devant un chevalet, tenant un porte-fusain dans sa main droite un peu en avant de lui, à hauteur de sa taille, l'autre appuyée sur la hanche, écartant un pan de la romantique redingote grise qui laissait voir un gilet brodé et un pantalon mastic, fixant l'artiste en train de le peindre (peut-être lui-même dans une glace) d'un regard sévère, pensif, sous la coiffure romantique qui retombait jusque sur son col, tandis que derrière lui (sur la portion de mur entre son corps et le montant incliné du chevalet) on pouvait voir une de ces têtes en plâtre aux yeux bombés et sans prunelles ... (95)

My reader may rest assured that I shall not attempt to transpose the reception of such a passage into Ingardenian terminology, for the result would be intimidating indeed ...

The *mise en abyme* of the production of the work is often encountered in the description of postcards such as the one 'représentant la rue d'un village montant en escalier entre des murs de pierres sèches une femme se tenant sur le seuil d'une maison la partie gauche du corps cachée par le montant vertical de la porte, *regardant le photographe un poing sur la hanche un seau à ses pieds* ...' etc. (24). And so just as the image frozen by the photographer's lens is sometimes seen to resume a movement or a gesture that had appeared to have been interrupted for all eternity and the instant captured by the camera to give way to the moment that had inevitably to *succeed* it,[21] so, too, is the reader often allowed to share in the moment that had to have *preceded* the one in which the photo had been taken:

> scène dont émanait on ne savait quoi d'insolite et même d'irréel ... : le thé offert, la classique assiette de petits gâteaux, le studieux jeune homme, le sévère docteur à lunettes ... – et à côté, sur le divan, la présence du modèle nu ... dont le cliché d'amateur, cette photo-souvenir prise avec la même absence d'artifice ou d'habileté que les maladroites photos de famille, accentuait encore la nudité: non pas bougé, comme le visage du Hollandais au premier plan ... , mais un peu flou – du fait sans doute de la profondeur de champ insuffisante –, et non pas dans une de ces consternantes postures prétendûment harmonieuses ou tentatrices, mais simplement appuyé sur un coude, le buste légèrement soulevé, en train, comme les autres personnages, de prendre le thé ... à demi allongée (probablement *encore dans la pose qu'elle tenait pendant les séances*), fixant l'objectif d'un regard surpris *parce qu'elle a sans doute été alertée par l'appel du Hollandais, le fatidique 'Vous y êtes Ne bougez plus'*, alors que lassée par la longueur des préparatifs elle a pris le parti de ne plus s'en occuper etc. (305–6)

In such instances, the referent of the image depicted on the postcard is no longer doubly 'suspended' or deferred on the level of the fiction (that is, within the fictional universe of *Histoire*), but becomes actualized for the reader by the text itself in the form of a normal fictive referent: the photographic image yields to its original. The task of concretizing what is depicted on the postcard is effected for us, or more precisely, the occasion of its concretization is no longer the linguistic evocation of a pictorial representation of the object concerned but a direct verbal description of the latter, which takes on all the attributes of any other fictive referent in any other novel and functions, provisionally at least, in exactly the same manner.

Sooner or later, however, the reader is brought back to the realization that the occasion for the evocation in question was its pictorial representation on the postcard. And here an important aspect of the description of the postcards should be mentioned that has been left aside so far: their function as material objects of communication. Not only are their postage stamps often described in detail but so are their cancellation marks: '... prenant aussitôt une autre carte et se remettant à écrire répondant confirmant sa prochaine arrivée à cette

---

21 See 70–1, for example.

amie espagnole dont elle classait aussi les cartes parmi les autres, timbrées celles-ci à l'effigie rose langouste (dans un cadre rond sur le pourtour duquel courait la mention SELLO POSTAL)' (35). Moreover the written messages they bear together with the photographs and the signature of the author of the messages, 'la laconique signature calligraphiée avec un soin de comptable au revers de paysages tropicaux' (24), for example, are also cited in the text of *Histoire*:

... ces cartes postales qu'il lui envoyait ne portant le plus souvent au verso dans la partie réservée à la correspondance qu'une simple signature au-dessous d'un nom de ville et d'une date par exemple:
'Colombo 7/8/08
Henri' (21)

Even the character of the handwriting is evoked:

... prenant dans son classeur une de ces autres cartes postales ... , et traçant à l'encre mauve de son écriture haute épineuse rigide la réponse ... (34)

... le texte au dos de la carte, de l'écriture épineuse et violette de l'amie espagnole disant:
No puedo escribirte de lo cansada que estoy. (129)

Finally, let me cite one of the longest of these descriptions, which features every detail that is to be found on the postcard:

... la carte oubliée sans doute dans le sac ... la fatidique semeuse [of the stamp] sur fond bistre aux longs cheveux flottant hors du bonnet phrygien immobilisée éolienne et agreste un bras en arrière serrant de l'autre contre sa hanche le sac de graines, à demi cachée par le cercle magique aux chiffres gras écrasés difficilement lisibles 21 h 30 1–6 BD DES ITAL messagère fécondante et magicienne, comme une de ces statues encore à demi ensevelies émergeant des fouilles sa robe aux remous d'argent ses pieds d'argent imparfaitement dégagés de la gangue de terre rougeâtre et fertile, Le Pavillon Tyrolien au Bois de Boulogne situé sur la route du Tour du lac est remarquable par son installation son service et sa cuisine entièrement tyrolienne Avec son orchestre national il est unique dans son genre à Paris Raphael Tuck et Fils Ltd Paris Collection Villes de France Fournisseurs de LL. MM. Le Roi et La Reine d'Angleterre Empereur et Impératrice des Indes Colombo Singapour
'Ceylan 25/9/07
Henri'
Kandy by Moonlight (60)

The *material* reality of the postcard is thus as important a part of the evocation as the message conveyed.[22] In short, it is always as paper objects that the postcards are first introduced so that the reader can never lose sight of their physical reality indefinitely. This is why he eventually finds himself obliged to transform the represented three-dimensional space contained within the photograph back into the represented two-dimensional space of the postcard. As a linear, sequential process whereby the two-dimensional space gives way to the three-dimensional and subsequently, vice versa, this is perfectly conceivable in terms of reading experience. It is only when a two-dimensional represented *real* space is required to coexist within the reader's mind with a three-dimensional represented *imaginational* space that the powers of the imagination are tested to the limit.

We now come to the final development of this complex analysis, which will explain the placing of this study on reference in *Histoire* in the penultimate chapter of the present work. For inasmuch as the problems that this novel has been seen to present have clearly been situated on the first level of the concretization of the fictive referents and that it is on this level that, as in the case of Blanchot's *Au Moment voulu*, the referential process is problematized, its examination might well have been undertaken before moving on to the second level of reference and the process of appropriation in Camus' *La Chute*.

The postcards featured in *Histoire* possess one important trait that distinguishes them from all the other pictorial representations in this novel. In their function as fictive referents, they are the only ones that paradoxically possess *real* referents, for the actual source of this work – what I would call not its 'inspiration' but its 'occasion' – consisted of 'real-life' postcards that the novelist had placed in front of him as he was writing his text. There is every reason to believe that they played the same role as the landscape that stretches out in front of the painter as he sits at his easel attempting to capture on his canvas the forms and hues of the countryside[23] – with one vital distinction, however:

22 This is equally true of the statues: 'fêlure lézarde déchirant le marbre qui de part et d'autre s'affaisse légèrement, les deux plans séparés formant un angle dièdre à grande ouverture, le marbre – ou la pierre – offrant cet aspect savonneux résultat d'une longue érosion' (129), although in their case, the reader is brought back from the imaginational space corresponding to what they represent to an awareness of the real space they occupy, which like the former is also three-dimensional.

23 The comparison with Malraux's novels could not be more striking. The descrip-

for this novelistic painter is contemplating what is already someone else's depiction of reality. In other words, the appropriate analogy is rather with those painters who set out to produce copies of other artists' works. Here, the a-temporal process of textual productivity that gives birth to the *mise en abyme* and that has been our concern up to this point gives way to the historical process of the work's genesis. The fact that the fictive referent has as its counterpart a real referent indistinguishable from it means that the referential process here leads us *out of* the text in a far more direct manner than is the case with virtually all other novelistic texts. The phenomenon is analogous to what one finds in the historical novel when historical figures are depicted – analogous but not identical for two reasons: first, because it is rarely the case that the historical figures were the starting-point and the *raison d'être* of the novel in question, and second, because it is self-evident that the novelist could not have been in the presence of the characters concerned while writing his novel.

In *Histoire*, the realization of the reference is, finally, deferred not on the first level, that of the fiction, but on the second level, that of the *appropriation of the text by its reader*. For the latter, the reference is blocked, irremediably impeded, in fact, or doubly suspended. The situation can best be elucidated as follows: the text of the novel with its imaginary universe gives way here to a new text to be concretized (before being deciphered and interpreted) in the form of a postcard whose referent – the pictorial image reproduced on it – may be fictional (when it takes the form of a painting), real (when it takes the form of a photo) or both at the same time (when it takes the form of a theatrical stage setting). What is more, the fictive referent is itself subject to a process of duplication, since the true referent of the passage of the text evoking the postcard was *not*, as the reader believed and as any reader unaware of the circumstances of the novel's genesis is obliged to believe, *the scenes, objects, or people* represented on the card but the *material object*, the *piece of paper* on which the image

---

tions in *La Condition humaine* and *L'Espoir*, as we have seen, create precisely such an impression, in spite of the fact that they are wholly imaginary in that if such landscapes and cityscapes actually existed in China or Spain, they had to have been recreated from memory by the novelist. In Simon's case, on the other hand, the reader can often let himself be caught up in the long descriptions of events arising from the coming-to-life, so to speak, of the scenes depicted on the postcards to the point that he eventually loses sight completely of the actual pictures on the postcards, to whose reality he sooner or later, as was noted earlier, has to return.

has been reproduced, in other words the postcard itself. Consequently, the reader is in exactly the same situation as the one that presided over the creation of the novel – that of the writer himself. He, too, is in the presence of the very same postcard(s). Not the least remarkable aspect of this state of affairs is the way in which the circularity characterizing auto-referentiality here manifests itself paradoxically on the level of the reference itself.

But at this point, we have reached the outside limit of the realm of referentiality and encroached upon a quite different topic: that of the transcoding of the pictorial into the linguistic and vice versa. For, as was hinted at earlier, the whole text of *Histoire* can be seen to be a kind of *interpretation* of the original postcards[24] inasmuch as translation and interpretation are necessarily contemporaneous if not synonymous. And what is at stake here is not the translation from one language or linguistic system into another but from one code into another as we are dealing with the *transliteration into a verbal text of a pictorial text*, of plastic images into words. In the end, *Histoire* possesses the status of a metatext and by the same token the present chapter assumes the character of a meta-metatext.

24 Some of the actual postcards are reproduced in Jean Ricardou's *Le Nouveau Roman*, 184.

9

The Lexical Referent:
Bataille's *Histoire de l'œil*

The reader of *Histoire de l'œil*,[1] originally published in 1928[2] under
what was obviously a pseudonym 'Lord Auch,'[3] could clearly have

1 Two chapters of my *Monde à l'envers / Texte réversible: La fiction de Bataille* are
devoted to *Histoire de l'œil*: chapter 4, 'L'Œil qui ne voit pas' (39–46) explores
the text with regard to the ontological fictional universe underlying the work,
and chapter 5, '*Histoire de l'œil*: texte ludique' analyses the role of the signifier
in the text. The present study, although based on the findings of the latter analysis,
approaches the work from a completely different perspective: that of its reception by the reader.
2 A note on chronology is necessary here. Although the present study is not concerned with tracing the chronological, i.e., historical, evolution of the problematization of reference in twentieth century French fiction, this, the last novel
studied, was written before *all* of the works previously analysed. However, it
was not until 1967 – the year Simon's *Histoire*, the most recent of the novels
considered in these pages, was published – after Bataille's death, that *Histoire
de l'œil* was published under the novelist's own name and in a normal commercial
printing. Of the three previous pseudonymous editions (see n. 3 below), the
1928 edition was limited to 134 copies, the 1944 edition to 1,999 copies and the
1952–3 edition to some 500 copies (See Michel Surya, *Georges Bataille: La mort
à l'œuvre. Biographie*, 116–7).
3 Lord Auch, *Histoire de l'œil* (Paris [René Bounel] 1928; re-edited: Paris: K. éditeur,
1944; Paris [J.J. Pauvert] 1952 or 1953); Georges Bataille, *Histoire de l'œil* (Paris:
J.J. Pauvert, 1967). (My source for the preceding bibliographical information is
Surya's *Georges Bataille*, 531.) Other editions are *Histoire de l'œil* in Georges
Bataille, *Premiers Ecrits 1922–40* (Paris: Gallimard, 1970), vol. 1 of the *Œuvres
complètes* and *Histoire de l'œil* (Paris: U.G.E., '10/18,' 1973). I cite the Folio edition
here; all emphasis within quotations is mine unless otherwise stated. The status
of the different editions cannot be established with any clarity from the brief
indications given by the editor of the *Œuvres complètes*, Denis Hollier (see vol.
1, 611); however, the Folio edition appears to be a later version than the text
published in the *Œuvres complètes* (where the Folio text is reproduced as an
appendix) in that it is the more concise of the two.

considered the story he was reading to be the pretext for an inventory of the various possibilities offered by eroticism. The fact that it had appeared under a pseudonym, a procedure common to so many pornographic publications, would certainly not have discouraged such an appreciation of the work – on the contrary. In one respect at least, moreover, that reader would not have been completely mistaken: here the fiction depicted obviously does not constitute the text's *raison d'être*. For one thing the sexual activities that take place, both by their variety and by their frequency, would not have been unworthy of the Marquis de Sade, and for another, there is more than a little doubt in the reader's mind concerning the practical feasibility of certain of the characters' exploits. In other words, the creation of a fictive universe and a series of characters to inhabit it is here not an end in itself but rather a pretext for something else. The identity of this 'something else' is less obvious than appears at first sight. A situation where an author writes a story the point of which is not that story, however, sets the resulting work apart from all the other novels examined so far. Or, more precisely, since Simon's *Histoire* is no more interested in the actual *events* it depicts than is *Histoire de l'œil* (while, on the other hand, retaining an indisputable interest in the *manner* of their depiction), what is remarkable in this novel is that, unlike Beckett's *L'Innommable*, which sets out to undermine the representational powers of language and thus frustrate any concretization on the part of its reader, a fictional universe is here at one and the same time created and subverted.

Such a process calls to mind the literary genre of the parody, and indeed are not many pornographic novels written in such a way as to give the impression that their author is making fun of this type of literature, tongue in cheek, so to speak? There is, indeed, every reason for him to do so: it is a natural reflex of self-defence. Nonetheless, once one takes into account the central place occupied by eroticism in *all* of Bataille's fiction and indeed in all the rest of his writings – not to mention his important work entitled *L'Erotisme*[4] – any parodic intent can be readily ruled out, at least as far as the primary motivation for the writing of this work is concerned. The fact remains that the story explicitly designated by and in its title is only a pretext. This is what gives it a unique status in these pages, for the ostensible reference, while functioning in a manner that is perfectly satisfactory in that it enables its reader to concretize the fictive referents and make

4 Paris: Editions de Minuit 1957

of them a coherent world, is nothing but a smoke-screen: here what we are faced with is, indeed, in the fullest sense of Barthes' expression, 'un *effet* de réel.'[5] Extraordinary as it may seem, the coherence of the world in question is a *lexical coherence*, throwing up onto the screen of the reader's imagination what is in the end only a mirage.

From the outset, it is clear that the *Histoire de l'œil* is not like any other story. Most stories do not take as their subject a material object or, as in this case, a part of the human anatomy. Stories are more generally stories of people, even though they may be fictional creations. That is not true, of course, of that other literary genre, poetry, where in the sixteenth century a poet would sing the praises of a particular aspect of his loved one's person under the title of 'L'Emblême du sein,' for example. Even in fiction, one might recall Diderot's *Les Bijoux indiscrets*. However, Bataille's eighteenth-century predecessor related the reminiscences that the most intimate parts of the female anatomy might have recounted had they possessed the capacity to do so. We find no such personification in Bataille's tale. The eye here remains resolutely but one part of the human anatomy.

The only other possibility is that the tale to be told concerns what becomes of the eye in question. And indeed we find that at one point in the story the eye of a corpse, removed from its socket, is subsequently lodged in the genital organs of one of the female characters:

'Elle me fit venir à côté du mort et, s'agenouillant, écarta les paupières, ouvrit largement l'œil à la surface duquel s'était posé la mouche.
– Tu vois l'œil?
– Eh bien?
– C'est un œuf, dit-elle en toute simplicité.
J'insistait, troublé.
– Où veux-tu en venir?
– Je veux m'amuser avec.
– Mais encore?
Se levant, elle parut congestionnée (elle était alors terriblement nue).
– Ecoutez, sir Edmond, dit-elle, il faut me donner l'œil tout de suite, arrachez-le.
Sir Edmond ne tressaillit pas mais prit dans un portefeuille une paire de ciseaux, s'agenouilla et découpa les chairs puis il enfonça les doigts dans l'orbite et tira l'œil ... Il mit le petit globe blanc dans la main de mon amie.

5 Roland Barthes, 'L'Effet de réel'; my emphasis

Elle regarda l'extravagance, visiblement gênée, mais n'eut pas d'hésitation. Se caressant les jambes, elle y glissa l'œil.' (115)

This extraordinary scene, in the full sense of that epithet, does indeed occur right at the end of the tale, in an episode that can be seen to be the climax of the series of scenes leading up to it. However, as Roland Barthes pointed out, such an account of the text is far from exhausting the meaning of the title: 'Comment un objet peut-il avoir une histoire? Il peut sans doute passer de main en main (donnant lieu alors à d'insipides fictions du genre *Histoire de ma pipe* ou *Mémoires d'un fauteuil*), il peut aussi passer *d'image en image*: son histoire est alors celle d'une migration, le cycle des *avatars* (au sens propre) qu'il parcourt loin de son être originel, selon la pente d'une certaine imagination qui le déforme sans cependant l'abandonner; c'est le cas du livre de Bataille.'[6]

Let us begin by examining what is involved in this journey from image to image. The first chapter is entitled 'L'Œil de chat'; the title establishes from the outset the principle by which objects sharing a common shape become associated in this text, since the title of the whole novel, which the reader has, of course, already read on the title-page, is *Histoire de l'œil*. The association between an eye and a plate explains why the very first scene depicts the young woman Simone indulging her curious penchant for sitting on plates. The plate in question, since it is filled with milk, also shares with the human eye the fact that it is white in colour like the eye surrounding its pupil: 'Simone mit l'assiette sur un petit banc, s'installa devant moi et, *sans quitter mes yeux*, s'assit et trempa son derrière dans le lait ... Elle ne bougeait plus; pour la première fois, je vis sa "chair rose et noire" baignant dans le lait blanc' (71). One appreciates the reason why mention is made here of Simone's eyes being fixed on the male narrator-protagonist: so that the eyes and the plate of milk exist side by side, that is, in close contiguity, within the concretization of the scene by the reader. As for the last sentence, the image of 'sa "chair rose et noire" baignant dans le lait blanc' that offers itself up for visualization in the fullest sense of that term resembles nothing so much as a painter's still life.

What is even more curious about this opening episode than the action depicted is the manner in which it is introduced into the novel.

6 'La Métaphore de l'œil,' 238. Barthes' emphasis. See my 'A Critique of Roland Barthes' Essay on Bataille's *Histoire de l'œil.*'

The passage cited is preceded by the following: '– Les assiettes, c'est fait pour s'asseoir, dit Simone. Paries-tu? Je m'assois dans l'assiette.' The full import of such a statement by the character is partially obscured by her rhetorical question 'Paries-tu?' in that her subsequent action can be seen to be a response to a self-imposed wager by which she dares herself to do the unimaginable. However, the fact is that *assiettes* (plates) are *not* made to be sat in, in spite of their common etymological origin, *s'asseoir* coming from the Vulgar Latin verb *assedere* and *assiette* coming from the past participle of the same verb *assedita*.[7] Since in modern French the etymological origin of the word *assiette* has largely been lost sight of and the modern meaning of the word has supplanted what was originally its only meaning, there are two ways in which the reader, upon reflection, may react to Simone's remark. One may, if knowledgeable enough, consider that Simone is consciously alluding to the common Latin origin of the two words, in which case one will be led to consider the girl to be uncommonly well-versed in etymological matters, or – and this is much more likely – one may believe that she is making a pun. (What is *not* possible – and this fact is crucial here – is to attribute the statement to the *author's* erudition and to his alone, for the remark is made in the character's own words and, moreover, in a most self-conscious manner with the intent to shock, or at least surprise her companion.) Now, for the character of a novel to indulge in punning is not particularly unusual or, indeed, even worthy of note. What is, on the other hand, wholly unexpected is for that character to translate the pun, once she has uttered it, into actions, that is, for her to *act out a play on words*. This means that the subsequent events going to make up the fiction are motivated and brought about by the play on and with words – a purely linguistic phenomenon. And the agent of this linguistic generation of the fiction is not the author or the narrator of the tale but one of the characters *in* the tale, whose actions are hence directly determined by the structures of language. Any fictional universe is, of course, dependent on the language of the text in question. The difference here, however, is twofold: first, it is as though the protagonist had taken on the role not of the narrator, but of the novelist himself; and second, the fiction evoked normally results from the status of the

---

7 This explains why the French word *assiette* originally had as its first meaning the *seat* or *seating* of a person (on a horse, for example) or of a piece of architecture. In modern French, it also has the technical meaning, within the context of the taxation system, of a *tax base*.

linguistic signs on the page as *signifieds* rather than as *signifiers*, for it is the former that play by far the greater role in the concretization of any form of prose fiction (poetry presenting quite different characteristics in this respect).

In the present episode, what we are witnessing is nothing less than the process by which the novel is produced and its fictional world given form and substance being turned upside down and inside out. The protagonist Simone is acting as though she were herself the novelist whose creation she nonetheless remains, while the object of her own verbal creation is not a novel but a 'real-life' event. At the same time, all of the aforementioned circumstances are themselves featured within the text of a novel.

The resulting situation as far as the concretization of the episode by the reader is concerned is not a simple one. On the first level, there is no doubt about the fictional existence of the referents here: what Simone is saying and what she does. It is the relation between the former and the latter that exercises a subtle effect on the status of the fictive referents involved. First, it should be noted that Simone's words are reported directly, without any intervention on the part of the fictional narrator. Now, as Tzvetan Todorov points out in his article 'Reading as Construction,' in any novel direct speech attributed to one of the characters is the only part of the text that is its own referent: it alone does not stand for any non-linguistic reality; its referent is itself in the form of a series of *signifiers*, oral in character.[8] In Todorov's words, 'Direct discourse is the only way to eliminate the differences between narrative discourse and the world it evokes: words are identical to words, and construction [= concretization] is direct and immediate.'[9] What we as readers conjure up then in our imagination are the words themselves as they are uttered by the character, as though she were speaking to us directly. There is no doubt that our focusing on words *as words* can only facilitate our becoming aware of a punning effect, of the fact that Simone is playing on words. And this awareness cannot fail to undercut the evocative power that the subsequent language of the text describing her sitting on the plate would normally possess, inasmuch as the latter would appear to be the direct result of that punning and hence the prolongation of the pun, which has to be

8 This still calls for a translation or a recoding, on the reader's part, of the *written* signifier that goes to make up the printed text into an *oral/aural* signifier, but the latter does not affect the content of the present analysis.

9 'Reading as Construction,' 70

verbal in character. The consequences for the process of concretization should by now be obvious. The fictive referents corresponding to Simone's actions cannot help but be undermined once the words in the text remain as words for the reader. These particular words do, of course, possess extralinguistic referents, but it is impossible for the reader to concretize at one and the same time a sequence of linguistic signifiers *and* the referents of those signifiers: the awareness of the first obliterates any awareness of the second and vice versa. In this interesting and complex manner, the reader experiences a definite *subversion* of the referential process that jeopardizes the fictional reality of the events concerned.

The second chapter, 'L'Armoire normande,' introduces another object that shares even more obvious formal properties with the eye: the egg. It begins thus: 'Dès cette époque, Simone contracta la manie de casser des œufs avec son cul' (75). Immediately, a further association is thus brought about: 'Elle se plaçait pour cela la tête sur le siège d'un fauteuil, le dos collé au dossier, les jambes repliées vers moi ... Je plaçais alors *l'œuf au-dessus du trou*: elle prenait plaisir à l'agiter dans la fente profonde.' Such activities are characterized as 'des jeux' (72) as in the present case: 'Sa mère surprit notre manège, mais cette femme extrêmement douce, bien qu'elle eût une vie exemplaire, se contenta la première fois d'assister au jeu sans mot dire ...' (75). Now, while it is difficult to see any association whatsoever between, on the one hand, *l'œil* and *les yeux*, and on the other hand, *les jeux*, one referring to an object and the other to an activity, that is no longer the case once we come upon the following sentence a few lines later: 'La vieille dame se rangea, nous regardant de ses *yeux* tristes, avec un air si désemparé qu'il provoqua nos *jeux*' (75). The relationship between 'l'œil' and its plural form 'les yeux' is, however, not on the level of their meaning and hence their respective referents but on that of their common phonetic identity, *y* being interchangeable with *j*. As in the case of the pun in the first passage examined, it is an association of *signifiers* that is here brought to our attention.

The next chapter 'L'Odeur de Marcelle,' offers little in the way of objects whose form could suggest that of the eye, with the sole exception of the moment we see the second of the two young female protagonists, Marcelle, 'abandonner de jolies fesses rondes à des bouches impures' (81). Indeed Simone will later remark that 'chacune de ses fesses était un œuf dur épluché' (92).

With its title 'Une Tache de soleil,' the following chapter introduces yet another circular object just as it will close by establishing a less obvious parallel: 'Il ne resta devant nous qu'une fenêtre vide, trou rectangulaire perçant la nuit noire, ouvrant à nos yeux las un jour sur un monde composé avec la foudre et l'aurore' (86). It is precisely the rectangular shape of the window that distinguishes it from an eye; and yet like the latter, the window not only opens but is transparent. Moreover, while it is, in fact, the eyelid that literally opens, through its transparency the eye, too, can be said to open, 'opening,' as it does for the onlooker, onto another world, that of a human consciousness. This analogy is, moreover, brought out in the text by an association through contiguity ('ouvrant à nos yeux'), that is, a physical proximity in the world of the fiction. In other words, here the analogy is once again between the fictive referents themselves.

The window plays a key role right from the first paragraph of this same chapter. It is the window of the bedroom of the country house in which Marcelle is imprisoned and through which Simone and the narrator will help her to escape with them. Attached to the bars of this window is a large white sheet that is blown about by the wind: '... le drap qui s'étalait dans le vent avec un bruit éclatant était souillée au centre d'une large tache mouillée qu'éclairait par transparence la lumière de la lune...' (84). It is not difficult to imagine the central *transparent* part of the sheet possessing a shape analogous to an eye or a window. But another circular object that, like the sun, is associated with transparency in that it is a source of light now appears on the scene of the fiction. It is the moon: 'En peu d'instants, les nuages masquèrent à nouveau le *disque lunaire*: tout rentra dans l'ombre' (84). This manner of imagining and concretizing the sheet with its wet, transparent centre had in fact already been suggested by the chapter's title 'Une Tache de soleil,' with its otherwise inexplicable transposition of the moon into the sun.

The same analogy between the window and an eye is repeated in the first evocation of the window in the first paragraph of the next chapter, 'Un Filet de sang,' with its 'vision du trou éclairé de la fenêtre vide' (87). The 'filet de sang' has itself come into being through its visual association with the 'tache de soleil' of the previous chapter's title, for the sun could well be perceived as 'bleeding.' Another circular form will present itself to the reader's imagination when there finally appears at the end of the chapter the trickle of blood as Simone is evoked lying unconscious: 'Je la trouvai inerte, la tête pendante: un mince filet de sang avait coulé à la commissure de la lèvre' (89). The hanging head will prove to be a productive image for the rest of this text as it anticipates the corpse of the priest at the end of the novel, which we saw depicted in the very first quotation above as well as that of the eyeball hanging out of its socket in the bullfighter's corpse, which we shall encounter shortly.

The next chapter introduces a new object in the form of the narrator's penis: '... à l'heure où le *soleil* oblique de six heures éclairait la salle de bains, un *œuf* à demi gobé fut envahi par l'eau et, s'étant empli avec un bruit bizarre, fit naufrage sous nos *yeux*; cet incident eut pour Simone un sens extrême, elle se tendit et jouit longuement, pour ainsi dire buvant mon *œil* entre ses lèvres' (91). Eggs reappear to feature in yet another game the narrator plays with Simone: 'Bientôt elle prit plaisir à me faire jeter des œufs dans la cuvette du siège, des œufs durs, qui sombraient, et des œufs gobés plus ou moins vides. Elle demeurait assise à regarder les œufs' (90) – in other words, with *les œufs dans les yeux*. And then to our amazement, the text confirms this latter reading, which could well represent the form the concretization has taken for the reader, who could have been led to picture the eggs reflected in her eyes – an interesting variant on the title of the present book, *Reflections in the Mind's Eye*: '... Simone me priait de la coucher sur des couvertures auprès du siège sur lequel elle penchait son visage, reposant ses bras sur les bords de la cuvette, afin de fixer sur les *œufs* ses *yeux* grands ouverts' (91).[10] For the first time in the text, not only are the analogous objects – the eggs and the eyes – associated with each other, but their two signifiers are as well. This passage is almost as disconcerting as the one in which Simone was playing on the words *assiettes* and *asseoir*. The reader cannot help but have the impression that Simone has been led to 'fixer sur les *œufs* ses *yeux* grands ouverts,' although he knows full well that Simone is not, in fact, dealing with the *words* in question but with the actual material *objects*,[11] since in this instance, contrary to the previous episode with the plate, the objects are not *named* within the fictional universe by any of the characters. For the moment, the association within the text of the eggs and the eyes has to be put down to some strange reciprocal attraction exercised by like objects. If we were here dealing with a *metaphor* rather than the relating of events in the plot of the tale, then that would be another story, so to speak – but we shall come back to metaphors later.

There is no denying, however, that Simone has a well-developed

---

10 Bataille's emphasis
11 If she were dealing with the words themselves, Simone would, in fact, have to become 'Simone,' *a name in a text*.

sense of the way words sound, as is revealed one paragraph farther on: 'Et, comme je lui demandais à quoi lui faisait penser le mot uriner, elle me répondit *Buriner*, les yeux, avec un rasoir, quelque chose de rouge, le soleil. Et l'œuf? Un œil de veau, en raison de la couleur de la tête, et d'ailleurs le blanc d'œuf était du blanc d'œil, et le jaune la prunelle. La forme de l'œil, à l'entendre [and to read this text, one might add!], était celle de l'œuf ... Elle jouait gaiement sur les mots, disant tantôt *casser un œil*, tantôt *crever un œuf ...*' (92).[12] We may well be taken aback by such verbal dexterity on the part of the protagonist. This confirms our previous disconcerting impression that Simone is acting to all intents and purposes as though she were the novelist who had devised the text we are reading. A number of the associated objects are encountered here: not only the egg and the eye but also the sun. It should, however, be noted that only the first sentence involves a pun, and that Simone does not have recourse to the plural form of *œil*, *yeux*, which is no doubt why the *signifiers* remain dormant in favour of the *signifieds*.

A few pages farther on, in the chapter entitled 'Les Yeux ouverts de la morte,' we come upon a passage that once again gathers together a number of objects interrelated by having a circular shape, but this time the passage does not take the form of direct speech, of words spoken by one of the characters, but is an evocation of what the narrator experiences: 'Je m'allongeai alors dans l'herbe, le *crâne* reposant sur une *pierre plate* et les *yeux* ouverts sur la Voie lactée, étrange *trouée* de sperme astral et d'urine céleste à travers la *voûte crânienne* des constellations: cette *fêlure ouverte* au sommet du ciel, apparemment formée de vapeurs ammoniacales devenues brillantes dans l'immensité – dans l'espace vide où elles se déchirent comme un cri de coq en plein silence – un *œuf*, un *œil* crevé ou mon *crâne* ébloui, collé à la pierre, en renvoyaient à l'infini les images symétriques' (97). The formal affinities the various objects here depicted share can only facilitate the reader's concretization of what the narrator sees above him, and no doubt what he imagines, too, since by the end of the evocation he would appear to be standing outside of himself looking down on his own head 'collé à la pierre.'

With the introduction of the bullfight in the next chapter, 'Animaux obscènes,' another round object appears in the form of the dead bull's testicles, which certain amateurs like to eat grilled, Sir Edmond tells Simone (102). This leads up to another bullfight they attend

12 Bataille's emphasis

together in the chapter devoted to 'L'Œil de Granero.' During the course of the bullfight, the relationship between the testicles and the eye is explicitly established: '... à la place où mon amie [Simone] devait s'*asseoir* reposaient sur une *assiette* les deux couilles nues; ces glandes, de la grosseur et de la forme d'un œuf, étaient d'une blancheur nacrée, rosie de sang, *analogue à celle du globe oculaire*' (104). As one might expect, Simone then attempts to sit on the plate but is prevented from doing so by the narrator, who takes the plate from the seat before forcing her to sit down. Interestingly, however, the sentence that narrates the event manages, by the very manner in which it is formulated, to draw attention, yet again, to the similarity of the two words or signifiers: 'J'enlevai l'*assiette* et l'obligeai à s'*asseoir*' (105). The sun also makes its appearance in this scene, as if called forth by its circular counterparts, the bull's testicles: 'Le rayonnement solaire, à la longue, nous absorbait dans une irréalité conforme à notre malaise, à notre impuissant désir d'éclater, d'être nus. Le visage grimaçant sous l'effet du soleil, de la soif et de l'exaspération des sens, nous partagions cette déliquescence morose où les éléments ne s'accordent plus' (105). The subsequent sequence of events is, however, even more disconcerting than if Simone had had her way:

'Ce qui suivit eut lieu sans transition, et même apparemment sans lien, non que les choses ne fussent liées, mais je les vis comme un absent. Je vis en peu d'instants Simone, à mon effroi, mordre l'un des globes, Granero s'avancer, présenter au taureau le drap rouge; puis Simone, le sang à la tête, en un moment de lourde obscénité, dénuder sa vulve où entra l'autre couille; Granero renversé, acculé sous la balustrade, sur cette balustrade les cornes à la volée frappèrent trois coups: l'une des cornes enfonça l'œil droit et la tête. La clameur atterrée des arènes coïncida avec le spasme de Simone. Soulevée de la dalle de pierre, elle chancela et tomba, le soleil l'aveuglait, elle saignait du nez ... L'œil droit du cadavre pendait. (106)

The character first bites into the testicle, thus bringing the latter into contact with her mouth, before inserting it into that other orifice, and both parts of the body can be seen to have a roughly circular shape corresponding to that of the testicle. This produces a potential visual effect that is curiously analogous to the *mise en abyme* and to which we shall return in a moment. The bullfighter's red cloak and the blood that goes to Simone's head have been prefigured by the redness of the sun, that association having already been encountered earlier in the text ('Une Tache de soleil' [83] 'Un Filet de sang' [87]). The association between the eye and Granero's head is then made for the first time ('l'une des cornes enfonça l'œil droit et la tête') as well as that between the sun and Simone's bleeding nose. And then the reader realizes what this whole scene has been leading up to: the image of the eye hanging from Granero's corpse's head, which had, in its turn, been foreshadowed by the earlier image of 'la tête pendante' (89). Moreover, the displacement of the eye from its socket makes the reader more aware of the circular shape the eye shares with the head, through the fact that in the concretization of the scene the two objects are separated from each other, each as a distinct object, while remaining in close contiguity. Even more remarkable is the way that, on the formal level of the text as text, the previous *mise en abyme* effect noted above finds itself de-composed, as it were, or deconstructed in that the microcosm of the ocular globe naturally contained within the macrocosm of the round head has emerged from its container and is set off against the latter. To put it in other terms, the two-dimensional figure of the *mise en abyme* has become a three-dimensional one, except that in the process, what began by being contained within the larger shape has come out of its container without, however, becoming completely detached from it.

This striking image is recalled and juxtaposed with the even more striking image of the 'displaced' bull's testicle that preceded it right at the beginning of the next chapter, the title of which evokes yet again that other *planetary* globe, 'Sous le soleil de Séville':[13] 'Deux globes de même grandeur et consistance s'étaient animés de mouvements contraires et simultanés. Un testicule blanc de taureau avait pénétré la chair "rose et noire" de Simone; un œil était sorti de la tête du jeune homme' (107). With the re-evocation of the testicle as it enters into the young woman's body, the *mise en abyme* is, so to speak, reinstated in the text, once one takes into account the shape of the orifice containing the foreign object. At this point it would be as well to stress that at first reading, we are unlikely to become aware of the formal properties (*mise en abyme*) latent in the images we are, and have been, picturing for ourselves in our mind's eye. It is only progressively, as we experience the tendencies of this text to subvert and undermine the fiction it is ostensibly offering up for concretization – some of which have already been remarked upon in the form of what

13 The common association of the Spanish city of Séville with oranges is doubtless far from coincidental here, thus adding yet a further object to those conjured up in relation to the image of the eye.

one might call intrusive signifiers, not to mention the character's apparent usurping of the role of the novelist, her creator – that the *textual* dimension of the reading experience will come to the fore with its potential not only to *displace* but to *replace* the world of the fiction: for awareness of words on the level of signifiers is incompatible with the process of concretization, words perceived blotting out, in advance, images imagined.

The next striking image we come across before the end of this chapter is, exceptionally for the present text, contained within a painting: 'À droite et à gauche de la porte, deux célèbres tableaux de Valdès Leal figuraient des cadavres en décomposition: dans l'orbite oculaire d'un évêque entrait un énorme rat...' (108). Now it is the eye that, instead of penetrating another object, the human body – from which, it must not be forgotten, it had been removed in the first place[14] – , is penetrated in its turn. More worthy of note, however, is the truly horrifying character of the image evoked; previous images we have focused upon have perhaps been more disturbing and disconcerting than horrifying. It, in fact, reaches into the deepest recesses of the human mind – those selfsame recesses that from time to time come to the surface in Malraux's novels[15] – provoking in the reader a visceral reaction of repulsion that necessarily, for that very reason, blinds him to anything as abstract or esoteric as the formal properties of a literary text. Here – for once, one is tempted to add – concretization reigns supreme and the impact of the 'reality' of the scene on the reader's mind is not to be denied. This *depicted* horrifying spectacle (painted on a canvas within the fictional universe of the characters and thus perceived by them, too, as a representational image of an imagined, or at least absent reality) is but a foretaste, for the reader, of what will finally be acted out, so to speak, in the 'real' world of the fiction when Simone draws back the eyelid of the priest's corpse 'à la surface duquel s'était posé la mouche' (115).

This final climactic epsiode of the book is preceded by the scene of the confessional: 'Après une longue attente, une très jolie femme quitta le confessionnal, les mains jointes, traits pâles, extasiés: la tête en arrière, *les yeux blancs*, elle traversa la salle à pas lents, comme

14 See the chapter 'L'Œil qui ne voit pas' (in my *Monde à l'envers*) for the ontological and existential implications and consequences of this situation.
15 Particularly in Tchen's dreams and nightmares as he relates them in *La Condition humaine*, for example. See also 'Le Monstre s'impose: l'univers de *La Voie royale* et du *Temps du mépris*' in Fitch, *Le Sentiment d'étrangeté*, 26–40, and Charles Moeller, 'André Malraux ou l'espoir sans terre promise.'

un spectre d'opéra' (109). Eyes rolled up to reveal their whites[16] can only serve to reinforce the resemblance between eyes and 'œufs durs' (90). This final episode evokes Simone masturbating as she makes her confession to the priest:

> – Le plus coupable, mon père, est que je me branle en vous parlant [says Simone].
> Quelques secondes, cette fois, de chuchotment. Enfin presque à voix haute:
> – Si tu ne crois pas, je peux montrer.
> Et Simone se leva, *s'ouvrait sous l'œil de la guérite* se branlant, se pâmant, d'une main sûre et rapide. (110)

The wicket of the confessional is likened to an eye looking at her, or rather looking at her genital organs, the two orifices facing each other in an improbable mute visual dialogue.

We now come to the closing chapter entitled, not surprisingly, 'Les Pattes de mouche.' After mention of the priest's 'couilles vides' and his 'yeux ... illuminés' (112), the orgy the poor man is forced to participate in with Sir Edmond, Simone, and the narrator reaches its climax with the death of the priest by strangulation, coinciding with the orgasm he experiences as Simone copulates with him. Whereupon, 'Une mouche, bourdonnant dans un rai de soleil, revenait sans fin se poser sur le mort. Elle la chassa mais, soudain, poussa un léger cri. Il arrivait ceci d'étrange: posée sur l'œil du mort, la mouche se déplaçait doucement sur le globe vitreux ... Elle me fit venir à côté du mort et, s'agenouillant, écarta les paupières, ouvrit largement l'œil à la surface duquel s'était posée la mouche' (114–15). We have now come full circle to the passage cited at the beginning of this analysis, which once again insists on the similarity between the eye and the egg for the coming together of which the whole text and the whole tale now appear to have served as a mere pretext:

> –Tu vois l'œil?
> – Eh bien?
> – C'est un œuf, dit-elle en toute simplicité.
> J'insistai, troublé.
> – Où veux-tu en venir?

16 The phenomenon of 'les yeux blancs' has a particular significance within Bataille's universe (see my 'L'Œil qui ne voit pas' in *Monde à l'envers*, in particular, 41–4).

– Je veux m'amuser avec.

– Mais encore?

Se levant, elle parut congestionnée (elle était alors terriblement nue).

– Ecoutez, sir Edmond, dit-elle, il faut me donner l'œil tout de suite, arrachez-le.

Sir Edmond ne tressaillit pas mais prit dans un portefeuille une paire de ciseaux, s'agenouilla et découpa les chairs puis il enfonça les doigts dans l'orbite et tira l'œil ... Il mit le petit globe blanc dans la main de mon amie.

Elle regarda l'extravagance, visiblement gênée, mais n'eut pas d'hésitation. Se caressant les jambes, elle y glissa l'œil ... Simone ... glissait l'œil dans la fente des fesses. Elle s'étendit, releva les jambes et le cul. Elle tenta d'im-mobliser le globe en serrant les fesses, mais il en jaillit – comme un noyau des doigts – et tomba sur le ventre du mort.

L'Anglais m'avait déshabillé.

Je me jetai sur la jeune fille et sa vulve engloutit ma queue. Je la baisai: l'Anglais fit rouler l'œil entre nos corps.

– Mettez-le moi dans le cul, cria Simone.

Sir Edmond mit le globe dans la fente et poussa.

A la fin, Simone me quitta, prit l'œil des mains de Sir [sic][17] Edmond et l'introduisit dans sa chair. (115–16)

Thereupon Simone draws the narrator to her and having ejaculated, he draws back from her to contemplate a spectacle worthy of the literature of the fantastic, from the pen of an Edgar Allan Poe, for example: 'Me levant, j'écartai les cuisses de Simone: elle gisait étendue sur le côté; je me trouvai alors en face de ce que – j'imagine – j'attendais depuis toujours – comme une guillotine attend la tête à trancher. Mes yeux, me semblait-il, étaient érectiles à force d'horreur; je vis, dans la vulve velue de *Simone*, l'œil bleu pâle de *Marcelle* me regarder en pleurant des larmes d'urine' (116).[18]

The reader now appreciates what the images of the 'tête pendante' (89) and of the eye hanging from the head of Granero's corpse (116) have been leading up to: the eyes of the narrator, bulging from disbelief, as though they themselves were on the point of coming out of their sockets to join the weeping blue eye that holds their fascinated gaze. What more fitting finale could one conceive of for the tale of the eye?[19]

17 Here the text departs from its usual spelling of 'sir Edmond' with a small *s*.

18 Bataille's emphasis

19 We shall come back later to the closing paragraphs, which follow this scene in the manner of an epilogue.

We have now followed the peregrinations of the 'eye' although in the literal sense they are limited to the last four chapters of the book, since it is only from the moment when the bullfighter's eye becomes dislodged from its socket that the eye sets out for its final resting place between the thighs of Simone. Until that moment at the bullfight, the eye had rather undergone a series of transformations under the bemused and fascinated gaze of the reader's inner eye – from an eye to an egg, to a window, to the wet centre of a flapping sheet, to a lunar disc, to the sun, to a hanging head, to the 'eye' of the penis, to a skull, to a bull's testicles, to the 'eye' of a confessional's wicket. Such transformations, by which the same shape is seen to match the contours of objects whose identities have nothing whatever in common, do not, of course, take place in any real world inhabited not by fictive referents but by actual three-dimensional, tangible objects. They *can* only be seen as reflections in the mind's eye; it is through the process of refraction exercised thereby that such a merging of ontologically independent objects can come about. But then is not any and every concretization of a fictional world by the reader of a novel a reflection in the mind's eye?

The answer is yes ... and no. It is, in the sense that the concretization is not wholly of the reader's making, being brought about by the language of the novel; and it is not, precisely inasmuch as it *is* nonetheless of the reader's own making since the imagined visual, audible, tactile images the reader experiences cannot be said to have pre-existed the act of reading. Here the interrelationship, the physical contiguity of the various objects – the eye, the egg, the testicles, and so on – produces a blurring of outlines[20] that is indispensable if their different identities are to be confused with one another. Moreover, the merging of their identities *has to* come about *if only for the sequence of events constituting the story line to be accounted for*. And yet this blurring effect[21] that softens the precise outlines of the objects in order to bring about their interchangeability, can only take place within the reading imagination. In other words, the affinities they share are

20 An analogous blurring effect or *réverbération formelle* is at work throughout Bataille's novels and is responsible for the formal attributes of his texts (see *Monde à l'envers*, 170–4).

21 Barthes does not fail to register this same phenomenon when, after examining 'le cycle des *avatars* (au sens propre) que [l'œil] parcourt loin de son être originel, selon la pente d'une certaine imagination qui le déforme sans cependant l'abandonner' ('La Métaphore de l'œil,' 238), he concludes that 'il s'agit de parcourir le tremblement de quelques objets ... de façon à échanger des uns aux autres les fonctions de l'obscène et celles de la substance' (245).

indeed in the eye of the beholder – just as the relationship between something-being-compared and what-it-is-being-compared-to is only explicable in terms of that other relationship between the perceived and the perceiver, since it is the perceiver who is doing the comparing. Now if the perceiver takes the form of the writer, then what we have is precisely the phenomenon of *metaphor*. And the fiction of *Histoire de l'œil* resembles nothing so much as an extended metaphor where the metaphoric paradigm has been laid out *syntagmatically* to form the very plot of the novel.

An interesting variant of precisely this principle is to be found in at least two different passages of this work. The first is brief and very much to the point here. It occurs during the episode where Simone and the narrator are rescuing Marcelle from the country house:

'Je l'embrassai [Marcelle] longuement sur le front et les yeux. Une de ses mains par hasard ayant glissé sur ma jambe, elle me regarda avec de grands yeux, mais avant de la retirer, me caressa d'un geste d'absente à travers le drap.

L'immonde barreau céda après un long effort. Je l'écartai de toutes mes forces, ouvrant l'espace nécessaire au passage. Elle passa en effet, je la fis descendre, *l'aidant d'une main glissée à nu entre ses jambes.* Elle se blottit dans mes bras sur le sol et m'embrassa sur la bouche. Simone, à nos pieds ... étreignit ses jambes, embrassant ses cuisses sur lesquelles tout d'abord elle s'était contentée de poser sa joue, mais ne pouvant contenir un frisson de joie, *elle ouvrit le corps* et, collant ses lèvres à la vulve, l'embrassa avidement. (95–6)

It is clear that the first two italicized sentences constitute a metaphorical evocation of Simone's oral rape of Marcelle's body: they lead up to it while at the same time expressing the violence of the physical effort involved. Thus one element of the fiction, an event, stands in a relationship of a metaphorical character to another quite distinct event. The first two sentences suggest a hidden meaning quite different from the one they ostensibly evoke as fictive referents: the image of sexual penetration. But almost immediately, their hidden reference manifests itself explicitly in the last sentence in the form of further, apparently disassociated fictive referents. Another way of putting this would be to say that the first two sentences acquire *retroactively* a metaphorical status *while nonetheless, on the level of the plot,* retaining their initial status as fictive referents like any other.

A few pages earlier in the tale, we come upon exactly the same phenomenon but in a more complex guise. The narrator is now in the park in front of the same country house: 'J'assurai mon *revolver* dans ma poche et j'entrai: c'était un salon semblable à n'importe quel autre. Une lampe de poche me permit de *passer dans une antichambre, puis dans un escalier*. Je ne distinguais rien, n'aboutissais à rien' (84). We note the importance of the revolver, a phallic symbol *par excellence*, and the difficulty the narrator has entering the house. The rest of the passage is curious indeed: 'J'étais d'ailleurs incapable de rien comprendre, envoûté; *je ne sus même pas sur le moment pourquoi je me déculottai* et continuai en chemise mon angoissante exploration. J'enlevai l'un après l'autre mes vêtements et les mis sur une chaise, ne gardant que des chaussures' (84). Although he does not understand the motivation for his actions, there is every reason to suspect that his 'distressing exploration' will end up assuming a sexual character and that the sexual symbolism will come to be explicitly materialized with the unfolding of subsequent events, as of course it does:

...je m'empressai de sortir; je sautai pas la fenêtre et me cachai dans une allée. Je m'étais à peine retourné qu'une femme nue se dressa dans l'embrasure de la fenêtre: elle sauta comme moi dans le parc et s'enfuit en courant dans la direction des buissons d'épines ... *je ne savais que faire du revolver*: je n'avais plus de poche sur moi. Je poursuivais cette femme que j'avais vue passer, comme si je voulais l'abattre ... *Ni dans mon intention, ni dans mes gestes, il n'était rien de saisissable*. Je m'arrêtai; j'étais arrivé au buisson ... *Exalté, revolver en main*, je regardais autour de moi: mon corps à ce moment se déchira; *une main ensalivée avait saisi ma verge* et la branlait ... les jambes nues d'une femme se collaient à mes jambes avec un soubresaut d'orgasme. Je n'eus que le temps de me tourner pour *cracher mon foutre* à la figure de Simone; *le revolver en main*, j'étais parcouru d'un frisson d'une violence égale à celle de la bourrasque, mes dents claquaient, mes lèvres écumaient, les bras, les mains tordus, *je serrai convulsivement mon revolver* et, malgré moi, *trois coups de feu terrifiants et aveugles partirent* en direction du château. (85)

The sexual symbolism of the opening three sentences of this passage could hardly be more obvious, and once again one notes the metaphorical evocation of events preceding their direct evocation. The greater complexity of this example lies in the fact that the revolver, far from being lost from sight once its real referent has been actualized in the act of ejaculation, spits out its bullets *after* the evocation of the ejaculation, thereby maintaining the secondary metaphorical level of the fiction beyond the point where it can usefully function: the orgasm it was earlier ostensibly and ostentatiously pointing to. Here we have, then, a doubling-up effect, whereby the fiction reproduces itself in the form of its own reflection *within the fiction.*

Seeing the text as having assumed the form of an extended metaphor creates further problems with regard to the reader's reception of the work. What he is then led to concretize is, in fact, not the latent fictive referents corresponding to the eye, the egg, the testicles, and so on, but rather mental images conjured up in the mind's eye *as* mental images produced by the imagination and posited as such (and not as mental images to be taken for perceptions of the equivalent of real-life objects). They are in fact already conceived as such *within the fiction* by the characters themselves, inasmuch as they are explicitly perceived as possessing analogous shapes and attributes, as we saw earlier: 'Deux globes de même grandeur et consistance s'étaient animés de mouvements contraires et simultanés. Un testicule blanc de taureau avait pénétré la chair "rose et noire" de Simone; un œil était sorti de la tête du jeune homme' (107). Here the character concerned happens also to be the narrator. As was also noted earlier, one of the protagonists in particular, Simone, could well be taken for the novelist himself:

Et, comme je lui demandais à quoi lui faisait penser ... quelque chose de rouge, le soleil. Et l'œuf? Un œil de veau, en raison de la couleur de la tête, et d'ailleurs le blanc d'œuf était du blanc d'œil, et le jaune la prunelle. La forme de l'œil, à l'entendre, était celle de l'œuf ...

Elle ajouta que ... chacune de ses fesses était un œuf dur épluché. (92)

However, what Simone produces through dwelling on such associations is not a novel but a series of events that she herself will go on to live out through the rest of the tale. Whence the paradox ...

But *is it*, in fact, a sequence of events such as normally go to make up any fictional narrative? There is reason to believe not. Within the very same passage was it not as much a question of the words themselves as of what they evoked: 'Et, comme je lui demandais à quoi lui faisait penser le mot uriner, elle me répondit *Buriner* ... Elle jouait gaiement sur les mots, disant tantôt *casser un œil*, tantôt *crever un œuf* ...' (92). The initial analysis of the concretization of the various objects by the reader already revealed the role of what was referred to as the 'intrusive signifier.' A good and not atypical illustration of the latter is found in the following sentence: '... comme nous regardions la fenêtre où claquait le drap, nous constatons, surpris, qu'une balle avait étoilé un carreau quand nous vîmes cette *fenêtre ébranlée s'ou-*

vrir ...' (85). The evocation of the same sheet with its wet circular-shaped centre analogous with a hole followed by the transformation of the square-shaped window into the round planetary body of a star – a transformation itself brought about by that other rounded object 'une balle' – could not better prepare us for reading 'ébranlée' as *branlée* and the window as a representation of the female genitals being encouraged to open up through masturbation. When we read earlier that '[Simone] penchait son visage, reposant ses bras sur les bords de la cuvette, afin de fixer sur les *œufs* ses *yeux* grands ouverts' (91), we might well have noticed that the intentionality expressed by the preposition 'afin de' and attributed to the character Simone could not have been more significant in that it was symptomatic of a far more fundamental intentionality underlying the workings of this whole text – even if, on the level of the fiction, it were as though Simone were attempting to make the real world conform to the world of metaphor governed by associations of all kinds, albeit linguistic (related to the signifier) as well as material (related to the signified). In fact, as we shall see, this last sentence will reveal itself to be the kernel from which the whole text emerges.[22]

Let us look again at the closing sentences of a passage cited earlier: 'La clameur *atterrée* des arènes coïncida avec le spasme de Simone. Soulevée de la dalle de pierre, elle chancela et tomba, le *soleil* l'aveuglait, elle saignait du nez ... *L'œil* droit du cadavre pendait' (106). Once we are sensitized to the workings of the signifier, we notice that the word *soleil* is preceded by the word *atterrée* and followed by the word *œil*. Now, the root of *atterréé* is none other than the synonym for *sol*, which is the first syllable of *soleil*; moreover, the word *l'œil* is disseminated and barely concealed within the word *soleil*, of which, without its initial letter, it is in fact the anagram.

Another key passage quoted previously is just as significant in this respect: '... à la place où mon amie [Simone] devait s'asseoir reposaient sur une assiette les deux couilles nues; ces glandes, de la grosseur et de la forme d'un œuf, étaient d'une blancheur nacrée, rosie de sang, analogue à celle du globe oculaire' (104). This sentence not only gathers together 'l'œuf,' 'la couille,' and 'l'œil,' it also reveals that the bull's testicles have come to figure in the fiction not solely because their form resembles that of the eye or even because, as Roland Barthes

---

22 Much in the manner that the whole text of Beckett's trilogy has been shown to emerge like a Japanese flower plunged in water from the one word *inventaire* (see *Dimensions, structures et textualité*, 149–63).

points out, 'l'usage courant ... donne le nom d'*œufs* aux testicules d'animaux.'[23] If the expression 'globe oculaire' has replaced the word 'œil,' it is because 'couilles' comes within two letters of constituting the anagram of 'oculaire,' not to mention the fact that *couille* is also the anagram of *œil* and *cul*, the latter term understandably playing a key role throughout this text.

But no mention has been made so far of the two paragraphs – the second of the two being but one sentence long – that bring the work to an end, coming as a kind of epilogue after the dramatic image of the final resting place of the eponymous eye:

Nous disparûmes ainsi sans fin de l'Andalousie, pays jaune de *terre* et de *ciel*, *infini vase de nuit* noyé de lumière, où, chaque jour, nouveau personnage, je violais une nouvelle Simone et surtout vers midi, sur le *sol*, au *soleil*, et sous les *yeux rouges* de sir Edmond.

Le quatrième jour, l'Anglais acheta un *yacht* à Gibraltar. (116)

This echo of the shadow of a fiction on the point of finally being extinguished for good is characterized by the tonal transition from yellow to red.[24] The pair of words 'terre' and 'ciel' announce that other pair, 'sol' and 'soleil' ('terre' being synonymous with 'sol' and 'ciel' standing in opposition to 'terre' just as 'soleil' stands in opposition to 'sol'), while at the same time being taken up again in 'soleil' in a disseminated form through the transition *-iel* > *-eil* and the shared phonetic identity of each of their initial letters. The form constituted, on the other hand, by 'infini vase de nuit' will first of all give rise to the circle shape of the 'soleil' and then subsequently to the circles of Sir Edmond's 'yeux rouges.' As for the word '*viol*ais,' it will call forth the scarcely concealed *voile* of the 'yacht.' But the most important series of seminal associations here is the following one: from 'terre' to 'sol' to 'soleil' (= 'œil') to 'yeux rouges,' – with, first of all, the progressive formation of the first syllable of '*sol*eil' (of which 'sous' represents a variant, thanks to anticipated contamination by the 'yeux' that immediately follow it) and then, 'l'œil,' which detaches itself from 'soleil' so as to produce Sir Edmond's 'yeux rouges,' which are, in their turn, further determined by the aforementioned common circular shape, on the level of the signifieds, that links the sun to the eye.

23 'La Métaphore de l'œil,' 240; Barthes' emphasis
24 For the process of association by colour, too complex to go into here, see my *Monde à l'envers*, 62–7.

Need one add that once the reader has become alerted to the extensive word-play of this novel and realizes that '*Histoire de l'œil*' is *also*,
and indeed before all else, 'Histoire de l'*œil*,' not to mention 'des *yeux*,'
then this text can never be the same again as far as the manner of its
reception is concerned. The characters' incessant 'jeux des œufs' and
the multiple variants thereon are then seen for what they really are:
des jeux de mots, just like those that Simone has been seen to indulge
in so wantonly. The signifiers, continually emerging from behind the
concretized images of the fiction like so many moths eating away at
a tapestry, finally succeed in undermining irreparably, for the reader,
any illusion of a fictional universe. Here the worm in the fruit of the
reader's enjoyment of what Jean Ricardou calls 'l'euphorie du récit'[25]
is none other than the linguistic signifier, and in particular one pair
of signifiers: *œil-yeux*, whose generative productivity for the novelist
and destructive potential for the reader can be traced through in some,
if not all, of its complexity in the accompanying diagram.

Here, indeed, in the beginning was the word ... What distinguishes
this remarkable text of Bataille is that *in the end*, too, there remains
only the word and the word alone – for that is the only possible
outcome of any reading of this text. Having been led to concretize,
not without some sense of incredulity, a world that has taken on all
the fanciful attributes that metaphorization can give rise to – in short,
belonging to the world of the fantastic in the full sense of that term –
the reader finally comes to the realization that what he has taken to
be a fictional universe is nothing but a giant metaphor-made-flesh, so
to speak. In this sense, *Histoire de l'œil* is nothing more and nothing
less than the literary process itself, laid bare. And the reader's concretization of the work is, of course, a part of that process.

Histoire de l'œil provides a fitting conclusion to the present series
of studies of twentieth-century French fiction, for here the only fictive
referent that remains as it draws to a close is a sequence of words, that
is, a text: there is no extra-textual, extralinguistic referent since,
outside this text, there is nothing ...

This represents then the ultimate thwarting of the referential process we set out to study in these pages. We have been dealing, therefore, with a work that lends itself in an exemplary and irrefutable
manner to a formalist approach. The study of it thus reveals the outer
limits of the hermeneutic interrogation of the literary work (even
more so than did Simon's *Histoire*, whose ultimate referent did lie

25 Jean Ricardou, *Le Nouveau Roman*, 31

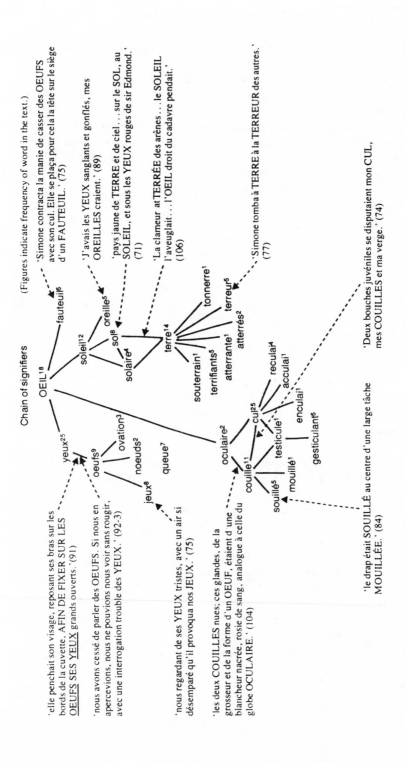

outside the novel), just as Camus' *La Chute* and, even more so, Beckett's *L'Innommable* brought home to us the inadequacy of any exclusively formal approach to the modern French novel. In this way, we may have succeeded in bridging the gap referred to in the introduction between the two main conceptions of the phenomenon of literature – formalist or structuralist, on the one hand, and hermeneutic or phenomenological, on the other. For I have demonstrated, paradoxically – and yet logically – both the pertinence *and* the inadequacy of either of these two approaches when it is to the detriment of any consideration of the other. And if this conclusion may be read as an unfashionable plea for eclecticism, so be it... For the critic, unlike the theoretician or indeed the poetician, always writes in response to the work he is interrogating.

Conclusion

In the preceding chapters we have seen various ways in which the referential function has drawn attention to itself in a number of significant twentieth-century French novels. In each case, the latent referentiality of the text in question posed problems for its reader. The problem was, however, posed at different levels or stages in the functioning of the reference. The progression mapped out through the course of the study of the eight novelists examined was clearly from the most to the least obvious as far as the problem of reference was concerned.

When the difficulty encountered by the reader involves the process by which he imagines the world of the novel in his mind's eye and his attempts to picture the characters and the events that they experience and that go to make up the story, as was the case with Bernanos's *Sous le soleil de Satan* and *L'Imposture* and Blanchot's *Au Moment voulu*, both the nature of the problem confronting the reader and the very fact that there *is* a problem will be most readily conceded. In other words, when it is the constitution of the fictional universe itself that takes a problematic turn and the reference in question is the generally accepted fictional mode of reference without whose recognition the novelistic characters and their universes would be taken for real(ity), then there can be, it seems to me, general agreement among readers that we do indeed have a problem. For the problem concerns the novelistic technique employed by its writer and the technical means brought to bear – its narrative devices, descriptive techniques, and imagery, for example – are without a doubt intersubjectively verifiable. While the content of a given act of imaginative concretization will necessarily differ from that of any other act of concretization, even by the same reader, without its existence being reduced to a purely subjective or psychic phenomenon, as Ingarden is at pains to point out and as Todorov's distinction between signification and symbolization serves to confirm, the thwarting of concretization can be readily ascertained since the reader will soon feel frustrated. Moreover, the difficulty he experiences in concretizing the work is encountered by the reader immediately, on the very first level of his perception and reading of the text. For before one can even get to the task of *interpreting* the novel – a task in which the reader's particular and personal skills and qualities inevitably come into play to distinguish his activity as an interpreter from that of any other reader – one has to have something to interpret ...

In the case of Beckett's *L'Innommable* and even more so in the case of Camus' *La Chute* the situation of the reader is very different as far as the functioning of the reference is concerned. There is no question for Camus' reader of doubting the fictional existence of the voluble narrator calling himself Clamence[1] and either his present world of Amsterdam or, upon first reading at least, his past Parisian environment. In other words, here there is no impediment to concretization. If this were not so, the reader would not feel concerned and increasingly threatened as his reading progresses. Only when one allows for the fact that the brackets placed around the world of the novel by the recognition of its fictionality finally fall away and that, in the words of Nelson Goodman, 'the so-called possible worlds of fiction lie within actual worlds' so that 'fiction ... applies truly neither to nothing nor to diaphanous possible worlds but, albeit metaphorically, to actual worlds'[2] can reference in the fictional mode be seen to be but a transitional stage on the way to reference's functioning as it always does and has to in order to merit the name. For if we speak of fictive *referents* rather than, say, imaginary *creations*, it is surely not because, where literature is concerned, the outcome of the process by which language refers to something outside of and other than itself has evaporated into thin air but simply because language itself has come to constitute a work of literature the initial thrust of which is, as Frye points out, always centripetal. As we saw in my opening chapter, the language of fiction and literary language in general no more lack a referent than does any other form of language for it is in the very nature of language to possess a referent: the use of language implies its user's referring

1 Except when, at the end of the work as we have seen, he has every reason to put in question the portrait he has painted of his past life
2 *Ways of Worldmaking*

thereby to the extralinguistic just as the presence of words denotes the absence of the reality they stand (in) for, so to speak, since, in Henri Meschonnic's words, 'le signe linguistique est un substitut des choses, et même leur mise à mort puisque, selon Hegel cité par Blanchot que cite Sartre, le signe – le nom – "les anéantit dans leur existence (en tant qu'existants)".'[3] Only when due allowance is made for the eventual and inevitable lifting of the initial suspension of disbelief whereby we, as readers, 'take to heart,' as fiction *and* in all seriousness, the experience furnished by our reading, drawing from it our own personal conclusions, can one account for the manner in which reference reaches out to encompass within its purview the actual, real world of its reader, who had thought to be out of harm's way, ensconced in the comfort of an armchair[4] hardly to be mistaken for Clamence's *malconfort* – or so it had seemed ... Here the Gadamerian concept of the fusion of horizons – the coming together and merging of the literary work's horizon and the horizon of the reader – is experienced for its own sake, as it were, at first hand.[5] It was Ingarden's concepts of represented real space and imagined real space on the one hand and imaginational and psychic space on the other that made possible the actual analysis of this phenomenon. The irony of the reader's situation is, of course, that the make-believe world he had sat back to contemplate is in reality, like the world of any novel, ultimately of his or her own making.

This final development, which fictional reference shares with all reference and which establishes its referential credentials, so to speak, constituting the finality of the process itself, is more readily recognizable in the guise of the reader's *appropriation* of the literary work. This being so, many might dispute that what was essentially being

---

3 Henri Meschonnic, 'Mallarmé au-delà du silence,' 20. Meschonnic is quoting from Hegel's *Le Système* of 1803–4, quoted by M. Blanchot in *La Part du feu*, 324, quoted by Sartre in 'L'Engagement de Mallarmé,' 190.

4 Michel Picard's observation that 'les espaces gigognes où se blottit le lecteur, son appartement, son salon, son fauteuil, sa robe de chambre, son adolescence et son enfance revivifiées, la ronde autour de lui des référents privilégiés (aux signifiés secrets) qu'il accroche distraitement mais fermement aux signifiés des descriptions, tout cela est lui-même – et n'est pas lui, puisqu'il joue, sur le texte d'un autre' (*Le Jeu de la lecture*, 110) takes on ironic overtones when applied to *La Chute*.

5 Usually of course, the process occurs during our reading of any novel but without coming to our attention. Here we are made aware of it in an inescapable manner. The process was operative, here, too, but without our being aware of it, right from our reading of the very first pages of the work.

discussed in relation to *La Chute* has anything to do with reference at all. Leaving matters of terminology aside, it would no doubt be generally agreed that what is at stake falls within that large and even more largely undelimitated and fashionable area referred to, with an appropriate nod towards its Germanic antecedents in *Rezeptionsesthetik*, as Reception Theory, even if the French varieties of this branch of literary studies[6] owe far more to poetics than to phenomenology or even hermeneutics in general and go no way whatsoever towards bridging the gap between the former and the latter. In fact, concretization is no less central to any account of the reception of the literary work than reference is. To put the stress on 'reference' is to insist on what is being spoken of, whereas to stress 'reception' is to focus on how what is being spoken of is heard and understood, in other words registered by the work's receiver. To speak of 'appropriation,' on the other hand, is to attribute to the work's addressee what is perceived to be a far more active role. It was no doubt to find a middle ground between the (relative) passivity of 'reception' and the (relative) activity of 'appropriation' that Gadamer chose to reactivate a term taken from traditional jurisprudence, that of 'application.' It is just such a middle ground that I consider most appropriate properly to represent and to account for the coming together of the literary work and its reader, the fusing of their two horizons into something other than what pre-existed the *act* of reading,[7] such as it is analysed in the philosophical mode in *Wahrheit und Méthode*.

Few would dispute, however, that Beckett's *L'Innommable* occupies its rightful place in the present study. For concretization poses the reader as much of a problem here as it does in Bernanos or Blanchot. It is not so much that one has difficulty in effecting the appropriate concretization called for by the fictive referents but that concretization is permanently frustrated and definitively undermined. Nonetheless, what creates the problem in the first place remains, as with the other two novelists, the actual character of the fictive referents

6 Here I am thinking particularly of Michel Charles' *Rhétorique de la lecture*, as well as Umberto Eco's *Lector in fabula*. This is far less true of Michel Picard's *Le Jeu de la lecture*, cited earlier on a number of occasions, although Roman Ingarden and Georges Poulet are absent from Picard's bibliography of works on reading.

7 Here I would reiterate Jean-Paul Resweber's word of warning (cited earlier) concerning this Gadamerian concept, against 'toute conception dialectique qui ferait, de l'horizon nouveau, la synthèse de l'horizon de l'auteur (thèse) et de celui de l'herméneute (anti-thèse)' (*Qu'est-ce qu'interpréter*).

concerned, the nature of the kind of reality being referred to. Here the reality involved is that of language[8] itself and the manner in which the mechanisms of language function on both the level of the signifieds and the level of the signifiers.[9] This is why I consider that as a text,[10]

8 At this point, given the conclusion to the chapter on Blanchot's *Au Moment voulu*, it is necessary to draw a fine but fundamental distinction between that novel and *L'Innommable*. This is because the whole fictional universe of Blanchot's *récit* constitutes, in a manner that remains to be clarified, a *representation*, no doubt necessarily metaphorical in character, of the 'space' of language – although that, too, remains to be determined, for the reading of the novel presented in these pages remains tentative; if it has subsequently to be radically revised then its fate will be no different from that of many other critics' readings of Blanchot's fiction (see, for example, Roger Laporte's *Maurice Blanchot*, where he writes the following: '… je ne vois pas pourquoi l'auteur n'aurait pas le droit … de condamner un travail qu'il estime complètement manqué. A cause de sa bêtise, sans parler d'autres raisons encore plus graves, j'ai donc depuis long-temps décidé d'interdire toute reproduction … de "Une passion," l'une des *Deux lectures de Maurice Blanchot* [la première est faite par Bernard Noël], ouvrage paru en 1973 aux éditions Fata Morgana' [61]). However, within the universe it offers up for concretization there live ordinary fictional characters like those of any other novel, relatively speaking at least. Beckett's novel, on the other hand, in no wise constitutes a representation of anything, unless it be that of the linguistic signifier (see note 9 below).

9 The working out of the signifiers was studied in minute detail across the trilogy in my *Dimensions, structures*, and confers on the three texts concerned their auto-referential character, thereby relating them to the Nouveau Roman gener-ally, i.e., to texts talking about texts. In the present context, this aspect of *L'Innommable* has been left aside for the obvious reason that the signifier does not – if at all – relate to the referent in the same direct and inextricable manner as the signified does. I have therefore focused on the signifieds. When the latter operate in the self-reflexive mode, as is the case with all shifters or deictics that, as Benveniste points out, necessarily, by their very nature and function within the linguistic system, 'réfléchissent leur propre emploi' ('La Nature des pro-noms'), then what is brought to the forefront of the reader's attention is the problematic character of language itself and the use we make/that is made of it and for which it has ostensibly been designed. The questioning of language, like reference itself, is of course as much a philosophical matter as an aesthetic one. It is because *L'Innommable* possesses these two facets, being self-reflexive both as a text and as a work thereby problematizing at one and the same time the production and the reception of language, that it represents, in my view, such a fundamental achievement. The metaphor of the writer's and reader's shadow employed earlier is, of course, a reflection of this duality. To my knowledge, there does not yet exist a coherent and self-consistent metalanguage, whether it be that of traditional criticism or that of contemporary poetics, enabling one to speak of both at the same time.

10 Here I opt deliberately for the term *text* rather than *work*, for it is debatable, given its refusal of concretization in any form whatsoever, whether Roman

it focuses on the activity of appropriation itself. At the same time it raises an even more fundamental question than that of the reception and appropriation of the literary work[11] as such: that of the acquisition and use of language, of how the linguistic system lends itself to appropriation by each one of us – not only as readers but also as writers and even thinkers.

This would make *L'Innommable* appear to override, as it were, the problematization of reference and hence the scope of this study – were it not for the fact that just as it has always appeared to me curious that one could presume to analyse the reading of novels, for example, without first having studied the process of reading itself,[12] it is clear that the appropriation of language is the most fundamental prerequisite to the appropriation of any literary work for which it is a veritable *sine qua non.* To problematize the former is thus inevitably to problematize the latter. Moreover, as was pointed out in the preface, like the relation that language entertains with reality through its reference, the relation it establishes with its user through the operations that linguistic shifters lend themselves to concerns that basic interplay between the linguistic and the non- or extralinguistic in all its forms. This does not, however, for all that, prevent me from conceding that consideration of *L'Innommable* places us on the outer limits of the problem of reference, even conceived of in the broadest sense of the term that has been chosen for the purposes of the present study. More precisely, what is highlighted thereby is nothing less than *the very possibility of reference*: it raises the question of whether language can ultimately relate or refer to *anything outside of and other than itself.* And given the fact that *L'Innommable* is neither a philosophical treatise nor an essay but a literary text, this questioning becomes the reader's questioning. Because the emergence and awareness of self-identity is intimately bound up with our use of language, the reader is thus led to initiate a process of self-questioning and self-

---

Ingarden would consider it to qualify on his terms as a *literary work.* If my hypothesis is correct, Beckett would, of course, have been the first to be delighted by such a judgment! (See the discussion of Beckett's overall aesthetic in the chapter 'Before and after Babel,' in my *Beckett and Babel,* 180–92.)

11 Once *L'Innommable* is considered in relation to *The Unnamable,* it can also be seen to address and thematize the problem of bilingualism (see 'Text[e] & Metatext[e]s,' in my *Beckett and Babel,* 141–61).

12 In his *Act of Reading,* Wolfgang Iser, for example, takes some account of scientific studies devoted to ocular movements during reading.

scrutiny. To paraphrase Emile Benveniste, *ego* is no more than 'qui dit *ego*.'[13]

This very possibility of language's referring to anything outside of itself had, of course, already been put in jeopardy in the most direct manner in *La Nausée*. What differentiates Sartre's novel from Beckett's, however, is that this putting-in-question takes place, in the first instance, in a discursive mode, since the fictional narrator and protagonist is led to formulate in his own words the problem of language's arbitrary relation to what it ostensibly signifies. Here the concretization of Roquentin's experience itself calls paradoxically for the thwarting of any such concretization, thereby undermining its own vehicle. For ultimately, concretization becomes reduced to what it cannot be: the mere perception of language for its own sake, as a series of signifiers, in that concretization entails by its very nature that language become, on the contrary, transparent. The concretization of language itself is, in fact, a contradiction in terms, for it means that direct visual perception has blocked off the reader's access to the evocative powers of his own imagination, upon which all concretization is dependent. Nonetheless, it is just such a process that is lived out by Roquentin in the pages of his diary. *La Nausée* is thus central to the concerns of this study, since it represents nothing less than the *fictionalization* of the problematization of reference and obliges its reader to experience at first hand the problematization of his own activity: the process of concretization. In the end the reader finds himself *succeeding*, inasmuch as he perseveres in his reading of the novel, where Roquentin *failed* – while at the same time, through his efforts to understand and appreciate Roquentin's failure, undermining his own success in making sense of the words he is reading and concretizing the world they bring into being.

The mention of the self-referentiality of language brings us to that epitome and logical outcome of the latter, the French Nouveau Roman and its self-reflexive text, what I referred to in relation to another writer not usually associated with the Nouveaux Romanciers as 'the narcissistic text.' And there is no doubt whatsoever that Claude Simon and his novel *Histoire*, like the rest of his novelistic output since *Le Vent* at least,[14] belong in that company. What, however, tends to

13 'De la subjectivité dans le langage,' in *Problèmes de linguistique générale 1*
14 The exceptions are his earlier novels *Gulliver, Le Sacre du printemps, Le Tricheur*, and *La Corde raide*.

distinguish Simon's fiction from that of most other Nouveaux Romanciers is the status of the fictive heterocosm within it. As Ralph Sarkonak has demonstrated with much critical finesse,[15] there is in his work
a delicate balance between representation and anti-representation,
between the *lisible* and the *scriptible*. In fact, his reader is called upon
to inhabit a world that is as distinctive as that of Marcel Proust,[16] no
less 'real' and equally fascinating. This is why to embark upon a study
of the way *Histoire* functions referentially is not quite as perverse an
undertaking as was suggested earlier. For I would maintain that its
reader does read that work referentially for the world it evokes, however much he may at the same time be aware of its *littérarité*, which
is at work undermining the very bases of that world.

There are two ways in which the place of the study of referentiality
in *Histoire* can be viewed. On the one hand, it can be seen to demonstrate that even within the Nouveau Roman consideration of reference
is neither an idle nor wholly futile occupation, the reason being that
any Nouveau Roman is read not only *as well as* being an object of
analysis for the poetician or the textologist but *before* becoming such
an object. Studies devoted to the actual reception of such works by
their readers have been singularly lacking to date.[17] For example,
thorough analyses of the manner in which the *mise en abyme* functions as a mirroring device *within* the text are common in critical
studies on the Nouveau Roman[18] (and indeed not only on the latter),[19]
whereas the way such a formal device is *read* or 'received' by the reader
has barely been deemed worthy of consideration let alone serious
study and analysis. My chapter on *Histoire* could, among other more
immediate concerns, be considered to contribute, however modestly,
to the elucidation of the reader's reception of the *mise en abyme*.[20]

15 See Sarkonak, *Claude Simon: les carrefours du texte.*
16 It should be added here that Proust's work provides a bridge between Simon's and
   Beckett's fiction, since Simon's main themes are eminently Proustian and Beckett has given us a very important monograph on Proust (see *Proust and Three
   Dialogues*).
17 See 'Reflexivity and Reading,' Lucien Dällenbach's recent attempt to broach this
   problem while remaining within a formalistic conception of the text – an
   attempt that is, in my view, thus doomed from the outset.
18 Starting of course with Dällenbach's classic study *Le Récit spéculaire*
19 See, for example, my study of Georges Bataille's *Le Bleu du ciel* ('*Le Bleu du ciel*:
   le texte réversible,' in *Monde à l'envers*, 135–60).
20 What will appear problematic about the present analysis to certain readers will
   be the subjecting of a *formal* device to *phenomenological* analysis. Rather than

Indeed the complexity of this aspect of *Histoire* makes it a prime candidate for such an analysis. On the other hand, the chapter on Simon can also be seen to show how the reference becomes progressively more difficult to actualize as it moves from postcards to paintings and photographs depicted thereon and thence to the 'animation' or bringing-to-life of the paintings and photographs, together with the evocation of the events leading up to the scenes depicted – not to mention the reception of all these different phenomena – until it finally collapses in a process of implosion. Concretization, in fact, becomes such a complex process calling for such extraordinary imaginative versatility that it stretches the bounds of feasibility. (Need it be added here that I am well aware that advocates of the genre – for the Nouveau Roman is tantamount to a new literary *genre*, as has already been pointed out in the case of Beckett – would no doubt point to the labyrinthine character of that analysis as proof of the impossibility or at least the futility of such a referential reading of this type of text?) In this way, one could claim that even in works such as Simon's that definitely eschew the project undertaken by so many other Nouveaux Romans, the systematic and self-conscious rejection of representation in favour of *anti*-representation, reference ends up by participating in and contributing to the same centripetal forces as the latter by turning in upon itself. Nothing, of course, could be less natural than such an outcome: it is no less than a betrayal of reference's *raison d'être*, which is by definition centrifugal (in relation to language), involving precisely what is other than that which is doing the referring and what lies beyond the parameters of the text.

In a sense, with regard to referentiality, *Histoire* reveals itself to be complementary to *L'Innommable*, for both ultimately subscribe to the subversion of the process. Whereas Beckett's novel does so through a frontal attack that in the end – as well as, of course, as we have seen, at the beginning – leaves nothing standing, Simon's novel manages to make the unilinear trajectory of reference deviate from its normal path and turn back on itself to create a closed circular system, so that what is normally a way out of the text reveals itself to be a way back

of the literary work or text, the value of such an exercise could well be considered to lie precisely in the bringing together of the two. I resorted to an analogous procedure elsewhere ('La Navette et l'ellipse chez Malraux') in an attempt to show how a formal textual feature could be related to the basic heuristic device of hermeneutics, the hermeneutic circle.

into it again. If Beckett offers nothing to escape to, Simon offers no way of escape. In this the penultimate novel considered, reference finally yields to self-reference and *lisibilité* to *scriptibilité* – albeit in an original and atypical manner, since the auto-referentiality concerned does not so much stand in opposition to referentiality as it paradoxically constitutes the upshot of the latter.

No less original is the transformation that Barthes' concept of the *scriptible* undergoes in Malraux's revolutionary novels, where it becomes transposed from the medium of writing to that of painting. The transformation of the *scriptible* into the *pictural* is none other than that of the materiality of language into the plasticity of paint, the signifier of the writer giving way to that of the painter. At the same time, Malraux's novels were seen to provide an unusual and less obvious variant on the situation obtaining in Simon's *Histoire:* that of a fictive referent that is itself a visual *representation* of a fictional reality.

The *scriptible* finally comes into its own in Bataille's *Histoire de l'œil.* Here self-reference attains its ultimate realization and marks the culmination of the progressive frustration of reference that has been mapped out in these pages and the definitive collapse of the fictional reality born of concretization. All reflection now disappears from the mind's eye of the reader as though replaced by the white eyes, pupils up-turned, of so many of this novelist's protagonists. The concretization of language posited in *La Nausée* now comes to pass for the reader himself as the language of the text congeals into that *matière langagière* that is held in the fascinated gaze of the reader of every French New Novel: the medium has finally become the message – but a message the content of which is its own vehicle. Everything – that is, the elements of an embryonic fiction that had struggled to materialize in the reader's imagination – has receded vertiginously back to its origin: mere words on paper as they offer themselves up to perception.

It should be clear by now that what has been the constant concern throughout the preceding pages is the interaction of the novel and its reader, what exactly happens – and the term *exactly* should be stressed here – when the two come together. Gerald Prince[21] and others[22] in his

---

21 'Introduction to the Study of the Narratee'
22 Michel Charles, for example, in *Rhétorique de la lecture*

wake have insisted that the reader is inscribed in the text.[23] 'Ainsi
s'épuise-t-on parfois,' as Michel Picard puts it, 'à chercher le lecteur
bel et bien *dans* le texte, prenant au sérieux les stratégies séductrices
d'un écrivain-araignée,' adding tellingly: '... c'est faire du lecteur un
fantôme, qu'aucune évocation ni aucun rituel ne feront accéder à la
vie.'[24] There is, in fact, no conceivable way that the reader, in his role
as reader, can actually come to life until we pick up the book and
begin reading it, bringing to it the sum total of our experience, both
of life *and* of literature, to that point. The process that then takes
place is not in any sense a contamination of the work in itself and for
itself. Novels are meant to be read and readers cannot be eliminated
from their reading. Why some readers should wish to believe they can
be has always been a source of wonderment to this particular reader.
It is no coincidence that critical commentaries and studies have traditionally been referred to as 'readings,' and it has taken the advent of
poetics to cultivate the tantalizing mirage of readerless readings. That
one should want to study the process one is thereby involved in in as
accurate and thorough a manner as possible, subjecting the outcome
to the criterion of intersubjective verifiability, is only natural given
the natural demands of intellectual curiosity. The need to understand – as the whole hermeneutic tradition tells us, beginning in the
modern period with Schleiermacher and culminating in Heidegger –
is and always will be at the core of the human as opposed to the
natural sciences. I have sought to demonstrate, texts in hand, that
this is possible, and it is clear that Roman Ingarden's founding of the
non-psychic and hence potentially verifiable nature of concretization
is of vital importance for the viability of such an endeavour.

The phenomenological approach[25] adopted in these pages is, it

23 See the title of the excellent anthology of reception-theory essays *The Reader in
the Text.*
24 *Le Jeu de la lecture,* 147, 148
25 The extensive critical writings of the Geneva School (Georges Poulet, Jean Starobinski, Jean Rousset, Jean-Pierre Richard and including the early work of the
only non-francophone among them, J. Hillis Miller) with which my earlier study
of Bernanos has marked affinities represent one of the most sophisticated and
fruitful examples of phenomenological criticism, which was largely responsible
for instigating the crucial debate around *La Nouvelle Critique* in France. Without them, moreover and paradoxically, Structuralism would have been unlikely
to have been able to impose itself so readily and rapidly on the French literary
scene. For the relationship between these critics and Blanchot's theory and practice of literature, see Sarah N. Lawall's fine exegesis in *Critics of Consciousness*

would appear, the only one adequately and properly equipped to address the particular topic that has been our concern: the interaction of ourselves and the novels we read. Once we finally close the novel in question and walk away from it – and only then – do we enter the realm of the strictly private and personal about which any attempted generalization will tend to be futile.

It should be clear by now that it was only the unique status of Beckett's *L'Innommable* that enabled the process of reference to be traced right through into that of the actual appropriation of the text by the reader. Inasmuch as *L'Innommable problematizes* appropriation in any and every shape and form, just as *La Chute* does likewise for the concept of the fusion of horizons, reference can be said to have been revealed to be *problematic*, but only – it must be stressed – with respect to these particular texts. This means that within this period of French literature, reference does indeed constitute a problem: its actualization no longer goes without saying, as it were. But that much was in a sense already common knowledge to the readers of the Nouveau Roman, not to mention the Nouveau Nouveau Roman. What this study has attempted to show, however, is the *precise manner* in which reference becomes problematized.

At the same time, a certain *theoretical* objective has, I trust, been attained, in that a case has been made for *a broader definition of the very concept of reference* in the novel. This results in what is in my view the necessary reintegration of fictional reference within the referentiality inseparable from language itself. Indeed, when all is said and done, this is precisely what *L'Innommable* is basically 'about.'

This development was made possible by the progression from the linguistic theory of reference of Maurice-Jean Lefebve to Roman Ingarden's phenomenological analysis of the structure of the literary work and its concretization through the act of reading (complemented by Jean-Paul Sartre's phenomenological study of the psychology of the imagination and Tzvetan Todorov's signification/symbolization dichotomy), and thence to Paul Ricoeur's crucial bringing together of the linguistic and the philosophical in his account of the appropriation of the literary work, with due acknowledgment (by Ricoeur himself, of course) to the philosophical hermeneutics of Hans-Georg Gadamer.

The 'reader' of the preceding chapters is, of course, not just any

---

and Poulet's chapter on Blanchot in *La Conscience critique*. See also Robert R. Magliola's *Phenomenology and Literature*.

reader. As was anticipated by my remarks in chapter 1, he has at times proved to be singularly matter-of-fact and literal-minded in the attempt to remain as close as possible to what is signified – as opposed to symbolized – by the texts of the novels studied. I could, of course, have identified from the outset the reader concerned as the author of these pages but that would have been to falsify the very thesis of this study. For the reader chosen was intended to be a partial, that is, incomplete reader rather than any hypothetical 'compleat reader,' or indeed any of those other species of reader postulated by contemporary theoreticians such as Riffaterre, Fish, Iser, et al. The former sought to focus on bringing to life through the powers of the imagination the world of the fiction, and in so doing, to scrutinize exactly what was involved and to what extent it was, or was not, possible. As we have seen for ourselves through the analyses not only of *La Chute* and *L'Innommable* but also of *Histoire de l'œil*, the piecing-together of the fictive heterocosm into a coherent Gestalt, far from being the end of what reading entails, is but the beginning. However, it is also a beginning that cannot be avoided, that is not merely the pretext but the necessary occasion for all that fiction does for us, its readers. The topic we have been studying comes together most evocatively in the title of this work: reflections in the mind's eye ... So our story has, in a sense, been none other than Bataille's 'histoire de l'œil.' Ultimately the preceding pages are indeed reflections on reflections in one particular mind's eye. If the mind is mine, however, the eye, like Bataille's peregrinating eye, could be anyone's ...

Bibliography

NOVELS

Bataille, Georges. *Histoire de l'œil*. Paris: Pauvert '10/18' 1970 (1st ed.: Lord Auch [pseudonym]. Paris: [René Bounel] 1928)

Beckett, Samuel. *En attendant Godot*. Paris: Editions de Minuit 1952

– *L'Innommable*. Paris: Editions de Minuit 1953

– *The Unnamable*. In *Three Novels by Beckett: 'Molloy,' 'Malone Dies,' 'The Unnamable.'* New York: Grove Press 1965

Bernanos, Georges. *L'Imposture*. In *Œuvres romanesques suivies de 'Dialogues des Carmélites.'* Paris: Gallimard, 'Bibliothèque de la Pléiade' 1961 (1st ed.: Paris: Plon 1927)

– *La Joie*. In ibid. (1st ed.: Paris: Plon 1929)

– *Journal d'un curé de campagne*. In ibid. (1st ed.: Paris: Plon 1936)

– *Monsieur Ouine*. In ibid. (1st ed.: Paris: Plon 1946)

– *Nouvelle Histoire de Mouchette*. In ibid. (1st ed.: Paris: Plon 1937)

– *Sous le soleil de Satan*. In ibid. (1st ed.: Paris: Plon 1926)

Blanchot, Maurice. *Aminadab*. Paris: Gallimard 1942

– *Au Moment voulu*. Paris: Gallimard 1951

– *Thomas l'obscur*. Paris: Gallimard 1941

– *Thomas l'obscur: nouvelle version*. Paris: Gallimard 1950

– *Le Très-Haut*. Paris: Gallimard 1948

Camus, Albert. *La Chute*. In *Théâtre, récits, nouvelles*. Paris: Gallimard, 'Bibliothèque de la Pléiade' 1962 (1st ed.: Paris: Gallimard 1956)

– *L'Etranger*. In ibid. (1st ed.: Paris: Gallimard 1942)

– *La Peste*. In ibid. (1st ed.: Paris: Gallimard 1947)

Constant, Benjamin. *Adolphe*. In *Adolphe, Le Cahier rouge, Cécile*. Paris: Gallimard, 'Folio' 1973

Gide, André. *Les Caves du Vatican*. In *Romans*. Paris: Gallimard, 'Bibliothèque de la Pléiade' 1958

Green, Julien. *Varouna*. Paris: Editions du Seuil, 'Points' 1984

La Fayette, Madame de. *La Princesse de Clèves.* Paris: Gallimard, 'Folio' 1972

Malraux, André. 'A l'Hôtel des sensations inédites,' *Marianne,* no. 13 (déc. 1933): 4

- *La Condition humaine.* In *Romans.* Paris: Gallimard, 'Bibliothèque de la Pléiade' 1947 (1st ed.: Paris: Gallimard 1933)
- *Les Conquérants.* In ibid. (1st ed.: Paris: Grasset 1928)
- *L'Espoir.* In ibid. (1st ed.: Paris: Gallimard 1937)
- *Les Noyers de l'Altenburg.* Paris: Gallimard 1948 (1st ed.: Lausanne: Editions du Haut-Pays 1943)
- *Le Temps du mépris.* Paris: Gallimard 1935
- *La Voie royale.* Paris: Grasset 1930

Sarraute, Nathalie. *Le Planétarium.* Paris: Gallimard, 'Folio' 1959

Sartre, Jean-Paul. *La Nausée.* In *Œuvres romanesques,* ed. Michel Contat et Michel Rybalka avec la collaboration de Geneviève Idt et de George H. Bauer, 3–210. Paris: Gallimard, 'Bibliothèque de la Pléiade' 1981 (1st ed.: Paris: Gallimard 1938)

Simon, Claude. *La Corde raide.* Paris: Editions du Sagittaire 1947
- *Gulliver.* Paris: Calmann Lévy 1952
- *L'Herbe.* Paris: Editions de Minuit 1958
- *Histoire.* Paris: Editions de Minuit, 'Folio' 1973 (1st ed.: Paris: Editions de Minuit 1967)
- *La Route des Flandres.* Paris: Editions de Minuit 1960
- *Le Sacre du printemps.* Paris: Calmann Lévy 1954
- *Le Tricheur.* Paris: Editions du Sagittaire 1945
- *Le Vent: Tentative de restitution d'un rétable baroque.* Paris: Editions de Minuit 1957

REFERENTIALITY AND RELATED LITERARY THEORY

Barat, Jean-Claude. 'Le Retour du référent,' *Fabula,* no. 2, 'Les Référents du roman' (1983): 123–30

Barthes, Roland. 'L'Effet de réel.' In *Littérature et réalité,* R. Barthes, L. Bersani, Ph. Hamon, M. Riffaterre, I. Watt, 81–90. Paris: Editions du Seuil 1982. (First published in *Communications,* no. 11 [1968])

Black, Max. *Models and Metaphors: Studies in Language and Philosophy.* Ithaca, NY: Cornell University Press 1962

Blanchot, Maurice. *L'Espace littéraire.* Paris: Gallimard, 'Folio idées' 1988 (1st ed.: Paris: Gallimard 1955)

Bleich, David. *Subjective Criticism.* Baltimore and London: Johns Hopkins University Press 1978

Crosman, Inge. 'Reference and the Reader,' *Poetics Today,* 4, no. 1, 'Reference and Fictionality' (1983): 89–97

Fabula, no. 2, 'Les Référents du roman' (1983)

Falk, Eugene H. *The Poetics of Roman Ingarden*. Chapel Hill: University of North Carolina Press 1981

Frege, Gottlieb. 'On Sense and Nominatum.' In *Readings in Philosophical Analysis*, ed. Herbert Feigl and Wilfrid Sellars, 85–102. New York: Appleton-Century-Crofts 1949

Gadamer, Hans-Georg, *Truth and Method*. New York: Seabury Press 1975

Gann, Andrew. 'The Scandal of Referentiality.' In *Social Values and Poetic Acts*, 115–31. Cambridge, MA: Harvard University Press 1988

Goodman, Nelson. *The Languages of Art: An Approach to a Theory of Symbols*. Indianapolis: Bobbs-Merrill 1968

– *Ways of Worldmaking*. Ann Arbor, MI: Harvester Press 1978

Hamburger, Käte. *Logique des genres littéraires*. Trad. de l'allemand par Pierre Cadiot, préface de Gérard Genette. Paris: Editions du Seuil 1986; *Die Logik der Dichtung*. Stuttgart: Ernst Klett 1977

Ingarden, Roman. *The Literary Work of Art: An Investigation on the Borderlines of Ontology, Logic and Theory of Literature*. Trans. with an introduction by George Grabowicz. Evanston, IL: Northwestern University Press 1973; *Das Literarische Kunstwerk*. Tübingen: Max Niemeyer Verlag 1965

Iser, Wolfgang. *The Act of Reading: A Theory of Aesthetic Response*. Baltimore and London: Johns Hopkins University Press 1978; *Der Akt des Lesens*. München: Wilhelm Fink Verlag 1976

– *The Implied Reader: Patterns of Communication in Prose Fiction from Bunyan to Beckett*. Baltimore and London: Johns Hopkins University Press 1974; *Der Implizite Leser: Kommunikationsformen des Romans von Bunyan bis Beckett*. Münich: Wilhelm Fink Verlag 1972

Jauss, Hans Robert. *Aesthetic Experience and Literary Hermeneutics*. Trans. by Michael Shaw. Minneapolis: University of Minnesota Press 1982

– 'Levels of Identification in Hero and Audience,' *New Literary History*, 5, no. 2 (1974): 283–317

– *Toward an Aesthetic of Reception*. Trans. by Timothy Bahti. Minneapolis: University of Minnesota Press 1982

Kerbrat-Orecchioni, Catherine. 'Le Statut référential des textes de fiction,' *Fabula*, no. 2, 'Les référents du roman' (1983): 131–8

– 'Le Texte littéraire: non-référence, auto-référence, ou référence fictionnelle?' *Texte* [Toronto], no. 1, 'L'Autoreprésentation: Le texte et ses miroirs' (1982): 27–49

Lavis, George. 'Le Texte littéraire, le référent, le réel, le vrai,' *Cahiers d'analyse textuelle*, 13 (1971): 7–22

Lefebve, Maurice-Jean. *Structure du discours de la poésie et du récit*. Neuchâtel: Editions de la Baconnière 1971

Linsky, Leonard. *Referring*. London: Routledge & Kegan Paul 1967

Meinong, Alexius. 'The Theory of Objects.' Trans. by Isaac Levi, D.B.

Terrell, and Roderick M. Chisholm. In *Realism and the Background of Phenomenology*, ed. Roderick M. Chisholm, 76–117. Glencoe, IL: Free Press 1960. (First published in *Untersuchungen zur Gegenstandstheorie und Psychologie*, ed. Alexius Meinong [Leipzig 1904] and republished in vol. 2 of Meinong's collected works)

Miller, Owen. 'Reading as a Process of Reconstruction: A Critique of Recent Structuralist Formulations.' In *Interpretation of Narrative*, ed. Mario Valdés and Owen Miller, 19–27. Toronto: University of Toronto Press 1978

Morot-Sir, Edouard. 'Texte, référence et déictique,' *Texte*, no. 1, 'L'Auto-représentation: Le texte et ses miroirs,' (1982): 113–42

Pavel, Thomas. *Fictional Worlds*. Cambridge, MA: Harvard University Press 1986

Picard, Michel. *Le Jeu de la lecture: Essai sur la littérature*. Paris: Editions de Minuit 1986

Picard, Michel, ed. *La Lecture littéraire* (*Actes du College tenu à Reims du 14 au 16 juin 1984*). Paris: Editions Clancier-Guénaud 1987

Pierrot, Alain. 'La Référence des énoncés métaphoriques,' *Esprit*, nos. 740–1, 'Paul Ricoeur' (juill.–août 1988): 274–89

Poetics Today, 4, no. 1, 'Reference and Fictionality' (1983): 73–107

Poulet, Georges. 'Phenomenology of Reading,' *New Literary History*, 1, no. 1 (Fall 1969): 53–68

Quine, W.V.O. 'Three Grades of Modal Involvement.' In *The Ways of Paradox*, 156–74. New York: Random House 1966

– 'Reference and Modality.' In *Reference and Modality*, ed. Leonard Linsky 17–37. London: Oxford University Press 1971

Revue des sciences humaines, no. 177, 'L'Effet de lecture' (1980)

Ricoeur, Paul. 'Appropriation.' In *Hermeneutics and the Social Sciences*, ed. John B. Thompson, 183–93. Cambridge: Cambridge University Press 1981

– 'The Hermeneutical Function of Distanciation,' *Philosophy Today*, 17, nos. 2/4 (Summer 1973): 129–41

– *Interpretation Theory*. Fort Worth: Texas Christian University Press 1976

– 'Metaphor and Reference.' In *The Rule of Metaphor*, 216–56. Translated from the French *La Métaphore vive* [Paris: Editions du Seuil 1975] by Robert Czerny with Kathleen McLaughlin and John Costello SJ. Toronto: University of Toronto Press 1977

– 'Metaphor and the Problem of Hermeneutics.' In *Hermeneutics and the Social Sciences*, ed. John B. Thompson, 165–81. Cambridge: Cambridge University Press 1981

– 'Phenomenology and Hermeneutics.' In ibid., 101–28

– 'Narrativité et référence.' In *Temps et récit*, vol. 1, 117–24. Paris: Editions du Seuil 1983

– *Temps et récit*. Paris: Editions du Seuil, vol. 1: 1983; vol. 2: 1984; vol. 3: 1985

– 'What Is a Text? Explanation and Interpretation.' In *Mythic-Symbolic*

Language and Philosophical Anthropology: A Constructive Interpretation of the Thought of Paul Ricoeur, ed. David M. Rasmussen, 135–50. The Hague: Martinus Nijhof 1971
- 'Writing as a Problem for Literary Criticism and Philosophical Hermeneutics,' *Philosophic Exchange*, no. 2 (Summer 1977): 3–15
Russell, Bertrand. 'On Denoting.' In *Readings in Philosophical Analysis*, ed. Herbert Feigl and Wilfrid Sellars, 103–15. New York: Appleton-Century-Crofts 1949
Sartre, Jean-Paul. *L'Imaginaire: Psychologie phénoménologique de l'imagination*. Paris: Gallimard, 'Folio idées' 1986 (1st ed.: Gallimard 1940)
Svenbo, Jasper. *Phrasiklein: Anthropologie de la lecture en Grèce ancienne*. Paris: Editions la découverte, 'Textes à l'appui' 1988
Todorov, Tzvetan. 'Reading as Construction.' In *The Reader in the Text*, ed. Susan Suleiman and Inge Crosman, 67–82. Princeton, NJ: Princeton University Press 1980. (Translated from the French 'La Lecture comme construction,' *Poétique*, no. 24 [1975]: 417–25)

LITERARY CRITICISM

Barthes, Roland. 'La Métaphore de l'œil.' In *Essais critiques*. Paris: Editions du Seuil, 'Tel Quel,' 1964
Beckett, Samuel. *Proust and Three Dialogues with Georges Duthuit*. London: Calder & Boyars 1969 (1st ed. *Proust*. London: Chatto and Windus 1931)
Bernal, Olga. *Langage et fiction dans le roman de Beckett*. Paris: Gallimard 1969
Blanchot, Maurice. *L'Espace littéraire*. Paris: Gallimard, 'Idées' 1955
- 'Où maintenant? Qui maintenant?' *La Nouvelle Nouvelle Revue française* (oct. 1953): 678–86
- *La Part du feu*. Paris: Gallimard 1949
Camus, Albert. *Carnets, janvier 1942-mars 1951*. Paris: Gallimard 1964
Carduner, René. *La Création romanesque chez Malraux*. Paris: Nizet 1968
Côté, Paul-Raymond. *Les Techniques picturales chez Malraux: Interrogations et métamorphose*. Sherbrooke: Naamen 1984
Dale, Jonathan. 'Sartre and Malraux: *La Nausée* and *La Voie royale*,' *Forum for Modern Language Studies*, no. 4 (1968): 335–46
Dearlove, J.E. *Accommodating Chaos: Samuel Beckett's Nonrelational Art*. Durham, NC: Duke University Press 1982
Durozoi, Gérard. *Beckett*. Paris: Bordas 1972
Fitch, Brian T. *Beckett and Babel: An Investigation into the Status of the Bilingual Work*. Toronto: University of Toronto Press 1988
- 'Clamence en chute libre: La cohérence imaginaire de *La Chute*.' In *Camus 1970 (Colloque organisé sous les auspices du Département des Langues et Littératures Romanes de l'Université de Floride les 29 et 30*

janvier 1970), ed. Raymond Gay-Crosier, 49–69. Sherbrooke, Canada: C.E.L.E.F. (Service de Diffusion, Faculté des arts, Université de Sherbrooke) 1970

– 'A Critique of Roland Barthes' Essay on Bataille's *Histoire de l'œil.*' In *Interpretation of Narrative*, ed. Mario Valdés and Owen Miller, 48–57. Toronto: University of Toronto Press 1976

– *Les Deux Univers romanesques d'André Malraux.* Paris: Lettres Modernes 1964

– *Dimensions et structures chez Bernanos: Essai de méthode critique.* Paris: Lettres Modernes 1969

– *Dimensions, structures et textualité dans la trilogie romanesque de Beckett.* Paris: Lettres Modernes 1977

– 'The Imagery of Malraux's *Royaume farfelu* and Its Significance for the Novels,' *Mélanges Malraux Miscellany*, 2, no. 2 (Autumn 1970): 20–9

– 'L'Innommable and the Hermeneutic Paradigm,' *Chicago Review*, 33, no. 2 (1982): 100–6

– 'Locuteur, délocuteur et allocutaire dans *La Chute* de Camus.' In *L'Analyse du discours / Discourse Analysis*, ed. Pierre R. Léon et Henri Mitterand, 123–35. Montréal: Centre Educatif et Culturel 1976

– *Monde à l'envers / Texte réversible: La fiction de Bataille.* Paris: Lettres Modernes 1982

– *The Narcissistic Text: A Reading of Camus' Fiction.* Toronto: University of Toronto Press 1982

– 'La Navette et l'ellipse chez Malraux: Le cercle herméneutique et la mise en abyme.' In *André Malraux: Unité de l'œuvre, unité de l'homme*, ed. Christiane Moatti et David Bevan, 95–105. Paris: La Documentation française 1989

– 'Participe présent et procédés narratifs chez Claude Simon,' *Revue des Lettres Modernes*, nos. 94–9, 'Un Nouveau Roman?' (1963): 199–216 (reissued as Lettres Modernes 'Reprint, érudition, poche' 1983)

– 'Un Référent fictif pas comme les autres: *Au Moment voulu* de Maurice Blanchot.' In *Roman, réalités, réalismes*, ed. Jean Bessière, 209–21. Paris: Presses universitaires de France 1989

– *Le Sentiment d'étrangeté chez Malraux, Sartre, Camus et S. de Beauvoir.* Paris: Lettres Modernes 1964 (reissued: Lettres Modernes, 'Reprint, érudition, poche' 1983)

– 'Le Statut précaire du personnage et de l'univers romanesques chez Camus,' *Symposium*, 24, no. 3 (Fall 1970): 218–29

– 'Temps du récit et temps de l'écriture dans *Au Moment voulu* de Blanchot.' Forthcoming in *Temps et récit romanesque*. Nice: Université de Nice, Faculté des lettres et sciences humaines, 'Cahiers de narratologie, no. 2' 1990

- 'Un Vide porteur d'échos et de mirages,' *Europe*, nos. 727–8 (nov.–déc. 1989): 112–17
- 'Une Voix qui se parle, qui nous parle, que nous parlons, ou l'espace théâtral de *La Chute*,' *Albert Camus*, no. 3 (1970): 59–79
Frohock, W.M. *André Malraux and the Tragic Imagination*. Stanford: University of Stanford Press 1952
Harris, Geoffrey T. *André Malraux: L'ethique comme fonction de l'esthétique*. Paris: Lettres Modernes 1972
Huyghe, René. *Dialogue avec le visible*. Paris: Flammarion 1955
Jeanson, Francis. 'Pour tout vous dire,' *Les Temps modernes*, no. 82 (août 1952): 354–83
King, Adèle. 'Structure and Meaning in *La Chute*,' PMLA, 77, no. 5 (Dec. 1962): 660–7
Lacouture, Jean. *André Malraux: Une vie dans le siècle*. Paris: Editions du Seuil 1973
Laporte, Roger. *Maurice Blanchot: L'ancien, l'effroyablement ancien*. Paris: Editions Fata Morgana 1987
Meschonnic, Henri. 'Mallarmé au-delà du silence.' In Stéphane Mallarmé, *Ecrits sur le livre (choix de textes)*. Paris: Editions de l'éclat 1985
Milner, Max. *Georges Bernanos*. Paris: Desclée de Brouwer 1967
Moeller, Charles. 'André Malraux ou l'espoir sans terre promise.' In *Littérature du xxe siècle et christianisme*, vol. 3, *L'Espoir des hommes*, 21–192. Paris: Casterman 1963
Morot-Sir, Edouard. 'Imaginaire de peinture et imaginaire romanesque dans l'œuvre d'André Malraux,' *Cahiers de l'Association internationale des études françaises*, no. 33 (mai 1981): 235–50
Noël, Bernard, and Roger Laporte. *Deux Lectures de Maurice Blanchot*. Paris: Editions Fata Morgana 1973
Quilliot, Roger. 'Un Monde ambigu,' *Preuves*, no. 110 (avril 1960): 28–38
Ricardou, Jean. *Le Nouveau Roman*. Paris: Editions du Seuil, 'Ecrivains de toujours' 1973
Robbe–Grillet, Alain. 'Nature, humanisme et tragédie.' In *Pour un Nouveau Roman*. Paris: Editions de Minuit 1963
Royce, Barbara J. '*La Chute* and *Saint Genet*: The Question of Guilt,' *French Review*, 39, no. 5 (April 1966): 709–16
Sabourin, Pascal. *La Réflexion sur l'art d'André Malraux: Origines et évolution*. Paris: Klincksieck 1972
Sarkonak, Ralph. *Claude Simon: Les carrefours du texte*. Toronto (Trinity College): Editions Paratexte 1986
Sartre, Jean–Paul. 'L'Engagement de Mallarmé,' *Obliques*, 'Sartre' (1979)
- 'Réponse à Albert Camus,' *Les Temps modernes*, no. 82 (août 1952), 334–53
Surya, Michel. *Georges Bataille: La mort à l'œuvre. Biographie*. Paris: Editions Garamont – Frédéric Birr, 'Librairie Séguier' 1973

Tucker, Warren. 'La Chute, voie du salut terrestre,' French Review, 43, no. 5 (April 1970): 737–44

Viggiani, Carl A. 'Notes pour le futur biographe d'Albert Camus,' Albert Camus, no. 1, 'Autour de L'Etranger' (1968): 200–18

VARIA

Barthes, Roland. S/Z. Paris: Editions du Seuil 1970

Beaugrand, Robert de and Wolfgang Dressler. Introduction to Text Linguistics. London and New York: Longman 1981

Benveniste, Emile. Problèmes de linguistique générale 1. Paris: Gallimard, 'Tel' 1966

Charles, Michel. Rhétorique de la lecture. Paris: Editions du Seuil 1977

Dällenbach, Lucien. Le Récit spéculaire: Essai sur la mise en abyme. Paris: Editions du Seuil 1977

– 'Reflexivity and Reading.' In Mirrors and After: Five Essays on Literary Theory and Criticism, 9–23. New York: Graduate School, City University of New York 1986

Eco, Umberto. Lector in fabula: Le rôle du lecteur ou la coopération interprétative dans les textes narratifs. Paris: Grasset, 'Livre de Poche: Biblio Essais' 1989

Fish, Stanley. Self-Consuming Artifacts: The Experience of Seventeenth-Century Literature. Berkeley, Los Angeles, London: University of California Press 1972

Frye, Northrop. Anatomy of Criticism. Princeton, NJ: Princeton University Press 1957

Gusdorf, Georges. Les Origines de l'herméneutique. Paris: Payot 1988

Holub, Robert C. Reception Theory: A Critical Introduction. London and New York: Methuen 1984

Jameson, Fredric. The Prison-House of Language: A Critical Account of Structuralism and Russian Formalism. Princeton, NJ: Princeton University Press 1972

Lawall, Sarah N. Critics of Consciousness: The Existential Structures of Literature. Cambridge, MA: Harvard University Press 1968

Lotman, Iouri. La Structure du texte artistique. Traduit du russe par Anne Fournier, Bernard Kreise, Eve Malleret, et Joëlle Yong sous la direction d'Henri Meschonnic. Préface d'Henri Meschonnic. Paris: Gallimard 1973; Struktura Khudožestvenogo Teksta. Moscou: Iskusstvo, 1970

Magliola, Robert R. Phenomenology and Literature: An Introduction. West Lafayette, IN: Purdue University Press 1977

Meschonnic, Henri. Pour la poétique II. Paris: Gallimard 1973

Palmer, Richard E. Hermeneutics: Interpretation Theory in Schleiermacher, Dilthey, Heidegger, and Gadamer. Evanston, IL: Northwestern University Press 1969

Poulet, Georges. *La Conscience critique*. Paris: Corti 1971
Prince, Gerald. 'Introduction to the Study of the Narratee.' In *Reader-Response Criticism: From Realism to Post–Structuralism*, ed. Jane P. Tompkins, 7–25. Baltimore and London: Johns Hopkins University Press 1980. (Trans. of 'Introduction à l'étude du narrataire,' *Poétique*, no. 14 [1973]: 177–96)
Resweber, Jean-Paul. *Qu'est-ce qu'interpréter: Essai sur les fondements de l'herméneutique*. Paris: Editions du Cerf 1988
Ricardou, Jean. *Le Nouveau Roman*. Paris: Editions du Seuil 1973
Schleiermacher, F.D.E. *Hermeneutik: Nach den Handschriften neu herausgegeben und eingeleitet von Heinz Kimmerle*. Heidelberg: Carl Winter Universitatsverlag, 'Abhandlungen des Heidelberger Akademie des Wissenschaften' 1959
– *Hermeneutics: The Hand-Written Manuscripts*, ed. Heinz Kimmerle, trans. James Duke and Jack Forstman. Missoula, MT: Scholar's Press 1977
Starobinski, Jean. *Les Mots sous les mots: Les anagrammes de Ferdinand de Saussure*. Paris: Gallimard 1971
Suleiman, Susan and Inge Crosman, ed. *The Reader in the Text*. Princeton, NJ: Princeton University Press 1980
Texte, ed. Brian T. Fitch and Andrew Oliver, no. 2, 'L'Intertextualité: Intertexte, autotexte, intratexte' (1983)
Todorov, Tzvetan. *Critique de la critique: Un roman d'apprentissage*. Paris: Editions du Seuil 1984
– *Symbolisme et interprétation*. Paris: Editions du Seuil 1978
Todorov, Tzvetan, ed. *Théorie de la littérature: Textes des Formalistes russes*. Paris: Editions du Seuil 1965
Tompkins, Jane P., ed. *Reader-Response Criticism: From Realism to Post-Structuralism*. Baltimore and London: Johns Hopkins University Press 1980
Van Dijk, Teun. *Some Aspects of Text Grammars*. The Hague, Paris: Mouton 1972

Index

Theory/Culture Series

DATE DUE

MAY 15 '00 X			
APR 1 9 2000			
APR 1 9 2000			
GAYLORD			PRINTED IN U.S.A